THE FORMS OF THE OLD TESTAMENT LITERATURE

*Now available

D1329486

MICAH

EHUD BEN ZVI

The Forms of the Old Testament Literature
VOLUME XXIB

Rolf P. Knierim, Gene M. Tucker, and Marvin A. Sweeney, editors

WILLIAM B. EERDMANS PUBLISHING COMPANY
GRAND RAPIDS, MICHIGAN / CAMBRIDGE, U.K.

© 2000 Wm. B. Eerdmans Publishing Co.
255 Jefferson Ave. S.E., Grand Rapids, Michigan 49503 /
P.O. Box 163, Cambridge CB3 9PU U.K.

Printed in the United States of America

05 04 03 02 01 00   7 6 5 4 3 2 1

ISBN 0-8028-4599-1

CONTENTS

ABBREVIATIONS AND SYMBOLS

I. MISCELLANEOUS ABBREVIATIONS AND SYMBOLS

b.	Babylonian Talmud
BCE	before the Common Era
ca.	*circa* (about)
cf.	compare
ch(s).	chapter(s)
diss.	dissertation
ed.	editor(s), edited by; edition
e.g.	for example
Eng.	English
esp.	especially
et al.	*et alii* (and others)
fem.	feminine
FS	*Festschrift*
HB	Hebrew Bible
Heb.	Hebrew
Intro.	Introduction
K	*Ketib*
lit.	literally
LXX	Septuagint
m.	Mishnah
Mak.	*Makkot* (talmudic tractate)
masc.	masculine
MT	Masoretic Text
Mur	Murabbaʿat text
n.	note
OT	Old Testament
Pesh.	Peshitta
pl.	plural
Q	*Qere*

repr.	reprint(ed)
rev. ed.	revised edition
sg.	singular
Sukk.	*Sukkot* (talmudic tractate)
Tg.	Targum
tr.	translator(s), translated by
v(v).	verse(s)
vol.	volume
Vg.	Vulgate
→	cross reference to another section of the commentary
//	parallel
§(§)	section(s)

II. PUBLICATIONS

AB	Anchor Bible
ABL	R. F. Harper, *Assyrian and Babylonian Letters,* 14 vols. (Chicago: Univ. of Chicago Press; New Haven: Yale Univ. Press, 1892-1914)
ABRL	Anchor Bible Reference Library
ANET	*Ancient Near Eastern Texts Relating to the Old Testament,* ed. J. B. Pritchard (3rd ed.; Princeton: Princeton Univ. Press, 1969)
ATD	Das Alte Testament Deutsch
ATR	*Anglican Theological Review*
ATSAT	Arbeiten zu Text und Sprache im Alten Testament
Aug	*Augustinianum*
AUSS	*Andrews University Seminary Studies*
BGBE	Beiträge zur Geschichte der biblischen Exegese
BHS	*Biblia hebraica stuttgartensia*
Bib	*Biblica*
BibInt	*Biblical Interpretation*
BibOr	Biblica et orientalia
BN	*Biblische Notizen*
BTB	*Biblical Theology Bulletin*
BZ	*Biblische Zeitschrift*
BZAW	Beihefte zur *Zeitschrift für die alttestamentliche Wissenschaft*
CahRB	Cahiers de la *Revue biblique*
CANE	*Civilizations of the Ancient Near East,* ed. Jack M. Sasson et al. (New York: Scribner, 1995)
CAT	Commentaire de l'Ancien Testament
CBET	Contributions to Biblical Exegesis and Theology
CBQ	*Catholic Biblical Quarterly*

DBHE	Luis Alonso Schökel, *Diccionario Bíblico Hebrew-Español* (Madrid: Trotta, 1994)
DCH	*Dictionary of Classical Hebrew,* ed. D. J. A. Clines (Sheffield: Sheffield Academic Press, 1993–)
ErIsr	*Eretz Israel*
ETL	*Ephemerides theologicae lovanienses*
FOTL	Forms of the Old Testament Literature
HAL	*Hebrew and Aramaic Lexicon of the Old Testament,* ed. W. Baumgartner et al. (tr. and ed. M. E. J. Richardson; Leiden: Brill, 1994–)
HAR	*Hebrew Annual Review*
HeyJ	*Heythrop Journal*
HSM	Harvard Semitic Monographs
HTR	*Harvard Theological Review*
HUCA	*Hebrew Union College Annual*
IB	*Interpreter's Bible,* ed. G. A. Buttrick et al., 12 vols. (Nashville: Abingdon, 1952-57)
IBHS	B. K. Waltke and M. O'Connor, *An Introduction to Biblical Hebrew Syntax* (Winona Lake, Ind.: Eisenbrauns, 1990)
ICC	International Critical Commentary
Int	*Interpretation*
ITC	International Theological Commentary
JBL	*Journal of Biblical Literature*
JCS	*Journal of Cuneiform Studies*
JM	P. Joüon and T. Muraoka, *A Grammar of Biblical Hebrew* (Subsidia biblica 14/I-II; Rome: Pontifical Biblical Institute, 1991)
JNES	*Journal of Near Eastern Studies*
JNSL	*Journal of Northwest Semitic Languages*
JR	*Journal of Religion*
JSOT	*Journal for the Study of the Old Testament*
JSOTSup	*Journal for the Study of the Old Testament* Supplement Series
JSS	*Journal of Semitic Studies*
JTS	*Journal of Theological Studies*
KAT	Kommentar zum Alten Testament
KJV	King James (Authorized) Version
NASB	New American Standard Bible
NCB	New Century Bible Commentary
NEAEHL	*New Encyclopedia of Archaeological Excavations in the Holy Land,* ed. E. Stern et al., 4 vols. (Jerusalem: Israel Exploration Society; New York: Simon & Schuster, 1993)
NICOT	New International Commentary on the Old Testament
NJPSV	New Jewish Publication Society Version
NRSV	New Revised Standard Version
NTT	*Norsk Teologisk Tidsskrift*
OBO	Orbis biblicus et orientalis

OTE	*Old Testament Essays*
OTG	Old Testament Guides
OTL	Old Testament Library
OTS	*Oudtestamentische Studiën*
RB	*Revue biblique*
REB	Revised English Bible
ResQ	*Restoration Quarterly*
RHPR	*Revue d'histoire et de philosophie religieuses*
RSV	Revised Standard Version
SAA	State Archives of Assyria Studies
SBLDS	Society of Biblical Literature Dissertation Series
SBLMS	SBL Monograph Series
SBT	Studies in Biblical Theology
ScrHier	*Scripta Hierosolymitana*
SEÅ	*Svensk exegetisk årsbok*
Sem	*Semitica*
SJT	*Scottish Journal of Theology*
SJOT	*Scandinavian Journal of the Old Testament*
SJT	*Scottish Journal of Theology*
SSN	Studia semitica neerlandica
TDOT	*Theological Dictionary of the Old Testament*, ed. G. J. Botterweck et al. (tr. D. E. Green et al.; Grand Rapids: Eerdmans, 1974-)
TBü	Theologische Bücherei
UF	*Ugarit-Forschungen*
VT	*Vetus Testamentum*
VTSup	*Vetus Testamentum* Supplements
WBC	Word Biblical Commentary
ZAH	*Zeitschrift für Althebraistik*
ZAW	*Zeitschrift für die alttestamentliche Wissenschaft*
ZDPV	*Zeitschrift des deutschen Palästina-Vereins*

Editors' Foreword

This book is the twelfth in a series of twenty-four volumes planned for publication. The series eventually will present a form-critical analysis of every book and each unit of the Old Testament (Hebrew Bible) according to a standard outline and methodology. The aims of the work are fundamentally exegetical, attempting to understand the biblical literature from the viewpoint of a particular set of questions. Each volume in the series will also give an account of the history of the form-critical discussion of the material in question, attempt to bring consistency to the terminology for the genres and formulas of the biblical literature, and expose the exegetical procedure in such a way as to enable students and pastors to engage in their own analysis and interpretation. It is hoped, therefore, that the audience will be a broad one, including not only biblical scholars but also students, pastors, priests, and rabbis who are engaged in biblical interpretation.

There is a difference between the planned order of appearance of the individual volumes and their position in the series. While the series follows basically the sequence of the books of the Hebrew Bible, the individual volumes will appear in accordance with the projected working schedules of the individual contributors. The number of twenty-four volumes has been chosen for merely practical reasons that make it necessary to combine several biblical books in one volume at times, and at times to have two authors contribute to the same volume. Volume XIII is an exception to the arrangement according to the sequence of the Hebrew canon in that it omits Lamentations. The commentary on Lamentations will be published with the second of two volumes on the book of Psalms.

The initiation of this series is the result of deliberations and plans that began some twenty years ago. At that time the current editors perceived the need for a comprehensive reference work that would enable scholars and students of the Hebrew scriptures to gain from the insights that form-critical work had accumulated throughout seven decades, and at the same time to participate more effectively in such work themselves. An international and interconfessional team of scholars was assembled and has been expanded in recent years.

Several possible approaches and formats for publication presented themselves. The work could not be a handbook of the form-critical method with some examples of its application. Nor would it be satisfactory to present an encyclopedia of the genres identified in the Old Testament literature. The reference work would have to demonstrate the method on all of the texts, and identify genres only through the actual interpretation of the texts themselves. Hence, the work had to be a commentary following the sequence of the books in the Hebrew Bible (the Kittel edition of the *Biblia hebraica* then and the *Biblia hebraica stuttgartensia* now).

The main purpose of this project is to lead the student to the Old Testament texts themselves, and not just to form-critical studies of the texts. It should be stressed that the commentary is confined to the form-critical interpretation of the texts. Consequently, the reader should not expect here a full-fledged exegetical commentary that deals with the broad range of issues concerning the meaning of the text. In order to keep the focus as clearly as possible on a particular set of questions, matters of text, translation, philology, verse-by-verse explanation, etc. are raised only when they appear directly relevant to the form-critical analysis and interpretation.

The adoption of a commentary format with specific categories for the analysis of the texts rests upon a conclusion that has become crucial for all form-critical work. If the results of form criticism are to be verifiable and generally intelligible, then the determination of typical forms and genres, their settings and functions, has to take place through the analysis of the forms in and of the texts themselves. This leads to two consequences for the volumes in this series. First, each interpretation of a text begins with the presentation of the *structure* of that text in outline form. The ensuing discussion of this structure attempts to distinguish the typical from the individual or unique elements, and to proceed on this basis to the determination of the *genre,* its *setting,* and its *intention.* Traditio-historical factors are discussed throughout this process where relevant; e.g., is there evidence of a written or oral stage of the material earlier than the actual text before the reader?

Second, the interpretation of the texts accepts the fundamental premise that we possess all texts basically at their latest written stages — technically speaking, at the levels of the final redactions. Any access to the texts, therefore, must confront and analyze that latest edition first, i.e., a specific version of that edition as represented in a particular text tradition. Consequently, the commentary proceeds from the analysis of the larger literary corpora created by the redactions back to any prior discernible stages in their literary history. Larger units are examined first, and then their subsections. Therefore, in most instances the first unit examined in terms of structure, genre, setting, and intention is the entire biblical book in question; next the commentary treats the individual larger and then smaller units.

The original plan of the project was to record critically all the relevant results of previous form-critical studies concerning the texts in question. While this remains one of the goals of the series, it had to be expanded to allow for more of the research of the individual contributors. This approach has proved to be important not only with regard to the ongoing insights of the contributors but also in view of the significant developments that have taken place in the field in recent years. The team of scholars responsible for the series is committed to following a basic design throughout the commentary, but differences of emphasis and even to some extent of approach will be recognized as more volumes appear. Each author will ultimately be responsible for his own contribution.

The use of the commentary is by and large self-explanatory, but a few comments may prove helpful to the reader. This work is designed to be used alongside the Hebrew text or a translation of the Bible. The format of the interpretation of the texts, large or small, is the same throughout, except in cases where the biblical material itself suggests a different form of presentation. Individual books and major literary corpora are introduced by a general bibliography referring to wider information on the subjects discussed and to works relevant for the subunits of that literary body. Whenever available, a special form-critical bibliography for a specific unit under discussion will conclude the discussion of that unit. In the outline of the structure of units, the system of sigla attempts to indicate the relationship and interdependence of the parts within that structure. The traditional chapter and verse divisions of the Hebrew text, as well as the versification of the *New Revised Standard Version,* are supplied in the right-hand margin of the outlines.

In addition to the commentary on the biblical book, this volume includes a glossary of the genres discussed in the commentary. Many of the definitions in the glossary were prepared by Professor Sweeney, but some have arisen from the work of other members of the project on other parts of the Old Testament. Each subsequent volume will include such a glossary. Eventually, upon the completion of the commentary series, all of the glossaries will be revised in the light of the analysis of each book of the Old Testament and published as Volume XXIII of the series. The individual volumes will not contain special indices, but the indices for the entire series will be published as Volume XXIV.

The editors acknowledge with appreciation the contribution of numerous persons and institutions to the work of the project. All of the contributors have received significant financial, secretarial, and student assistance from their respective institutions. In particular, the editors have received extensive support from their universities. Without such concrete expressions of encouragement the work scarcely could have gone on. At Claremont, the Institute for Antiquity and Christianity has from its own inception provided office facilities, a supportive staff, and the atmosphere that stimulates not only individual but also team research. Emory University and the Candler School of Theology have likewise provided tangible support and encouragement. The editors are particularly indebted to Jacqueline E. Lapsley of Princeton Theological Seminary for her extraordinary editorial assistance in the preparation of this volume while she was a graduate student at Emory University, and to Dr. and Mrs. J. E. Williams for their generous financial support of our work.

ROLF P. KNIERIM
GENE M. TUCKER
MARVIN A. SWEENEY

Author's Preface

Several people and institutions made the writing of this book not only possible but also an enjoyable experience. It is a pleasant duty to mention some of them. I was honored and delighted when Rolf P. Knierim and Gene M. Tucker invited me to write a commentary on the book of Micah. I wish to express my thanks to Rolf and Gene, the editors of this series at that time. I would also like to thank a new editor of the series, Marvin A. Sweeney, for his support and for our interesting conversations about prophetic literature.

I have learned and continue to learn much from my teacher and friend, Gene. He has provided me with support, encouragement, and much insight. In his role as editor of the series, he has carefully read and improved the manuscript of this commentary.

At different professional meetings during the last few years I presented papers on matters that directly relate to this commentary or that have strongly influenced my thinking about the book of Micah. I owe a particular debt of gratitude to my colleagues in two program units of the Society of Biblical Literature, "Prophets and History" and "Composition of the Book of the Twelve," for their constant input and frequent challenges. In addition, I have benefited much from the feedback and encouragement that I have received from my colleagues at the Hebrew Scriptures section of the Pacific Northwest Society of Biblical Literature and the Canadian Society of Biblical Studies.

I am indebted to my students at the University of Alberta, who have been most precious companions of mine in the learning journey that led to this commentary, to their enthusiasm and insight. Sonia Atwal, my research assistant, has provided invaluable help.

This commentary would have never been completed without the incredible dedication of the people at interlibrary loan at the University of Alberta and the university's support of this service.

I am thankful also to the Social Sciences and Humanities Research Council of Canada, which has supported the research leading to this commentary with a much-needed grant.

Most of all, my thanks are due to Perla, my wife, for her love, friendship, and unfailing support. My children, Amos, Naamah, and Micha, continue to inspire me, and I continue to be warmed by their love. I would like to dedicate this volume to them.

EHUD BEN ZVI

Chapter 1

INTRODUCTION TO THE BOOK OF MICAH, A PARTICULAR INSTANCE OF YHWH'S WORD

J. I. Alfaro, *Justice and Loyalty: A Commentary on the Book of Micah* (ITC; Grand Rapids: Eerdmans, 1989); L. C. Allen, *The Books of Joel, Obadiah, Jonah and Micah* (NICOT; Grand Rapids: Eerdmans, 1976); L. Alonso Schökel and J. L. Sicre Díaz, *Profetas,* vol. 2 (Madrid: Cristiandad, 1980); M. Alvarez Barredo, *Relecturas Deuteronomisticas de Amós, Miqueas y Jeremías* (Publicaciones del Instituto Teológico Franciscano, Serie Mayor 10; Murcia: Espigas, 1993); D. Barthélemy et al., *Critique textuelle de l'Ancien Testament,* vol. 3 (OBO 50/3; Fribourg: Éditions Universitaires, 1992); J. Calvin, "Commentary on Micah," in *Commentaries on the Twelve Minor Prophets* (5 vols.; tr. J. Owen; Grand Rapids: Eerdmans, 1950) 2:147-409; O. García de la Fuente, "Notas al texto de Miqueas," *Aug* 7 (1967) 145-54; D. G. Hagstrom, *The Coherence of the Book of Micah* (SBLDS 89; Atlanta: Scholars Press, 1988); D. R. Hillers, *Micah* (Hermeneia; Philadelphia: Fortress, 1984); idem, *Treaty-Curses and the Old Testament Prophets* (BibOr 16; Rome: Pontifical Biblical Institute, 1964); Ibn Ezra (see *Miqraot Gedolot*); A. S. Kapelrud, "Eschatology in the Book of Micah," *VT* 11 (1961) 392-405; T. Lescow, "Redaktionsgeschichtliche Analyze von Micha 1–5," *ZAW* 84 (1972) 46-85; idem, "Zur Komposition des Buches Micha," *SJOT* 9 (1995) 200-222; L. M. Luker, "Beyond Form Criticism: The Relation of Doom and Hope in Micah 2–6," *HAR* 11 (1987) 285-301; M. Luther, "Lectures on Micah" (tr. R. J. Dinda), in *Luther's Works,* vol. 18, ed. H. C. Oswald (St. Louis: Concordia Pub. House, 1975) 207-77; M. L. Margolis, *Micah* (Philadelphia: Jewish Publication Society, 1908); R. Mason, "Micah," in *Micah, Nahum, Obadiah* (OTG; Sheffield: JSOT Press, 1991) 9-53; J. L. Mays, *Micah* (OTL; Philadelphia: Westminster, 1976); S. A. Meier, *Speaking of Speaking: Marking Direct Discourse in the Hebrew Bible* (VTSup 46; Leiden: Brill, 1992); P. D. Miller Jr., *Sin and Judgment in the Prophets* (SBLMS 27; Chico, Calif.: Scholars Press, 1982); A. J. Petrotta, *Lexis Ludens: Wordplay and the Book of Micah*

(American University Studies 7/105; New York/Bern: Lang, 1991); Radaq (see *Miqraot Gedolot*); Rashi (see *Miqraot Gedolot*); B. Renaud, *La formation du Livre de Michée* (Gabalda: Paris, 1977); E. J. Revell, *The Designation of the Individual: Expressive Usage in Biblical Narrative* (CBET 14; Kampen: Kok Pharos, 1996); W. Richter, *Biblia Hebraica transcripta: Kleine Propheten* (ATSAT 33.10; St. Ottilien: Eos, 1993); W. Rudolph, *Micha — Nahum — Habakuk — Zephanja* (KAT 13/3; Gütersloh: Gütersloher Verlagshaus Gerd Mohn, 1975); C. S. Shaw, *The Speeches of Micah: A Rhetorical-Historical Analysis* (JSOTSup 145; Sheffield: JSOT Press, 1993); K. W. Shoemaker, "Speaker and Audience Participants in Micah: Aspects of Prophetic Discourse" (Ph.D. diss., Graduate Theological Union and Univ. of California, Berkeley, 1992; UMI order 9322138); H. Shy, *Tanhum Ha-Yerushalmi's Commentary on the Minor Prophets* (Jerusalem: Magnes, 1991); J. M. P. Smith, "Micah," in Smith, W. H. Ward, and J. A. Bewer, *Micah, Zephaniah, Nahum, Habakkuk, Obadiah and Joel* (ICC; Edinburgh: T. & T. Clark, 1911, repr. 1965) 5-156; R. L. Smith, *Micah–Malachi* (WBC 32; Waco: Word, 1984); G. Stansell, *Micah and Isaiah: A Form and Tradition Historical Comparison* (SBLDS 85; Atlanta: Scholars Press, 1988); A. van der Wal, *Micah: A Classified Bibliography* (Amsterdam: Free Univ. Press, 1990); Sh. Vargon, *The Book of Micah* (Ramat Gan: Bar-Ilan Univ. Press, 1994) (Heb.); R. Vuilleumier, "Michée," in Vuilleumier and C. A. Keller, *Michée, Nahoum, Habacuc, Sophonie* (CAT XIb; Geneva: Labor et Fides, 1971; 2nd ed. 1990) 5-92; J. de Waard, "Vers une identification des participants dans le livre de Michée," *RHPR* 59 (1979) 509-16; J. A. Wagenaar, "Ordeel en Heil: Een Onderzoek naar Samenhang tussen de Heils- en Onheilsprofetieën in Micha 2–5" (diss., Utrecht, 1995); A. Weiser, *Die Propheten Hosea, Joel, Amos, Obadja, Jona, Micha* (ATD 24; Göttingen: Vandenhoeck & Ruprecht, 1955; 8th ed. 1985); J. Wellhausen, *Skizzen und Vorarbeiten: Die kleinen Propheten übersetz, mit Noten* (Berlin: Reimer, 1892); C. Westermann, *The Basic Forms of Prophetic Speech* (tr. H. C. White; Philadelphia: Westminster, 1967); idem, *Prophetic Oracles of Salvation in the Old Testament* (tr. K. Crim; Louisville: Westminster/John Knox, 1991); H. G. M. Williamson, "Marginalia in Micah," *VT* 47 (1997) 360-72; I. Willi-Plein, *Vorformen der Schriftexegese innerhalb des Altes Testaments* (BZAW 123; Berlin: de Gruyter, 1971); J. T. Willis, "The Structure of the Book of Micah," *SEÅ* 34 (1969) 5-42; H. W. Wolff, *Micah* (tr. G. Stansell; Minneapolis: Augsburg, 1990); A. S. van der Woude, "Micah in Dispute with the Pseudo-Prophets," *VT* 19 (1969) 244-60; idem, "Three Classical Prophets: Amos, Hosea and Micah," in R. Coggins, A. Philips, and M. Knibb, eds., *Israel's Prophetic Tradition: Essays in Honour of P. Ackroyd* (New York: Cambridge Univ. Press, 1982) 32-57; M. Zeidel, "Micah," in *Tere Asar im Perush Da'at Miqra*, vol. 2 (Jerusalem: Mosad HaRab Kuk, 1970) (Heb.).

Every work of a scholar is interwoven with some of her or his previous other works. I have been working on questions related to the production and reading and rereading of prophetic texts in ancient communities for a while. So, at times, this commentary on Micah deals with matters that I have discussed elsewhere at some length or with matters that directly relate to issues discussed in these works. The following works are at one point or another referred to in this commentary. They are gathered here because they, too, are not included in the bibliographic lists attached to each of the following sections in this commentary.

Ehud Ben Zvi, *A Historical-Critical Study of the Book of Zephaniah* (BZAW 198; Berlin/New York: de Gruyter, 1991); "Isaiah 1,4-9, Isaiah, and the Events of 701 BCE in Judah: A Question of Premise and Evidence," *SJOT* 5 (1991) 95-111; "Understanding the Message of the Tripartite Prophetic Books," *ResQ* 35 (1993) 93-100; "Prophets and Prophecy in the Compositional and Redactional Notes in I-II Kings," *ZAW* 105 (1993) 331-51; "Inclusion in and Exclusion from Israel as Conveyed by the Use of the Term 'Israel' in Postmonarchic Biblical Texts," in S. W. Holloway and L. K. Handy, eds., *The Pitcher Is Broken: Memorial Essays for Gösta W. Ahlström* (JSOTSup 190; Sheffield: JSOT Press, 1995) 95-149; "Studying Prophetic Texts against Their Original Backgrounds: Preordained Scripts and Alternative Horizons of Research," in S. R. Reid, ed., *Prophets and Paradigms: Essays in Honor of Gene M. Tucker* (JSOTSup 229; Sheffield: JSOT Press, 1996) 125-35; "Twelve Prophetic Books or 'the Twelve': Preliminary Considerations," in P. House and J. W. Watts, eds., *Forming Prophetic Literature: Essays on Isaiah and the Twelve in Honor of John D. W. Watts* (JSOTSup 235; Sheffield: JSOT Press, 1996) 125-56; *A Historical-Critical Study of the Book of Obadiah* (BZAW 242; Berlin/New York: de Gruyter, 1996); "The Urban Center of Jerusalem and the Development of the Literature of the Hebrew Bible," in W. G. Aufrecht, N. A. Mirau, and S. W. Gauley, eds., *Aspects of Urbanism in Antiquity* (JSOTSup 244; Sheffield: Sheffield Academic Press, 1997) 194-209; "Micah 1:2-16: Observations and Its Potential Implications," *JSOT* 77 (1998) 103-20; "Looking at the Primary (Hi)story and the Prophetic Books as Literary/Theological Units within the Frame of the Early Second Temple Period: Some Considerations," *SJOT* 12 (1998) 26-43; idem, "Wrongdoers, Wrongdoing and Righting Wrongs in Micah 2," *BibInt* 7 (1999) 87-100; idem, "A Deuteronomistic Redaction in/among 'The Twelve.' A Contribution from the Standpoint of the Books of Micah, Zephaniah and Obadiah," in L. S. Schearing and S. L. McKenzie, eds., *Those Elusive Deuteronomists* (JSOTSup 268; Sheffield: Sheffield Academic Press, 1999) 232-61; idem, "When a Foreign King Speaks," in M. P. Graham and S. L. McKenzie, eds., *The Chronicler as Author: Studies in Text and Texture* (JSOTSup; Sheffield: Sheffield Academic Press, forthcoming 1999); idem, "Introduction: Writings, Speeches, and the Prophetic Books — Setting an Agenda," in E. Ben Zvi and M. H. Floyd, eds., *Writings and Speeches in Israelite and Ancient Near Eastern Prophecy* (Symposium; Atlanta, Ga.: Scholars Press, forthcoming).

Note: The main work on Micah published after the completion of this manuscript is: W. McKane, *Micah: Introduction and Commentary* (Edinburgh: T & T Clark, 1998).

Structure

3

The book of Micah is a written text that shows a great deal of literary sophistication. It may rightly be called a BOOK, though the term does not appear in the text, because of its written character and because it is a self-contained literary unit, with a clear beginning and conclusion, that shows a significant degree of textual coherence and distinctiveness.

The book of Micah is not merely a "book" but a PROPHETIC BOOK. A "prophetic book" is a book that claims an association with the figure of a prophet of the past, in this case Micah, and that is presented to its readership as YHWH's word. As such the book claims to communicate legitimate and authoritative knowledge about YHWH. The book of Micah is one of the fifteen prophetic books in the HB/OT. These books vary in size (cf. Isaiah with Obadiah) and in some basic structural characteristics. For instance, the book of Jonah is on the whole a narrative, unlike all others, and the books of Isaiah and Jeremiah contain substantial narrative sections, unlike, for instance, the book of Micah.

Yet these books share a significant literary and theological feature: the inclusion of a strong textually inscribed request to their primary readership to understand each prophetic book as distinct from the others, as a unit by itself (see Ben Zvi, "Twelve Prophetic Books"). It is for this reason that the book of Micah is studied here as a unit in and of itself, rather than as a subunit of the "Book of the Twelve."

As a written text, the book of Micah is aimed primarily at those competent to *read* it (see Setting). Moreover, the book of Micah was not produced to be read once and then put aside, but rather to be read and reread and meditated upon (cf. Josh 1:8; Hos 14:10 [NRSV 9]; see Sir 38:34–39:3). It is a book that claims to be and was composed to be treated as an authoritative writing for its readership, that is, as Scripture. The book is explicitly characterized by its title as *YHWH's word.* The book claims that it provides the readers who are competent to read it both knowledge originating in the divine (i.e., YHWH's word) and valid knowledge about the divine (i.e., an authentic representation of YHWH's positions, actions, plans, and indirectly of YHWH's character). To be sure, if the community of readers to which the book was aimed accepts such claims, they will find the book worthy of reading and rereading, of copying and recopying. As a result, the book will be transmitted from one generation of readers to the next. Conversely, if the book had not been read and reread, and, accordingly, copied and recopied, then it is most likely that the book would not have been preserved.

The book of Micah, like any ancient book, is also a *product,* that is, a text whose production and subsequent transmission involved a number of activities, for instance, writing and composition, likely editing, and surely copying, distribution, and archiving as well as reading, rereading, and studying. All of these activities required, directly and indirectly, social and economic resources (see Ben Zvi, "Urban Center"). The required resources were allocated to these activities because of, first, the social roles that the production and study of prophetic books (as well as, e.g., those included in the Pentateuch or in other sections of the HB/OT) had in ancient Israel; second, the related authority and legitimacy of these particular books from the perspective of the community (see Ben Zvi, "Urban Center"). I discuss these issues at length in many of the following sections on Setting and Intention. It suffices at this point to mention that these books shaped, reflected, and reinforced: (1) the story of postmonarchic Israel (i.e., the Jerusalemite-centered communities of the Achaemenid period) about itself, (2) those communities' self-understanding, (3) their understanding of the divine economy and their place in it, (4) their understanding of the attributes and past and future actions of YHWH, and (5) hope for a great and glorious future, in opposition to their actual position in worldly terms. In addition to all these theological or ideological roles, one may mention that these texts provided the literati who wrote, copied, read, reread, and studied them with a necessary social role, that of intermediaries or brokers of the divine knowledge present in the written word and not directly accessible to those who are unable to read that written word competently. It is worth remembering in this regard the words in Sir 38:34–39:3, particularly given that the social circumstances of Sirach stand closer to the social conditions to the Achaemenid postmonarchic communities with which one is to associate the book of Micah as we know it than to those existing in monarchic Judah or Israel.

The observation made above that the book of Micah was meant to be read and reread again and again is of major importance, because the way people reread texts differs significantly from their first reading of the same texts. For instance, rereaders, and particularly those who meditate on the text, are aware of the entire text even as they reread its first line. They may make connections between different units not only according to their sequence in the book but in multidirectional and cross-linked paths. They are also likely to find signposts that remind them of particular issues dealt with in the book as a whole. Moreover, texts that are suitable for continuous rereading show at least some degree of double meaning, ambiguity, and literary sophistication. Furthermore, the continuous rereading of YHWH's word — within a community that accepts the text as such — involves a particular mode of reading: careful reading, studious and meditative (cf. Josh 1:8; Hos 14:10 [NRSV 9]; Sir 38:34–39:3) as opposed to rushed reading. This approach to the act of reading and rereading is consistent with the presence in the text of multivalent expressions, added (and frequently multiple) connotations, puns, and networks of various readings informing each other.

It stands to reason that those who composed texts to be reread continuously and in this manner and who succeeded in this endeavor were most likely aware of the literary requirements of a text meant to be read and reread and meditated on. I address these issues at length in this commentary.

This commentary is a form-critical and a historical-critical one. Thus, for instance, the term *the reader* in this commentary does not refer to any possible reader of the text in the last two millennia, and certainly not to any hypothetical, transhistorical reader. Given the historical focus of this commentary, "the reader" and related terms (e.g., "readership") refer here only to the readers or, better, rereaders among whom and above all for whom the book of Micah was originally composed, that is, the "primary readership" at which this book was aimed, and the original communities of readers of the book. To be sure, I am not advancing any theological or ideological claim about the priority of the understanding of these ancient readers over any other group of readers located at any other point in time and within any other kind of social environment. The point is, first, that actual reading and rereading of a text imply a reader; second, the social identity, the world of knowledge, the theology and ideology of this reader all influence the process of reading and rereading carried out by this reader. Moreover, the ancient reading and rereading of the book of Micah was not a personal but rather an interpersonal affair that involved a community of readers or rereaders. Thus a commentary on a book and the message that it carries within a readership has to be explicit about the identity of the readership to which it is referring. Here that readership is located in postmonarchic Israel. (On the date of the book of Micah see Setting.)

[An editorial comment: Although the terms *reader* and *readership* may be used for any rereader and rereadership, its use here might mislead some of the readers of this book if these terms do not remind them that most of the reading of the book of Micah, and other biblical books, was in fact rereading. Yet a constant use of terms such as *rereader* and *rereadership* — or *(re-)reader* and *(re-)readership* — may be fastidious for some readers of this commentary. Thus the editorial policy adopted here, except in this introductory unit, is to refer to them as "reader," "readership," and the like for the most part, but still, as a signpost to the importance of the issue at stake, the terms *rereader* and *rereadership* will appear a few times in each section.]

The most basic structure of the book of Micah is simple, with three main sections: a title, the body of the book, and a conclusion. The title (1:1) serves to introduce the book to its rereaders. The title characterizes the book as YHWH's word, associates it with Micah, and anchors it in a particular time (→ 1:1).

The body of the book (i.e., 1:2–7:20) consists of READINGS, literary units with textually inscribed markers (such as openings, conclusions, inner-textual coherence, thematic focus) that were likely to signal to the intended re-readership of the book that they are supposed, or at least invited, to read and reread these units as such. It is worth stressing that although one may assume that the rereading of each of these READINGS proceeded one by one and probably sequentially as ordered in the book, the awareness of the other READINGS in the book strongly informed the reading of each one, creating a net of interwoven meanings. In other words, rereaders as opposed to a first reader are not ignorant of what lies ahead in the book; they know it and it informs their reading.

In addition, some units in the book could have been and were most likely reread in different manners. Careful rereading and studying allow the exploration of multiple alternatives in case of actual or potential textual polyvalence. Moreover, some verses or sections thereof could serve and most likely did serve at times as double-duty texts, even at the structural level. In other words, one or more verses were likely read as an integral part of two subsequent READINGS. For instance, 7:18-20 is part and parcel of a particular READING (7:7-20) but also stands as the conclusion of the entire book; 5:1 (NRSV 2) belongs to two different but subsequent readings, 4:8–5:1 (NRSV 5:2) and 5:1-5 (NRSV 2-6). Similar circumstances may obtain within a particular reading, as double-duty verses or expressions are present in the book of Micah (→ 1:5), as well as in other prophetic books (cf. Ben Zvi, *Obadiah,* 124-28, et passim). All in all, these features lead to a plurality of meanings, which created a tapestry of meanings that as a whole conveyed the meaning of the text to those communities of rereaders.

To be sure, these literary circumstances as well as numerous cross-references that go beyond the borders of one READING (e.g., 3:12 and 5:7 [NRSV 8]) and various links binding together subsequent READINGS (e.g., 3:1-2 and 4:1-5) indicate that these READINGS are not independent units. They all belong together to the book of Micah; moreover, very often their particular *Sitz im Buch* plays a most significant role in the shaping of their meaning or meanings.

It is worth mentioning that no textually inscribed markers indicate that the readership of the book was asked to reread the book or any READING within it in a manner governed by their own awareness of either any proposed redactional history of the book, or by the place of the relevant READING in a text other than the present book of Micah, be it a hypothetical forerunner of Micah or any other text. Indeed, it is far more likely that communities of rereaders will continually reread a certain book that they accept as YHWH's word in a way that is governed by the actual text of the book and its textually inscribed demands than by the text of an alternative — and hypothetical — book that they are not reading, rereading, copying, and studying.

Most of the READINGS in the book of Micah seem clustered in three SETS OF READINGS that show various degrees of textual coherence and general inner structure (e.g., notice the concluding READING in 1:2–2:13; or the textual links binding together 4:1–5:14 [NRSV 15]). Only one READING seems to stand alone, constituting as it were a set of its own. Significantly, this particular READING leads to and concludes with the explicit reference to the most significant event in the late monarchic period from the perspective of postmonarchic Israel, the destruction of Zion/Jerusalem and the temple (3:12).

The book of Micah itself closes, as expected, with a conclusion (7:18-20). A significant feature that is shared among the prophetic books in the HB/OT is the presence of a conclusion that provides, in one way or another, hope to Israel, that is, to the readership of the book (cf. Sir 49:10). In addition, the particular language often used in these conclusions of prophetic books contributes to the creation of a distinctive ring that serves to characterize and demarcate the relevant book as a literary unit (see Ben Zvi, "Twelve Prophetic Books," 141-42, 151, 153). The conclusion of the book of Micah (7:18-20) fulfills these two roles.

Arguments in favor of all the statements made above are discussed in the rest of this commentary. The interaction between this type of commentary and the more common historical-critical commentaries of the book of Micah (e.g., by Wolff, Hillers, Mays) is consistently discussed as well.

Genre

The genre of the book of Micah is, as mentioned above, PROPHETIC BOOK, a literary work of some length that is written so as to be read and reread, that presents itself as YHWH's word, and that is associated with a prophetic personage. The production, copying, reading, and rereading of these texts require the channeling of social resources for that purpose and the instruction and maintenance of bearers of high literacy. (On these issues → 1:1, particularly Setting and Intention, and the discussions on these issues in the following sections of this commentary.)

According to the long tradition that describes YHWH as "speaking" and "saying" rather than as "writing," YHWH's words are presented in the world of the written book of Micah as oral utterances. The same holds true for the human, prophetic voice that carries YHWH's words and whose own voice is constructed as associated and even at times intertwining with the divine (→ 1:2-16, et passim; see Ben Zvi, "Observations"). This situation corresponds with, for instance, the immense majority of cases in the books included in the Pentateuch, where both YHWH and the human speaker or speakers who communicate YHWH's words are described as "speaking" and "saying" rather than writing. (In fact, YHWH does not write anything except the two tablets in the Pentateuch.) One should stress, however, that these "oral utterances" exist in the *written* world of books, be it Genesis, Leviticus, or Micah. Indeed, it is *the written book* that is described as "YHWH's word" in Mic 1:1, and if YHWH's Torah is understood as pointing to some of, some portion of, or all the books in the Pentateuch, then YHWH's Torah will also be communicated by a written text, to be read, reread, and studied.

To be sure, the almost absolute literary and probably theological constraint of presenting and imagining YHWH as a speaking rather than writing personage, and the lighter but significant constraint to present the voices associated with YHWH's as also speaking voices, neither deny nor affirm the likely existence of prophets and other intermediaries who expressed orally what they thought or felt to be the word of YHWH in the monarchic period. Indeed, comparative studies show that there is no reason to deny their existence.

The setting of those intermediaries and the setting of the book of Micah are, however, surely different, because the latter setting involves literati writing, copying, and studying written texts that they identify with YHWH's word. It is most significant that the book of Micah (and pentateuchal books, for instance) develops a substantial gap between, on the one hand, the world of actual production and consumption (i.e., reading, rereading, and studying) of the book of Micah (and of the pentateuchal books), and, on the other hand, the world described in these books. This gap shapes an image of particular and foundational periods in Israel's past as substantially different from what was experienced by the literati responsible for these writings and their transmission. In one period YHWH's voice resonated orally; in their times YHWH's word is a written text.

It is probable that these literati confronted some flesh-and-blood prophets and oral intermediaries of divine knowledge in their days too. But, as I discussed elsewhere, it is most unlikely that these literati, who were deeply involved in the creation and development of a "written revelation," would have accepted the authority of these contemporaneous prophets — or new Moseses for that matter — and their new revelations (see Ben Zvi, *Zephaniah,* 349-53).

Setting

The social setting in which the book of Micah — as a whole — was produced is characterized by an authorship and readership able to produce, read, and reread this text. The following studies on the particular READINGS demonstrate that both the authorship and readership are to be found among literati or bearers of high literacy. These people are usually associated with urban centers and with social and political circumstances that allow for the training and maintenance of cadres of literati and for the production, reading, and rereading of their works.

The emphasis on explanations of the catastrophe that befell monarchic Jerusalem, the explicit reference to the exile in Babylon (4:10), other references to exile and loss of the land (e.g., 2:4, 10), to the gathering of the exiles (e.g., 2:12-13; 7:12), and salvation after exile (e.g., 4:10; 7:11-13) point to a postmonarchic setting for the book as a whole. I agree with the overwhelming majority of redaction-critical studies of the book of Micah that maintain that significant sections of the book, and hence the book as a whole, are post–586 BCE. (See, e.g., Wolff, *Micah;* Mays; Renaud; Alvarez Barredo; Willis, esp.

40-42.) Contrary to these redaction-critical studies, however, this commentary has its starting point in the book of Micah as it stands, rather than on the putative words of the prophet Micah ($\rightarrow$ 1:1 and the bibliography there).

The strong Jerusalem/Zion-centered theology or ideology that permeates the book and social, political, and economic considerations associated with the resources necessary for the production of highly literate works (including the preparation and maintenance of cadres of literati (i.e., the intended readership of these works) suggests that if an urban, political, and religious center is to be found for the activity of these literati, then Jerusalem (rather than Mizpah, the main urban center in Judah during the Neo-Babylonian period) is the first candidate to take into account. (There is no reason to assign the text to exiles in Babylon; notice the explicit reference to Babylon as "there" in 4:10; see Willis, 40-42.) The circumstances in the temple community around Jerusalem, particularly in the Persian II period (ca. 450-332 BCE), were conducive to the type of literary activity that may have led to books such as the book of Micah (see Ben Zvi, "Urban Center").

The world shaped within the book, as opposed to that in which the book was composed, read, and reread, is set in the monarchic period, from the reign of Jotham to that of Hezekiah. But, significantly, the setting created within the world of the text in each of these READINGS is not clearly anchored to any particular event during that period, nor to any place or circumstances in particular. Thus, on the one hand, the ancient readership was asked to read and reread the text (= YHWH's word) against the background of the circumstances of this portion of the monarchic period, as they knew or imagined it; on the other hand, the same readership was clearly asked not to strongly historicize the text, not to read it in a way that was strongly influenced by any particular event in their recollection of the past.

The monarchic setting of the world of the book communicates to the postmonarchic readership that some of the events foreseen by the speaker or speakers in the text have come to pass. Since the events already fulfilled point to judgment and destruction, and those yet to be fulfilled to salvation for Israel, the pattern of partial fulfillment serves to enhance the authority and validity of the text, and accordingly its ability to provide hope to Israel in general, and surely to the direct readership of the book.

The monarchic setting of the book communicates also an image of the monarchic period and of a prophet Micah. I must stress, however, that these images are triply removed from actual, historical circumstances in that section of the monarchic period. First, these are literary and theological texts; even if they are relatively contemporaneous with the historical setting that they attempt to describe, they are not snapshots of social reality and of social roles. They represent what their authors want, or at best allow, their readers to think of these circumstances (cf. Carroll, 206-8). Second, as I show in the commentary, the book of Micah does not show much interest in historical, particular events or attempt to convey a strong sense of mimesis. Rather than asking the readers to historicize its READINGS, the book is written so as to read them against their *Sitz im Buch* and against the most general circumstances. Third, the book was written centuries later, and under substantially different conditions, than those described in the world of the text. At best, it characterizes a monarchic prophet of old, Micah, according to the way in which he was imagined by the community of literati within which the book was composed, read, and reread. The same holds true for the social conditions referred to in the book (cf. Davies, 51). In sum, the study of the setting described in the book of Micah cannot be taken as a reliable source for understanding the history of monarchic Judah from Jotham to Hezekiah (see also Ben Zvi, "Wrongdoers"; idem, "Observations").

For the study of the settings of the different READINGS, in terms of both the world of the book and that of the intended readership, see the particular discussions under Setting in this commentary.

Intention

The most general, and primary, intention of the book as it stands is to instruct the intended community of rereaders about YHWH and in particular about YHWH's relationship to Israel, to Jerusalem, and to the Jerusalemite center, to explain YHWH's punishment of Israel in the past, and to communicate hope by pointing to an ideal future. See the particular discussions of Intention in this commentary.

Although it is not the primary intention of the book of Micah, the book also contributed to the construction of a world in which YHWH's word is a written text to which only the literati have *direct* access. Thus the text, and above all the literati who can read it to themselves and to the vast majority of the population who are unable to read it, become brokers of divine knowledge (see, e.g., Ben Zvi, "Observations," and further discussions in this commentary). In that world, the literati turn into mediators between YHWH, the patron and as such provider of knowledge, and Israel, the client who needs that knowledge to maintain its ways and to fulfill its obligations to the patron.

Bibliography

R. P. Carroll, "Prophecy and Society," in R. E. Clements, ed., *The World of Ancient Israel* (Cambridge: Cambridge Univ. Press, 1991) 203-25; P. R. Davies, "The Audiences of Prophetic Scrolls: Some Suggestions," in S. B. Reid, ed., *Prophets and Paradigms: Essays in Honor of Gene M. Tucker* (JSOTSup 229; Sheffield: JSOT Press, 1996) 48-62.

Chapter 2

THE INDIVIDUAL UNITS

SUPERSCRIPTION, 1:1

Structure

The expression "YHWH's word" characterizes the contents of the book as a whole. It is a textually inscribed marker that provides the rereaders of the book with a most significant interpretive key: they are asked to read the ensuing text in a way that is governed by a characterization of the book as nothing less than YHWH's word. This expression clearly identifies (or makes an unequivocal claim concerning) the genre of the following text. Since this particular genre carries a claim to legitimacy and authority, the explicit identification of the text with this genre, from the outset, communicates both legitimacy and authority. The expression as a whole may be seen as answering the implied question of why a person should read this text, and why such a person should care about what the text says.

"YHWH's word" is clearly a generic characterization since more than one prophetic book is so presented to its readers (see Hos 1:1; Joel 1:1; Zeph

1:1; cf., e.g., Jer 1:1). The present book is set apart from similar books that are not only explicitly included in the same literary and religious category but also carry the same expression in their superscription by means of a set of relative clauses. Thus Mic 1:1 claims that the following text is not only YHWH's word but YHWH's word that (1) came to Micah the Morashtite and (2) was in the days of Jotham, Ahaz, and Hezekiah, kings of Judah. The association of YHWH's word with a particular personage is the first and most salient way that served to set apart one prophetic book from another. No prophetic book was ever associated with more than one main prophetic character, no matter how many redactional layers and authors may have been at work during the composition and redaction of the book (cf. Ben Zvi, "Twelve Prophetic Books").

This being the case, it is obvious that a combination of the subject ("YHWH's word") and the first relative clause ("that came to Micah the Morashtite") may have functioned for generations as a code expression (signifier) pointing to the book of Micah (the signified of the signifier). Against this background it seems clear that "YHWH's word that came to Micah the Morashtite" was considered the title of the book. (See, e.g., already Tanhum HaYerushalmi [Shy, 140-41].)

The interpretation of this expression as the title of the book rests on the fact that the information included in "YHWH's word that came to Micah the Morashtite" is enough to characterize this book within the biblical repertoire, but also the tendency to refer to a text by its first words, a tendency found in Mesopotamian literature (and later on in Jewish biblical literature). Significantly, such a tendency is already suggested by the way in which particular speeches (or types of speeches) are referred to in 1 Kgs 22:28//2 Chr 18:27; Jer 7:4; 23:38; Ezek 22:28.

Moreover, it is unlikely that it is by accident that the full (and precise) expression rendered by "YHWH's word that came to X" (X = the prophet) occurs only in four related texts in the HB/OT: Hos 1:1; Joel 1:1; Mic 1:1; and Zeph 1:1. That the occurrence of this seemingly natural expression in biblical Hebrew is restricted to the first words of these four prophetic books suggests strongly that its presence there is dependent on conventions and expectations associated with that literary context. It is reasonable to assume that for the intended audience of these books (and their actual first readers) the aforementioned combination of the main and first relative clauses functioned as a clear marker about the character of the book that provided them with the most significant interpretive key as they embarked in reading the book, and at the same time as a "title" to refer to the book in settings other than its reading or rereading.

Many have proposed that a combination of the present main and first relative clauses (i.e., "YHWH's word that came to Micah the Morashtite") constituted (or could have constituted) the original title or superscription of a literary precursor of the book of Micah (e.g., Mays, 37; Nogalski, 127) and that the other clauses in Mic 1:1 were added at later stages in the redaction of the book. Alternative hypotheses about the redactional history of 1:1 have also been advanced (cf. Wolff, *Micah*, 33). These proposals are certainly possible, but they are still unverifiable; indeed, they are hypothetical at best, and highly speculative at worst. Moreover, none of these proposals arises from linguistic "difficulties" within the text of 1:1, nor is any of them necessarily related to the likely way in which the (present) book of Micah was read (and reread) by the community of rereaders for which it was composed.

The precise phrasing of the aforementioned combination (i.e., *dbr yhwh 'šr hyh 'l X*, "YHWH's word that came to X") is noteworthy. None of the prophetic books in the HB/OT begins with a sentence like "YHWH's word *(dbr)* which he spoke *(dbr),*" despite the obvious paronomasia created by this phrasing, and despite the strong preference for paronomasia in the HB/OT in general, and in Micah 1 in particular (cf. 2 Kgs 1:17; 15:12; 20:19; Isa 16:13; 37:22; 39:8; Jer 30:4; 45:1; on Micah 1, see esp. Petrotta, 65-89, also 118-23). The likelihood of an explanation of this absence in terms of a simple accident (i.e., pure coincidence) is not only questionable from the outset but further diminished by the fact that in this particular literary context the word "saying" *(l'mr)* is not found in any of the prophetic books after the usual combination of *dbr yhwh* ("YHWH's word") and a verbal form of *hyh* despite the fact that this syntagma is well attested (for instances in which *qtl* forms of *hyh,* usually "be," are involved see Gen 15:1; 1 Kgs 18:1, 31; Ezek 29:1, 17; 30:20; occurrences of *wyqtl* forms of *hyh* in these textual circumstances are numerous in biblical literature generally and in prophetic literature particularly; *l'mr* occurs in Jonah 1:1, but Jonah opens with a narrative introduction, not a superscription). Therefore the mentioned patterns of occurrence cannot be considered accidental. Even if they may have been influenced by certain linguistic conventions (cf. Meier, 143, 159-61, passim), these peculiar and consistent patterns of nonoccurrence precisely at the opening of prophetic books are not likely to be simple vehicles that provide no information about the theological and ideological world of the writers and readers responsible for the composition of these prophetic books. But what kind of information do they provide?

It is reasonable to assume that the consistent absence of these forms in this precise literary context either points to or expresses (and conveys to the readers of these books) a position consistent with a differentiation between the concepts of "YHWH's word" and YHWH's (direct) speech, *verbal* communication. One may contrast this feature with the Neo-Assyrian use of the expression "the word of X" — X being a person of authority, mainly the king — as an opening statement in official letters (see *ABL,* 288-87, 399-403; cf. Meier, 319). In other words, prophetic *books* were supposed to be considered "YHWH's word," that is, knowledge (or vision) that originates in the divine (see discussion of the third relative clause), or perhaps divine instruction, torah (see Isa 2:3; Mic 4:2), but not a report of divine speech-acts (cf. Jer 1:2 with 1:4), though the latter may be (and often are) embedded in a prophetic book.

It is true that one may maintain that this observation points to what had to be obvious for the readers of prophetic books. Still, that this differentiation clearly influenced the language used in the books points to a level of awareness of the differentiation that is not necessarily obvious.

The first observation that one may make about Micah, the prophet with whom this book is associated, is that he is a man. It is probably not by accident that all the prophetic books of the HB/OT are associated with male prophets, though the existence of female prophets in Israel was accepted (see Judg 4:4; 2 Kgs 22:14; Neh 6:14). It is noteworthy in this regard that in other ancient Near Eastern cultures female prophets may have outnumbered male prophets (see Parpola, xlviii-lii, cvi n. 258). It is possible that the association of the prophetic books in the HB/OT solely with male prophets is related to their being *books*. This feature may be related to the sense of partial overlap among the authoritative voices of the prophetic character in these books, those of the implied and actual authors of these books, and the literati who read, reread, proclaimed, and explained them to those unable to read. The last two groups seem to have been overwhelmingly male (see Nehemiah 8; Sir 38:34–39:3). This sense of overlapping voices connoted authority to the literati as mediators of divine knowledge and contributed to the attainment of the social roles for which the prophetic books were composed, read, and reread (→ Mic 1:2–7:20).

The reference to Micah as a Morashtite conveys — and shapes — a perspective shared by the authorial voice and the intended audience that is external to Moresheth, because a person is rarely called in his or her hometown by reference to the town itself. Gentilics are most often used as helpful identifying markers by and within a social group in which most of the people do not bear such a gentilic (cf., e.g., Mason, 23). Although we cannot be sure of the implied perspective reflected in the choice of the words "Micah the Morashtite," this perspective is more likely to be Jerusalemite than any other alternative, because Jerusalem was the most likely urban center of the cadres of sophisticated writers and rereaders within which and for which the book of Micah was written. Jerusalem was also the most likely center for channeling the resources necessary for the development and maintenance of these cadres. Finally, the clear Jerusalem-centered character of the book is congruent with this position. (On these issues cf. Ben Zvi, "Urban Center," and bibliography there.)

In addition, the particular characterization of Micah by a gentilic fulfills a similar role to that of a patronymic (notice that no patronym is given in Am 1:1; Mic 1:1; and Nah 1:1; the same holds true, e.g., for Elijah and Ahijah). In both cases, in a way typical of a traditional society, the mentioned personage is further identified by his or her name and by a social characterization (e.g., family, profession, or gentilic). The actual selection of a particular social characterization (e.g., priest, prophet, Morashtite, son of X, "empty slot" [as in Obadiah]) obviously contributes to the general image of the personage that the rereaders are asked to construe on the basis of the information given by the text and their own world of knowledge.

Micah (just like Amos and Nahum) is thus presented to the audience of the book as a non-Jerusalemite who conveyed a truly divine message that expresses and authoritatively teaches a clear Jerusalem-centered theological position (cf. Ben Zvi, *Obadiah,* 38-39). Significantly, all the prophetic books in which the main prophetic personage is characterized by association with a city or town point to locations other than Jerusalem.

Micah's/Micaiah's appellative is "the Morashtite" in Mic 1:1 and in Jer

26:18 (cf. Mic 3:12). Yet, whether the relation between the information given in Mic 1:1 and Jer 26:18 concerning the place of origin of Micah is one of dependence, interdependence, or of dependence on an accepted tradition about Micah, the message conveyed to the readership of prophetic books by the explicit reference to Micah as the Morashtite (and to Nahum as the Elkoshite, and the like) remains as explained above.

Van der Woude has proposed that the present book of Micah represents a Deuteronomistic and Josianic combination of the writings of two prophets, Micah of Moresheth and another prophet whose name "may have been Micah as well," and who was from the northern kingdom of Israel and contemporaneous with Micah of Moresheth ("Three Classical Prophets," esp. 48-53). To the northern prophet (Deutero-Micah) van der Woude attributes Micah 6–7 (cf. Alonso Schökel and Sicre Díaz, 2:1033-35; and already Burkitt).

But 1:1 does not tell its readers that such is the case. To the contrary, 1:1 asks them to associate the entire book with the figure of Micah the Morashtite. Moreover, as mentioned above, no prophetic book is associated with more than one central prophetic figure. (See Ben Zvi, "Twelve Prophetic Books.")

The geographical place alluded to by the gentilic "the Morashtite" is probably Moresheth-gath (cf. 1:14), a place that is usually identified with Tell el-Judeideh (see Broshi; on this tell see Gibson). Yet one should notice that the text in 1:14 does not single out this town from the many others mentioned there and in the immediate textual environment, nor bring in any way to the forefront a "personal" association between the speaker in the text and this precise town. Indeed, the text seems to allow — or perhaps even to hint indirectly at — more than one potential understanding of the gentilic "the Morashtite," even if the possibilities are kept within the narrow limits of the list of towns in ch. 1. It is not by chance (and certainly not the result of lack of knowledge of Hebrew; see Tanhum HaYerushalmi [Shy, 140-41]; cf. Hillers, *Micah,* 13) that there is a long tradition of interpretation that associates this gentilic with the town of Maresha (cf. Mic 1:15; see Tg., Pesh., Tanhum HaYerushalmi, R. Kara, Rashi, Radak).

The second relative clause (i.e., "that came in the days of Jotham, Ahaz, and Hezekiah, kings of Judah") requests the intended (and the actual) readers of the book to understand this singular instance of YHWH's word as anchored in the particular circumstances of a period considered to be part and parcel of their past. Of course, such a reference implies that this audience has a particular image of that specific period — if this was not the case, then the reference would have been meaningless. Thus one may say that this second relative clause activates the knowledge of the past held by the community of readers and situates this knowledge as an interpretive key for their reading of the book.

The period referred to by 1:1 includes the reigns of Jotham, Ahaz, and Hezekiah. That the past is organized in terms of regnal periods and that the precise expression used in 1:1 is "in the days of X" (X being the ruler or its equivalent, and during the monarchy, the king) is only to be expected (cf. Gen 14:1; 26:1; Judg 5:6; 8:28; 1 Sam 17:2; 1 Kgs 10:21; Isa 1:1; 7:1; Jer 1:2, 3; Zech 14:5; Esth 1:1; Ezra 4:7; 1 Chr 4:41; etc.). Neither the organization of time in such a way nor the presence of the aforementioned expression requires the assumptions that the text was written by a Deuteronomistic group, nor that a Deuteronomistic editing of an existing book has taken place (for a different approach see, among others, Nogalski, 127).

It is worth stressing that the ancient audience was asked to read and re-read the text (= YHWH's word) against the background of the circumstances of the period as they knew or imagined it, not against the "most likely historical circumstances." It follows then that it is not what happened during, for instance, Ahaz's days, but what was generally thought to have happened at that time that counted in this regard. Thus the question is not how can we reconstruct today the most likely historical circumstances from the reign of Jotham to Hezekiah, but how can we reconstruct what the writers and readers of the book of Micah thought of the period from Jotham to Hezekiah?

First, it is reasonable to assume that the image of the past in the community for which the book was written was shaped, at least in part, by the book of Kings or a possible forerunner, or, alternatively, the sources behind it. (Reading Kings or its forerunner cannot be equated with being a "Deuteronomist," as the example of the Chronicler shows clearly.) One may notice also the historical perspective of the note in Jer 26:17-19.

Second, the precise language of the second relative clause deserves attention because it resembles in many ways those found in Isa 1:1 and Hos 1:1. One may easily notice, for instance, the lack of the conjunctive *waw* in the series of names of kings, and the reference to Hezekiah as *yĕḥizqîyâ;* this king is named *yĕḥizqîyâ* only in Hos 1:1 and Mic 1:1. Coincidence is probably not the best explanation for these data. The similarities here are more likely due to either literary interdependence (i.e., the three were written more or less at the same time and by the same group of literati) or literary dependence (one was written first, and the others follow the example). Whether one prefers interdependence over dependence or vice versa — that it is impossible actually to assess which of the clauses was the first to be written does not undermine the argument for dependence — it seems most likely that the language of the three temporal clauses (or at least two of them) indicates a commonly accepted link among the clauses and among the books that they introduce. Significantly, these three books are not only bound together by a formal expression but they are all associated with the same period in the history of Israel/Judah (as is the book of Amos, which shares some other features with this triad of temporal introductions; for a different approach, see Andersen and Freedman, 146-49). Such a construction of the past associates no instance of "YHWH's word" with the reign of Manasseh, in sharp contrast to the regnal periods preceding and following his. This lack of association both reflects and shapes an image of Manasseh's reign that is consistent with that advanced in Kings (and with the relatively more benevolent approach to Ahaz present in Kings as opposed to Chronicles; cf. Ackroyd). Incidentally, one may contrast the social construction of a past characterized by a lack of *ḥāzôn* ("vision") during Manasseh's days with the position advanced by Wellhausen (*Prolegomena,* 486) and others in regard to the association of some sections of Micah (6:1–7:6) with the time of Manasseh.

It is certainly significant that, despite the clear temporal reference in the second relative clause, Micah is identified with Micaiah the son of Imla from 1 Kings 22 already in biblical times (see 1 Kgs 22:28; 2 Chr 18:27; for the interchange between the names "Micah" and "Micaiah" see Jer 26:18, *K*). It seems difficult to explain this identification away by resorting to a supposed lack of knowledge of Mic 1:1 on the part of those responsible for 1 Kgs 22:28 and 2 Chr 18:27 (one may notice the existence also of later instances of this identification; see, e.g., *Lives of the Prophets* 6; *Pesiq. Rab Kah.* 16.4). Since the issue of Micah's image in texts other than the book of Micah seems beyond the scope of this analysis, it suffices to mention here that (1) the "letteral" meaning of the text (i.e., the "literal-as-written" meaning of the text, as opposed to other possible understandings of "literal"; see Loughlin, 324-25) was not necessarily always the only generally accepted understanding (cf. Loughlin); and (2) a partial solution to the problem may be hinted at in the association of anything that is understood as "in the spirit of Micah" with Micah the Morashtite (cf. Cohen).

The third relative clause, the *ḥzh* ("saw") clause, is the first of many clauses and expressions in the book that not only may be understood in more than one way, but that seem to have conveyed their respective messages by means of a set of seemingly "separate" meanings shedding light on each other. On the surface, one may ask whether the clause refers back to Micah or to YHWH's word.

Yet there is no reason to prefer an "either-or" over a "both-and" reading of the clause in this context. Indeed, the latter is much more likely. First, double-duty expressions (whether both are at the same communicative level or one conveys the primary message and the other connotes a secondary message) occur in Micah in general and in Micah 1 in particular (→ 1:2-16, passim). Second, it is contextually and grammatically possible to understand the clause as informing the readers of the book that (a) the text is a particular case of "YHWH's word," namely, the one that Micah "saw [*ḥzh;* on this term see below] concerning/against Samaria and Jerusalem," that is, it further characterizes this particular text; and (b) that Micah the Morashtite is the one who prophesied *(ḥzh)* concerning/against Samaria and Jerusalem, that is, it further characterizes Micah. Third, there are no textually inscribed markers that may have signaled to the readers of the book that they should disallow either of the two understandings. Indeed, the text seems to be written so as to suggest both. Fourth, not only are the two readings not contradictory, but they seem to express the same information from a different perspective. Fifth, it is exactly this sense of sameness between the meanings that reinforces an association between Micah and the text, and of both of them with YHWH.

The root *ḥzh/y* ("see") occurs several times in the introductions of the prophetic books, both as a nominal form (i.e., *ḥzwn*) and as a Qal verbal form (see Isa 1:1; 2:1; 13:1; Am 1:1; Mic 1:1; Hab 1:1). In these instances it carries more significance than what the usual translations ("vision," "which he saw," or the like) seem to convey. For example, *ḥzwn* indicates neither a "simple vision" nor visual information. Contextually it points to a message that is reportedly rooted in the divine, and therefore communicates a claim for the legitimacy and social authority of itself. Moreover, *ḥāzôn* functions as a genre marker and as a part of the title of written books (see Isa 1:1; Obad 1:1 Nah 1:1; 2 Chr 32:32). The verbal form ḥāzâ in Mic 1:1 is probably better translated as "prophesied." (Cf. Isa 13:1 and Hab 1:1, where a prophet "prophesies" [ḥzh/y] a maśśā'; on ḥzh/y and ḥāzôn in the introductions of prophetic books, see Ben Zvi, *Obadiah*, 11-14.)

The precise syntagm ḥzh 'l (and the entire expression 'šr ḥzh 'l, "which he prophesied against or concerning"; see below) occurs only in prophetic literature and only in introductory contexts (see Isa 1:1; 2:1; Am 1:1; Mic 1:1). It seems therefore that this section of the introduction also conveys or reflects (or both) unequivocal contextual information about the genre of the ensuing text (cf. ḥzh l in Ezek 13:16; Lam 2:14). In this case 'l likely pointed to a meaning akin to "against," though potential readings such as "on account of" and "concerning" cannot be disregarded, at least at the level of connotation. The latter level is certainly significant in a text written so as to be read, reread, and meditated on, and such is the case of the prophetic books. (For the preposition 'al governing the object of interest with psychological predicates, such as thinking, grieving, and prophesying, see *IBHS*, 11.2.3.c.)

The reference to Samaria and Jerusalem is somewhat unexpected, for Samaria stands there in the traditional slot of "Judah" (cf. "Judah and Jerusalem," e.g., Isa 1:1; 2:1). The pair Samaria-Jerusalem appears also in Isa 10:11; Ezek 23:4; and Mic 1:5 (cf. 2 Kgs 21:13). In all these cases the pair is associated with trouble and sin for Jerusalem. It is reasonable to assume that the same perspective was connoted by the pair in Mic 1:1. If so, the introduction already helps to create a scheme about Jerusalem and, by extension, Judah, or perhaps Israel in a theological or ideological sense (→ 1:2-16) and what may befall her. Such a scheme creates an opening that is consistent with one of the most common, generic features of the prophetic books: the tendency to open (directly or indirectly, e.g., Amos) with judgment against Israel, and to conclude with some kind of message of hope. Significantly, as the nations are mentioned in Amos to draw attention to the judgment of Israel, so Samaria plays a similar role here (cf. Dell, 53-54).

Scholars who follow redaction-critical approaches tend to consider this relative clause as a redactional addition of a second level, an editorial comment that was attached to the rest of v. 1, which in itself is perceived as a Deuteronomistic addition to the "original" text of Micah. This second-level addition is associated with circles close to those who edited the book of Isaiah, who wrote Zion psalms, and who were influenced by Deuteronomistic ideas. (See, e.g., Alvarez Barredo, 83-84; cf. Willi-Plein, 70. On the issues raised by these approaches, see above.)

Genre

Micah 1:1 introduces the book to its readers. It conveys to them a clear message about the genre of the book (namely, "YHWH's word," likely connoting the meaning "YHWH's instruction") and its authority. In addition, it particularizes the book in relation to similar instances of "YHWH's word" by associating it with the figure of Micah the Morashtite. It also informs the readers about the background against which they are supposed to read the prophecy, and suggests its main topics. All these elements together provide a frame of reference, a scheme that not only allows but also strongly informs the subsequent reading of the text. In sum, from a functional vantage point, one may consider 1:1 the INTRODUCTION of the book of Micah.

It is customary to refer to 1:1 and similar written introductions as SUPERSCRIPTIONS. Such a characterization is correct if one keeps in mind that 1:1 and similar passages should be considered the superscription not to the book but to the main body of the book (in this case, 1:2–7:20). Mic 1:1 and similar SUPERSCRIPTIONS are an integral — and most significant — part of their respective books. Indeed, they provide the rereaders with authoritative, interpretive keys that, to a large extent, govern the set of potential interpretations that the texts are allowed to carry. Not only do they not stand apart from the book (a position that is implied in the distinction between superscript and script), but it is misleading to characterize them in such a way.

Congruent with its role within the book as a whole, 1:1 is presented to the readers of the book of Micah as a unit by itself. It is because it stands apart and "looks" at 1:2–7:20 as a whole that it clearly communicates to the readers that it characterizes that section of the book in its entirety. As such, one can consider it the SUPERSCRIPTION of 1:2–7:20.

The position that 1:1 is the SUPERSCRIPTION of the book and should be considered apart from it is perhaps defensible from the viewpoint of those who consider 1:1 (and similar texts) as secondary (redactionally or theologically, or both) to the rest of the book, or its main ("authentic") sections (see, e.g., Hillers, *Micah,* 14-15). But if the standpoint is that of an attempt to understand how the book of Micah was read by the ancient community for which it was composed, then a separation between superscript and script seems difficult to maintain. Mic 1:1 introduced the book of Micah to its readers; it was not only integral to the book (as it was being read by the community), but a most significant interpretive point for their understanding of the text being read.

Setting

The social setting of the actual writing (and reading) of the INTRODUCTION of the book of Micah is similar to that of the writing (and reading) of the entire book: within a social group that can be characterized by high literacy, by an interest in prophetic literature, in its authority, and in the theological and ideological message (claimed to be divine) that this literature conveyed. Although it is likely that this group cherished, shaped, and reshaped tradition about a prophet Micah, it is still worth stressing that within this group, YHWH's word that came to Micah *signifies* a written book, to be read, reread, and studied.

The authorial voice responsible for the introduction seems also to evoke and reflect a scribal milieu, one in which people refer to and classify written works by titles that carry, among other things, genre information (cf. Tucker; and cf. "Instruction of the Mayor of the city, the Vizier Ptahhotep," translated by M. Lichtheim, *Ancient Egyptian Literature* [3 vols.; Berkeley: Univ. of California Press, 1973-80] 1:62). Significantly, the authorial voice, the intended rereadership, and the actual writers and audience seem familiar with such classifying and cataloguing activities.

Intention

The main role of 1:1 is to introduce the book to the readers or, in other words, to help them develop their first concept about what the book is about. This first concept is then highly influential in the shaping of their reading of the book. The emphasis here is on the basic and most categorical proposition that the text is a particular instance of YHWH's word (or, perhaps, YHWH's instruction). The issue of authority and the related question of why this text is supposed to be read and reread (and copied, edited, etc.) are addressed by this proposition.

It is worth stressing also that YHWH's word or teaching is individualized by a reference to a human personage called Micah, and that this personage and YHWH's word are explicitly anchored in a certain section of the construed image of the past shared by the community of writers and readers within which the book was not only composed but also first read and reread. This past is explicitly marked as the days of Jotham, Ahaz, and Hezekiah.

Micah 1:1 also directly characterizes Micah as a Morashtite, and indirectly so characterizes the authorial voice and its intended audience, because the reference to Micah as a Morashtite conveys and shapes a perspective shared by the authorial voice and the intended audience that is external to Moresheth. Significantly, Micah is presented as another authoritative character from the monarchic period who was a non-Jerusalemite conveying a Jerusalem-centered theology (cf. Amos; on Obadiah see Ben Zvi, *Obadiah*, 38-39).

Micah 1:1 also prepares the readers of the book for a message of judgment against Samaria and Jerusalem. The unexpected binding of these two cities — along with the formal equivalence that suggests some degree of likeness between them — already conveys a negative characterization of monarchic Jerusalem and creates an expectation for a reference to its wrong ways and to its divine punishment.

Bibliography

P. R. Ackroyd, "The Biblical Interpretation of the Reigns of Ahaz and Hezekiah," in W. B. Barrick and J. R. Spencer, eds., *In the Shelter of Elyon: Essays on Ancient Palestinian Life and Literature in Honor of G. W. Ahlström* (JSOTSup 31; Sheffield: JSOT Press, 1984) 247-59; F. I. Andersen and D. N. Freedman, *Hosea* (AB 24; Garden City, N.Y.: Doubleday, 1980) 142-47; M. Broshi, "Tell Judeideh," *NEAEHL*, 3:837-38; F. C. Burkitt, "Micah 6 and 7: A Northern Prophecy," *JBL* 45 (1926) 159-61; R. P. Carroll, "Prophecy and Society," in R. E. Clements, ed., *The World of Ancient Israel* (Cambridge: Cambridge Univ. Press, 1991) 203-25; N. G. Cohen, "From Nabi to Mal'ak to

'Ancient Figure,'" *JSS* 36 (1985) 12-24; P. R. Davies, "The Audiences of Prophetic Scrolls: Some Suggestions," in S. B. Reid, ed., *Prophets and Paradigms: Essays in Honor of Gene M. Tucker* (JSOTSup 229; Sheffield: JSOT Press, 1996) 48-62; K. J. Dell, "The Misuse of Forms in Amos," *VT* 45 (1995) 45-61; S. Gibson, "The Tell ej-Judeideh (Tel Goded) Excavations: A Re-Appraisal Based on Archival Records in the Palestine Exploration Fund," *Tel Aviv* 21 (1994) 194-234; O. Grether, *Name und Wort Gottes im Alten Testament* (BZAW 64; Giessen: Töpelmann, 1934); G. Loughlin, "Using Scripture: Community and Letterality," in J. Davies et al., eds., *Words Remembered, Texts Renewed: Essays in Honour of John F. A. Sawyer* (JSOTSup 195; Sheffield: Sheffield Academic Press, 1995) 321-39; J. Nogalski, *Literary Precursors to the Book of the Twelve* (BZAW 217; Berlin: de Gruyter, 1993); S. Parpola, *Assyrian Prophecies* (SAA IX; Helsinki: Helsinki Univ. Press, 1997); G. M. Tucker, "Prophetic Superscriptions and the Growth of a Canon," in B. O. Long and G. W. Coats, eds., *Canon and Authority: Essays in Old Testament Religion and Theology* (Philadelphia: Fortress, 1977) 56-70; H.-M. Wahl, "Die Überschriften der Prophetenbücher," *ETL* 70 (1994) 91-104; J. Wellhausen, *Prolegomena to the History of Ancient Israel* (tr. A. Menzies and J. Black; Cleveland: Meridian, 1957).

PROPHETIC READING ABOUT
DIVINE JUDGMENT AND EXILE, 1:2-16

Structure

I. Divine judgment: presentation and explanation		2-7
A. Call to hear		2a
B. First explanation of the call		2b
C. Main explanation of the call: destructive theophany		3-4
D. Main explanation for the theophany		5
E. Divine announcement of judgment corroborating and		
further developing the preceding explanation		6-7
II. A threefold set of proper responses to the divine judgment		8-16
A. Mourning behavior and motive clause		8-9
1. Mourning behavior: short narrative		8
2. Motive clause for mourning behavior: Jerusalem		9
B. Dirge/taunt about objects of divine judgment and		
ambiguous corollary		10-15
C. Call to mourn and motive clause: exile		16

The focus of critical studies of this unit has often been on proposed forerunners of 1:2-16 and their respective historical circumstances. These forerunners are usually reconstructed according to principles of thematic or stylistic consistency, as these principles are perceived from the vantage point of a particular scholar, group of scholars, "school," or a particular "spirit of the times."

Thus, for instance, due to considerations of thematic consistency, Mays, Wolff, and many others assign v. 2 to a later redactor because of the prominent reference to a universal audience. Similarly, the reference to Judah and Jerusalem in v. 5b is considered an addition, or even a replacement of an original verset pointing to Samaria and Israel, because the original text is thought to be focused exclusively on the former. These considerations lead to proposals of a reconstructed original text that are, of course, consistent with the assumptions from which they arise (see, e.g., Hillers, *Micah,* 18-19; Mays, 45). Considerations of consistency in style and above all lexical repertoire lead scholars such as Jepsen, Schneider, and Nogalski to assume the presence of Hoseanic language (as opposed to what they consider to be the expected language of Micah) in Mic 1:6-7. Because of their different approaches to the redaction history of Micah as a whole, they explain their shared observations in different ways (see Jepsen; Schneider, 31-34; Nogalski, 138-40; cf. Peckham, 292-94). At times, arguments from an expected type of consistency in style and contents are brought together. For instance, Wolff maintains that "v. 13b fits neither the style nor the mood of its context," and accordingly he assigns it to a later redactor (see Wolff, *Micah,* 50; cf. Renaud, 55-56). As a result, a new text of v. 13 is brought about by the excision of v. 13b. This new text is, of course, more consistent with the mentioned principles, as understood by Wolff and others, and accordingly is considered to be more faithful to the original Hebrew text.

As these critical approaches are implemented in regard to 1:2-16 as a whole, the obvious result is a set of reconstructions of a proposed original text. These reconstructed texts usually share a common text (1:2-16 or a proposed text-critical version of 1:2-16) and "grow" out of it mainly by the deletion of those sections in the text that are marked out as secondary according to a set of principles of consistency (for misgivings concerning this procedure, see Hillers, *Micah,* 3-4). The resulting texts are then associated not with "Micah" the literary character created within the world of the book of Micah, but with "Micah" the historical prophet. This association is explicitly or implicitly grounded in an understanding of 1:1 (or a proposed, original version of it) as a reliable piece of historical information about monarchic Judah, and on an understanding of the reported (or constructed; see below) speeches in the proposed forerunner of 1:2-16 as, at least basically, a faithful representation of actual speeches delivered by the prophet Micah (and of God?) in the real world, in the time setting indicated by the superscription. Micah's authorship, either directly or vicariously (i.e., mediated by his students/disciples/tradents of his [living] words), is also often assumed. That is, the prophetic voice in the reconstructed text, its implied author, and its actual author tend to coalesce with the character mentioned in 1:1 (or any of its proposed original forms), and all of them (interpreted in a mimetic way) converge into and point to the "real-world," 8th-century prophet Micah. Headings such as "Micah, the man," or "Micah, the prophet," in critical studies attest explicitly to these tendencies in research (see, e.g., Wolff, *Micah the Prophet;* Mays, 15-21; Mason, 23-26).

Among others, the following "original" texts were "recovered" from 1:2-16 and associated with the historical prophet Micah: (1) vv. 3-5a, with the exception of *kî hinnēh* ("for behold") in v. 3, and vv. 8-16, with the exception of vv. 12b, 13b, and (perhaps) 16 (Mays); (2) vv. 6, 7b-13a, 14-16 (Wolff);

(3) vv. 10-13a, 14-15 (which were associated with 2:1-3*, 4*, 8-10; see Otto; cf. Lescow, "Komposition," which interacts with Otto's proposals). In sharp contrast, Hillers and Allen, to mention two, associate most if not all of 1:2-7/9, along with the rest of the section, with Micah, the 8th-century prophet.

The historical backgrounds of the proposed first texts have also received much attention in current research. For instance, Mays writes that "its [vv. 8-16] language gives the impression of composition while the invasion [Sennacherib's] was in full movement" (Mays, 53-54), whereas others associate these verses with the eve of the 701 campaign (Na'aman, "House of No-Shade," esp. 526-27), or including v. 16, the aftermath of this campaign (see Hillers, *Micah,* 30). Still others favor a date ca. 720 or 714-711 (e.g., Allen, 242; cf. Fohrer; Rudolph), or relate it to the Syro-Ephraimite conflict, and accordingly date it ca. 734 or slightly earlier (see, e.g., Donner; Freedman; Shaw, *Speeches,* 32-67, esp. pp. 56-67). Despite their differences, it is worth stressing that these scholars share in the main a common approach to the text. They tend to agree that the references or allusions made by the textually inscribed speaker to events such as the destruction of a city or town were directly and unequivocally related, at least in the original text, to actual, particular, historical events that happened either shortly before or soon after the composition of the text. Moreover, the temporal references conveyed by the speaker to the addressees in the world of the text tend to be interpreted mimetically, that is, in direct and univocal relation to the world outside the text. To illustrate, if the speaker's words in the text are understood to describe the fall of Samaria as standing in the future from the perspective of the utterance in the text, then the claim is often made that these words or this text were actually composed or uttered before the historical event, in this case, the fall of Samaria (e.g., Allen, 241; de Moor, 182; Alonso Schökel and Sicre Díaz, 2:1034; cf. Rudolph). This methodology leads to redactional models such as the one advanced by Renaud (48-49), according to which Micah the prophet composed 1:3-7* before the fall of Samaria, and after the event he reused his own old text by setting it within the frame of another text, the one communicating a threat toward Jerusalem, 1:3-7* + 8-16* (also cf. Alonso Schökel and Sicre Díaz, 2:1042-43; de Moor, 184-85).

One may notice, in short, that these approaches tend to focus their attention on a set of possible, but still speculative, reconstructions of the words of the historical Micah; these reconstructions are in the main achieved by selective deletions from the present text on the grounds of (1) perceived rules of stylistic, thematic consistency, and (2) an approach to the text that presupposes that its original version must have been consistent with an assumed high degree of direct correspondence between the world in the text and that of monarchic Judah in the 8th century. At times, similar attention is devoted to the work of the proposed subsequent editors of the book, that is, those who have added at different times the material that the scholar has "deleted" from the present text, according to the principles mentioned above.

My point of departure in this study is different. For all purposes, I focus on the text of the book of Micah, that is, a written text. I aim first at elucidating *its* (not *his*) likely message to *its* implied audience, and then the role that this book (and its reading) may have had in the community/ies within and for which the book of Micah — and not a possible but still speculative forerunner — was written.

Thus, within the limits of this section in the book (i.e., 1:2-16), I focus attention not on what portion of it could or could not have been uttered or composed by an 8th-century prophet, but on the way in which the intended rereader of the book was likely to approach the text of 1:2-16. What were the most conspicuous features and markers that would have helped the intended rereader to make sense of this text?

From this perspective, the first observation relevant to the structure of 1:2-16 seems to be that it begins with a call to hear that is reminiscent perhaps of a judicial setting (see below) and concludes with a call to mourn. These and other calls to perform some kind of activity in this unit are expressed by imperatives. Indeed, eight of the twenty-six imperatives in the book of Micah occur in this unit (e.g., v. 2: *šim'û* ["listen"], *haqšîbî* ["listen"]; v. 10: *hitpallĕšî* ["roll yourself over," *Q*]; v. 13: *rĕtōm* ["harness"]; v. 16: *gōzzî* ["cut off your hair"]). Of course, the readers of the book are not directly addressed by these imperatives, but nevertheless they are impressed by them. In other words, the imperatives fulfill an important affective function (cf. the concentration of imperatives in Deuteronomy; see also the discussion under Setting).

Calls to hear, expressed by imperative forms of *šm'*, are common introductory elements in the HB/OT in general and in prophetic literature in particular (see, e.g., Deut 6:4; Judg 5:3; 2 Kgs 7:1; Isa 1:2; 7:13; 48:1; Jer 10:1; Am 3:1; 4:1; 5:1; Mic 3:1; Prov 4:1; Job 34:2; cf. the "atypical" case of Lam 1:18). Further, the presence of these forms in Mic 1:2; 3:1; and 6:1, 2 may well mark main structural or discursive sections within the context of the entire book (cf. Hagstrom, 11-27, and the literature there).

In most instances in the HB/OT, the imperative calling to hear is immediately followed either by a vocative (i.e., by a reference to the one who is called to hear) or by a reference to the object of the "hearing," that is, what is to be heard (see Isa 48:1; Jer 10:1; Hos 5:1; Am 3:1; 4:1; 5:1; Mic 3:1). In any case, the main speech to be heard in the world of the book is placed in the text in close proximity to the imperative (e.g., Deut 6:4). Significantly, in Mic 1:2 the "slot" of what is to be heard seems to be left open. In fact, in this verse the call to hear is not followed at all by the main speech that those summoned by the call were supposed to hear (cf. Joel 1:2; Mic 3:1; 6:1; etc.). Instead of the expected address, the text in Mic 1:2 first advances an explanation for the call to hear (the *waw* that opens v. 2b is epexegetical; see *IBHS*, 33.2.2). Whereas this explanation provides a context for the anticipated address, and indeed may increase the expectation for the main address, it certainly cannot replace it — unless the readers of the text are so familiar with this defamiliarization of expectations that they immediately construe the implied address from the provided context. Then in vv. 3-4 the text follows and develops a second explanation; yet these verses do not provide the explicit or main address. Of course, this literary setting creates an open-ended situation that directs the attention of the readers.

This is only one example of the many "open ends" that occur in this

READING (i.e., 1:2-16; on the genre READING, see Genre below), and even within the narrower limits of its opening alone. For instance, the text is unclear about the role of the nations. Are they summoned (1) as witnesses (against Israel); (2) to be judged; (3) because they should implement the judgment; (4) because they will be negatively affected by Israel's judgment (which would suggest that they will suffer because of Israel's sin); or (5) any combination of these alternatives? The issue involves the long-standing debate about the meaning of *bākem* ("against you," NRSV; "among you," REB). In addition, the related issue of the extent of the area to be affected by the devastating theophany is also unclear (the issue involves the precise meaning or meanings of *'ereṣ,* "land/earth," in vv. 2 and 3). The same holds true about the exact identity of speaker and audience, and the rhetorical situation within the world of the text (notice the shift from 2nd to 3rd person created by *kullām,* "all of them," in v. 2; cf. Judg 16:18; NRSV "all of you" represents an "emendation" of MT's "all of them"). Nor is the nature and location of YHWH's holy place (heavenly abode, Zion/Jerusalem, both?) referred to in v. 3 unequivocal. (On these issues and some of their potential implications, see Ben Zvi, "Observations," and the bibliography there.)

Each of these at least potential ambiguities may or may not lead to "lasting equivocality" or to "polysemy," but in any case they serve to channel the attention of the rereaders. Significantly, as it becomes clear from the examples above, the attention of the readers is not simply channeled but channeled to issues of central importance in the theological or ideological discourse of the social group in which the book of Micah was written and for which it was written. Moreover, even if these issues are resolved or left open, they are addressed directly or indirectly in the ensuing text. Finally, the presence of ambiguities is most likely a precondition for the continuous rereading of the prophetic book by the community, and accordingly a genre requirement (see Ben Zvi, *Obadiah,* 4, et passim).

[An editorial comment: The use of the word "Zion" does not completely overlap that of the word "Jerusalem" in the HB/OT. Zion tends to be used more in cultic texts, in relation to Jerusalem as the city of YHWH and of YHWH's dwelling; moreover, it communicates a theological quality that is not always present in the word "Jerusalem" (see Stolz, 1072-73). Yet within the discourse of the period and that embedded and expressed in the book of Micah, Jerusalem and Zion are also one. Thus this volume often uses "Zion/Jerusalem" or "Jerusalem/Zion" to convey this understanding that the city is Jerusalem, in all its qualities including those fully in the realm of the material world, and it is also Zion, in all the qualities conveyed by that word in the discourse of the postmonarchic authors, readers, and rereaders of the book of Micah.]

That the call to hear is addressed to all the peoples and to the earth or land and all that are in it, along with the presence of *lĕʿēd* ("[be] a witness"), suggests that the text was written to evoke in its rereaders first an image of a cosmic judicial or trial setting, with YHWH as the implied judge (cf. Hos 4:1; Mic 6:1-2; Mays, 40). If this is so, then it is reasonable to assume that this setting either evoked or, better, reflected their image of a human court. One may mention that *lĕʿēd* ("[be] a witness") in itself is also likely to have carried multiple, connoted meanings; cf. with *lĕʿad*, "for the booty" (cf. Gen 49:27; Isa 33:23; Zeph 3:8); and with *lāʿad*, "forever," in Isa 30:8; 64:8; Am 1:11; Mic 7:18; and see Ben Zvi, "Observations."

Yet the text here is neither a transcript of an actual judicial or ritually enacted lawsuit (if the latter existed at all in ancient Israel; cf. the related discussion on whether there was a "prophetic lawsuit genre"; see Daniels and bibliography there) nor an attempt to convince its readers that such is the case, even within the literary world of the text. Indeed, the contrary holds true. The text explicitly defamiliarizes the "typical" court scene so as to disallow a mimetic reading of the text. (Cf. Dell's study of the "misuse" [*sic*] of forms in Amos.) A few examples will suffice. Contrary to expectations in a trial, the role of those who have been summoned to hear remains unclear, and so is the identity of the accused. Moreover, as mentioned above, the text following the call to attention presents an explanation for the call rather than the expected accusation (cf. Hos 4:1; Mic 3:1, 9; 6:1-2). Furthermore, whereas the call to attention and the expression *lĕʿēd* ("[be] a witness") contribute to the general flavor of the scene, so does the combined effect of the reference to *ʾereṣ ûmĕlōʾāh* ("O earth and all that is in it"; cf. Pss 24:1; 89:12 [NRSV 11]; also cf. 96:11; yet see also Isa 34:1) and to *hêkal qodšô* ("his holy temple"; cf. Jonah 2:5-8 [NRSV 4-7]; Hab 2:20; Pss 5:8 [NRSV 7]; 11:4; 79:1; 138:2). Yet the combined effect of the latter phrase was likely to lend a hymnic tone to the unit (cf. Mays, 40), and thus prepare the reader for the theophany described in the immediately following verses.

In part because of the aforementioned reasons, this commentary does not follow the traditional understanding of Mic 1:2-7 as a lawsuit, with v. 2 as a summons to witness, v. 5 as an indictment, and vv. 6-7 as a sentence. One may note also that this understanding fails to integrate fully the theophany (vv. 3-4) within the lawsuit pattern (cf. Stansell, 13). This situation has led to a number of redaction-critical explanations, which although possible remain by necessity hypothetical. In addition, given the many textually inscribed cohesive markers that link vv. 2-7 to the following verses (see below), an approach to the text that sets vv. 2-7 apart from the others is tantamount to reading against the grain of the text. Although such an approach is certainly not "wrong" in itself, it is not helpful for reconstructing either the ways in which the prophetic book was read or its theological message. Redaction-critical methods would, of course, focus on the text before the text, and for them such considerations do not apply; yet the weakness of these methods is the speculative character of their reconstructed textual history.

As mentioned above, the first explanation for the call to hear contributes to the judicial flavor of the text, yet also to its defamiliarization. The reference to *hêkal qodšô* ("his holy temple") is evocative of, and most likely activated in the readers, both the concept of heavenly abode and of Zion/Jerusalem as the holy abode of YHWH (cf. Jonah 2:5-8 [NRSV 4-7]; Pss 5:8 [NRSV 7]; 79:1; 138:2 with Ps 11:4; Hab 2:20). Significantly, the implied Jerusalem-centered perspective conveyed by this association is clearly at work and is communicated to the readers in the following sections of this READING (see Mic 1:8-16, esp. vv. 9, 12; see below).

The main explanation of the call is in terms of a theophany that involves a massive upheaval. Whether the imagery used for the theophany evolves out of that of an earthquake, a mighty storm, or even a marching army (cf. Crenshaw, 45; Shoemaker, 108), it can be correctly characterized as "stock imagery" (see Hillers, *Micah,* 20). Given the limitations inherent in stock imagery, it is striking that the language used here is clearly and closely related to that of the surrounding subunits in the text. Accordingly, it communicates to the readers a strong sense of cohesiveness within the text. The cumulative weight of, for instance, *qodšô* ("his holiness") and *mĕqômô* ("his place," vv. 2, 3), *'ereṣ* ("land," "earth," vv. 2, 3), *bāmôt* ("high places," vv. 3, 5), *yārad* ("come down," vv. 3, 12; cf. v. 4), and *'ēš* ("fire," vv. 4, 7) cannot be disregarded or explained as accidental. Further, only one word clearly stands out in v. 3 and has no direct relation with the any of the other units in Micah 1: *dārak* ("tread [on]"). Yet the presence of a verbal form from *drk* was almost required by the use of the expression *bāmôtê 'āreṣ* ("the high places of the earth"; see Crenshaw; for other positions see McKane, esp. 423-24). Significantly, the presence of the latter expression serves to support and to communicate clearly the cohesiveness of the text.

In addition, the language and imagery of v. 5 (e.g., the reference to "melting mountains" and to "wax" in this context) are reminiscent of psalmic literature (e.g., Pss 22:15 [NRSV 14]; 68:3 [NRSV 2]; 97:5) and are clearly suitable to a reference to *'ēš* ("fire"; cf. Ps 68:3 [NRSV 2]). One may mention also that the anaphoric character of *kol-zō't* ("all of this [is for]") contributes to that cohesiveness of the text (and cf. similarly the role of *'al-zō't,* "for this," in v. 8). (On textual cohesion in general, see, e.g., Renkema, 34-40; de Beaugrande and Dressler, 48-83.)

Given that the theophanic description is an integral and cohesive part of a larger text, and taking into account that it is preceded by vv. 1 and 2, this theophanic description does not create in the audience an expectation of salvation to Israel that is to turn around suddenly into punishment to their surprise (for a different approach see Stansell, 23), but it points to the cataclysmic power and divine source of the judgment against Israel and Judah, a judgment that leads to and culminates in exile (v. 16). Moreover, it already suggests to readers that this judgment implies an unnatural break in the proper divine order. Further, one may notice that even YHWH is imagined as coming out of YHWH's place because of the behavior of Israel (vv. 5-7).

Two observations concerning this theophany: (1) like many other texts (e.g., Psalm 1), this one reflects and communicates a worldview in which "fluidity" carries negative associations, and "stability" or "lack of movement" conveys positive associations (cf. Lack); (2) it also includes another, at the very least potentially, polysemic expression, *bāmôtê 'āreṣ* ("high places of the earth/world/land") that shows a built-in, denoted or connoted, ambiguity in regard to both nouns, and certainly as a whole (cf. Eng. "high places of the land/earth"). Moreover, the literary trajectory from *'ereṣ* in v. 2 to *'āreṣ* in v. 3, and from *bāmôtê 'āreṣ* ("high places of the earth/world/land") in v. 3 to *bāmôt yĕhûdâ* ("high place of [the land of] Judah") in v. 5 could not have been missed by the competent rereaders for whom the book was written. This trajectory leads the readers to an ongoing narrowing of their possible understanding of *'ereṣ*. (On these issues see Ben Zvi, "Observations.")

The flow of the unit seems to be governed by a consistent, implied, and perhaps didactic question, "Why?" which leads from explanation to explanation (cf. the role of *bĕpešaʿ* X ["for the transgression of X"] in Prov. 12:13; 28:2; 29:6; see structural outline above). At this stage in the text, the question is why this destructive theophany takes place at all. The answer is given in v. 5. Such an answer is also explicitly and strongly linked to the preceding text by *ʿal-zōʾt* (notice also the reference to *bāmôt yĕhûdâ*); that is, there are textually inscribed cohesive ties that ask the rereaders to approach v. 5 in the context of the preceding unit.

It is clear from the explanation advanced in v. 5 that the aforementioned massive upheaval, *all* of it, was unequivocally due to the transgression(s) and sins of Israel (on "Israel" see below). But on whose understanding? If v. 5 is approached from the perspective of v. 4, then one may assume that the "prophet" is the speaker; yet if one approaches v. 5 from the perspective of v. 6, then the most likely speaker is YHWH. Thus v. 5 turns into a Janus verse, looking both to what precedes and to what follows. Accordingly, this verse creates a gray area of overlap between the speech of two characters, YHWH and the "prophet," which in turn shapes in the readers a sense of association — or even loose identification — between the two (cf. vv. 8-9; cf. Dempsey, 83; on these issues see also Ben Zvi, "Observations." Gray areas occur in other sections of Micah as discussed, e.g., in the Structure section of the commentary concerning 2:1-5, 6-11; 3:1-12).

Significantly, this is not the only equivocal or, better, multivalent element in this seemingly unequivocal explanation. For instance, depending on one's understanding of the referent of *bāmôtê ʾāreṣ*, the nations are envisaged as either suffering because of Israel's sins (cf. Zeph 1:18) or not (see discussion of v. 2 above). In addition, who is/are/were the referent/s signified by "the house of Israel" in v. 5? On the surface, the parallelism between *bĕḥaṭṭōʾwt bêt yiśrāʾēl* ("for the sins of the house of Israel") and *bĕpešaʿ yaʿăqōb* ("for the transgressions of Jacob") seems to suggest an identification between "Jacob" and "the house of Israel," and since *pešaʿ yaʿăqōb* is then identified as Samaria, the text may seem to suggest an identification of "the house of Israel" with the northern kingdom of Israel (i.e., to the exclusion of Judah). Yet the structure of the verse and the explicit choice of words in the verse point clearly to the equivalence between *pešaʿ yaʿăqōb* in v. 5aα and 5bα. Such an equivalence clearly suggests the one between "the house of Israel" and "Judah" (at the center of the latter stands Jerusalem). Such a suggestion is eventually reinforced by the transformation of the meaning conveyed by the term "Israel." First, in the present instance, it points to an ambiguous referent. Then it points to Judah in v. 14, because the most likely referent of *malkê yiśrāʾēl* (lit. "kings of Israel") is "kings of Judah" in this verse (cf. 2 Chr 20:34 [contrast with 1 Kgs 22:46 (NRSV 45)]; cf. also 2 Chr 21:2; 28:19, 27; 33:18). Further, in Mic 1:15 as part of the expression *kĕbôd yiśrāʾēl* ("the glory of Israel"), "Israel" refers to a theological concept (or perhaps to Judah?), certainly not to the northern kingdom alone. This usage of language obviously reveals a theology or ideology that identifies Judah with Israel. Such a theology is only possible if "Israel" is already more of a theological and ideological concept than a narrowly defined "geographical-political" one. (On these issues see Ben Zvi, "Observations"; idem, "Inclusion.")

If, or when, v. 5 is read with the prophet in mind as the speaker, it becomes clear that the power to summon all the nations to observe the coming theophany, and to know the reason for its coming, points to the extent of the authority claimed by, or attributed to, the human speaker in this text. It is not surprising, therefore, that the text is shaped so as to strengthen the argument in support of this claim. Among the literary devices that contribute to this goal are the general introduction to the book and the close association between the character of the prophet and of YHWH that is conveyed by the aforementioned gray area of overlap between their speeches. The presence of a reported divine speech that assumes the truth-value of the words of the human speaker may also fulfill this literary and theological function. YHWH's direct speech in vv. 6-7 may be approached in this light. This speech is written in such a way that it presumes the presence of the preceding verses in the text, not only from a general contextual position but even from a formal viewpoint; see, for instance, the *wqtl* form, which is not supposed to open an independent narrative (e.g., A. Nicacci, *The Syntax of the Verb in Classical Hebrew Prose* [tr. W. G. E. Watson; JSOTSup 86; Sheffield: JSOT Press, 1990] 82).

Thus the text on the one hand acknowledges a differentiation between the two voices but on the other hand stresses the basic unity of their message and, accordingly, legitimizes and empowers the human voice in the text. This is not surprising because the message of the book — namely, of YHWH's word — is conceived from the outset as one to be conveyed by both the divine and the human voice in the text, as an analysis of the prophetic books explicitly called "YHWH's word" shows.

Even within this small unit of speech (vv. 6-7) stylistic features present elsewhere, either in Micah 1 or in the rest of the book, are easily recognizable. For instance, this is the first case in Micah of an explicit rhetorical question. Such a literary device is widely used in the book as a whole (e.g., 3:1; 4:8-9; 6:3, 6-7, 10-11; 7:18; cf. Shaw, *Speeches,* 54, and bibliography there). Within the world of the text, these questions help the speaker to draw the attention of the addressees. Yet these questions may — and most likely were intended to — fulfill a similar role in regard to those "overhearing" these reported speeches by means of their reading of the written text (cf. the case of "hear!" vs. "read!"; cf. below, Setting). Moreover, patterns of repetition of one type or another are pervasive in Micah 1. They are most conspicuous in vv. 10-16, but also are present in vv. 4, 8, and 6-7 (see *'āśîm šĕmāmâ* ["I will lay desolate"] and notice the triple repetition of *'etnan* ["wages"] in v. 7; *śamtî šōmrôn* ["I will make Samaria"] in v. 6; cf. the double *peša' ya'ăqōb* ["the transgressions of Jacob"] in v. 5; on these issues see Petrotta, 65-89).

Verses 6-7 move from the general imagery of the destruction of Samaria — namely, the destruction of the urban center and the reincorporation of its area into the general agrarian landscape — to an explanation of the reason for this divine action by means of a seemingly factual report of future and sure destruction. This accords with the pervasive tendency to attach an implicit or explicit motive clause at the end of each section dealing with a reported action.

The references to *pĕsîleyhā* ("her images"), *ʿăṣabbeyhā* ("her idols"; cf. Pss 115:4; 135:15), and *ʾetnan zônâ* ("wages of a prostitute"), all in v. 7, obviously point to sinful cultic behavior, as considered from the usual perspective informing the HB/OT. The first two terms occur also in Isa 10:10-11, another text that first associates Samaria with Jerusalem within the setting of punishment, and then clearly shows that Jerusalem is different (cf. Micah 1; see below). The third term present in Isa 10:10-11, *ʾĕlîleyhā* ("her gods"), is not present in Mic 1:7, and it might be inappropriate in the context of Micah. Yet, especially given the pervasive presence of puns and plays on dominant sounds in 1:2-16, one cannot but notice the conspicuous presence of a word such as *ʾêlîlâ* ("I will wail"; of course, the point made here is based on the sounds present in this word, not on its meaning) at the beginning of v. 8. Significantly, *ʾêlîlâ* and the two words immediately following it in v. 8, *ʾêlĕkâ šêlāl* ("I will go stripped," *K*), create a textual environment characterized by an unmistakable repetition of sounds.

The third item present in Mic 1:7, as opposed to Isa 10:10-11, is *ʾetnanneyhā* ("her wages"). Significantly, the reference to *ʾetnanneyhā* here is associated with the development of the accusation against Samaria, as it leads to the phrase *ʾetnan zônâ* (cf. Deut 23:19). This accusation activates (among other things) the "traditional" yet problematic biblical topos of the unfaithful city/woman, the polemic associations of prostitution and cult in regard to Samaria (e.g., Hosea), and the well-known polemic concerning the "idolatrous" character of the cult of the northern kingdom (not only *pĕsîleyhā* but also *ʿăṣabbeyhā* is significant in this regard; see, e.g., Pss 115:4; 135:15).

In addition, the three references to *ʾetnan* in Mic 1:7 along with that to *tannîm* ("jackals"; again, the point here is based on the dominant sounds present in this word) in v. 8 serve to convey a sense of textual cohesion based on the conspicuous repetition of consonants. Given the pervasiveness of patterns of repetition of sounds in ch. 1, it is most reasonable to assume that these repetitions bore meaningful messages to the intended audience of this text and contributed to its textual cohesiveness.

The combined occurrence of words from the root *glh* ("uncover/go into exile"; cf. v. 16), and especially from *qbṣ* ("gather") and *šûb* ("return") in vv. 6-7 within a context of judgment, are also worth noting. (For text-critical issues concerning vv. 6-7, and esp. the question of *qbṣh* see Barthélemy et al., 3:713-16 and bibliography; cf. Watson, "Allusion.")

On the surface the description of YHWH's judgment in vv. 6-7 concerns only Samaria. It is also true that a reading of this text that is absolutely decontextualized will necessarily lead to that conclusion. But it is highly unlikely that the intended readers of ch. 1 would have read this text in a decontextualized manner, the more so given the explicit formal and linguistic ties that link these verses to those surrounding them and to the READING as a whole. Thus there is no doubt that v. 1 and then v. 4 must have alerted the readers of the book that the punishment of Samaria is not meant to be the high point of the text, but only a useful and heavily connoted literary corridor that will lead them to the main chamber, namely, the fate of a sinning Judah and above all Jerusalem. I must stress that the presence of such a literary corridor delays the expected description of the punishment, but at the same time conveys a sense of inevitability to it and heightens the expectations of the readers. For these reasons and, of course, from the perspective of the present text, it seems inappropriate to classify this reference to Samaria's judgment as a "sentence" and to relate it to a divine lawsuit against it. The issue for the rereaders of 1:2-16 is never really Samaria, but Jerusalem. (For the proposal that the choice of words in 1:6 stresses the similarity between the fates of Samaria and Jerusalem in 3:12 see, e.g., Wagenaar, "Hillside.")

The divine action calls for a response. A threefold response is presented to the readers of the text as proper behavior in these circumstances. This response includes mourning, lament, and further mourning. Yet at each stage the text is crafted to provide to the readers not only a reference concerning a type of appropriate behavior but also additional divine knowledge about central theological issues. To illustrate, the first mourning unit leads to a motive clause that brings to the forefront the issue of Jerusalem and its particular fate. The following lament or taunt is composed around puns on words and assumes an intended rereadership that is most appreciative of them. Yet this somewhat ironic parade of towns to be punished by YHWH also communicates and reflects the distinctive status of Jerusalem vis-à-vis all other cities, though from a slightly different perspective (see below). Finally, the last call to mourning brings to the surface the issue of the exile and, within this context, the reasons behind it.

Verses 8-9 are also Janus verses in that they provide a necessary bridge between vv. 6-7 and 10-15 (cf. Dempsey, 83). They are obviously linked by their contents to the lament in vv. 10-15 and are clearly tied to the preceding unit by 'al-zō't ("for this"; cf. Ps 32:6). They are usually attributed to the human speaker (for a recent exception see Beal), but no clear syntactical or grammatical markers are present to urge the readers to shift their understanding of who is speaking from YHWH (vv. 6-7) to the prophet at the beginning of v. 8. The idea that such a metaphorical reference to YHWH (as lamenting and walking "stripped and naked" as a sign of mourning, and the like) is unthinkable is correct in relation to later understandings (cf. Tg.), but not necessarily true in regard to the discourse of a "biblical" community (see, e.g., Isa 63:10; see Gerstenberger and Schrage, and the long-standing point about YHWH's pathos made by Heschel, 151-52, 226, et passim). Indeed, it is reasonable to assume that also in this case the readers faced a gray area, even if admittedly they might have considered the prophet to be the more likely speaker. One may note that if one emends makkôteyhā ("her wounds") to makat yh(wh) ("YH[WH]'s wound"; so, e.g., Elliger, BHS), then the gray area disappears. Yet there is no textual support for such an emendation, nor is it likely. See, for instance, Barthélemy et al., 3:717, and the bibliography there.

The most salient feature of v. 8 is perhaps its language (see Ben Zvi, "Observations") and the patterns of repetition found in its first versets (see Wolff, Micah, 43); the most conspicuous element in the message conveyed by v. 9 concerns the implied status of Jerusalem. Significantly, v. 9 explicitly introduces a new motive for the preceding mourning activities: the disaster (i.e., YHWH's judgment, which is here described as the "incurable wound," as it is the case elsewhere in the HB/OT [see Jer 15:18] and in other ancient Near Eastern texts; see Hillers, *Treaty-Curses,* 64-66) has come to Judah and "reached" Jerusalem. The heightening sequence leading finally to Jerusalem and the reference to Jerusalem as *š'ar 'ammî* ("the gate of my people"; cf. Obad 13) reflect clearly and above all communicate the Jerusalem-centered theological perspective that informs and shapes the text. Yet this unequivocal claim about the theological and ideological status of Jerusalem is coupled with an equivocal claim about its reported fate. Is this *'ad* ("to") inclusive of Jerusalem (cf., e.g., Gen 13:3; 50:10; Judg 11:16; 2 Kgs 18:8) or is this an exclusive "to"? In other words, what does the text say about Jerusalem itself? Did the divine punishment fall on the city or not?

Given the context of the following verses, the first *'ad* in the verse was most likely understood as inclusive. This consideration and the repetitive pattern clearly present in the verse most likely suggested to the readers that Jerusalem was also under the divine judgment. Yet the full expression *nāga' 'ad* ("it has reached/touched to") might have suggested to them the opposite conclusion. This expression plays not only on the pair *makkâ* ("wound/blow")–*nāga'* (in the nominal form, "affliction/blow"; cf. Exod 11:1 with 1 Sam 4:8; and notice the somewhat similar semantic relation between the pair *pāsîl/pesel* ["image"] and *'āṣāb* ["idol"]; see, e.g., Pss 115:4; 135:15) but is suggestive of a situation that comes near X, almost at X, but does not reach X (cf. Ps 107:18). Hence, again, it is most likely that the readers were left to ponder.

But if so, were the readers supposed to understand this text as Micah's (or YHWH's or both) reference to the events of 701, or to those of 586, or to another event of the same kind? Alternatively, was it an equivocal reference written so as to suit more than one referent, and as such to be understood by the intended audience of this READING?

To be sure, if the Micah of the text was imagined by the intended reader as one who *must* have prophesied about political events that *must* have occurred in the span of time described in v. 1, then the events of 586 are out of the question, and a decision should be made among those of 734-732, 722, 712, or 701. (On the concept and use of "intended reader" in historical-critical studies of religious literature, cf. Kraemer.) But is this the case? The prophetic books describe prophets as people who certainly may prophesy concerning events far in their future, at least from the perspective of the historical background ascribed to them by the superscriptions. For instance, the book of Isaiah, as a whole, asserts that a prophet who was active during the reigns of Uzziah, Jotham, Ahaz, and Hezekiah (cf. Micah) prophesied about people and events of a much later period, such as Cyrus and the return from the exile (cf., e.g., Mic 4:6; 7:12). Moreover, the fact remains that the text does not provide its readers with any clear marker to anchor it to any historical event (see also below). Indeed, the opposite is true: the text leaves them to ponder whether Jerusalem fell under YHWH's judgment or was "saved" when the wave of destruction stopped just before it (cf. also 2 Sam 24:16; 1 Chr 1:15).

The next unit is the lament, which also serves as a taunt, in vv. 10-15.

The text is difficult at many points, and as expected in such cases, many textual emendations have been proposed. (On these issues see, e.g., Barthélemy et al., 3:720-25, and the bibliography there; see also Petrotta, 65-85, and the works mentioned there). Several redactional proposals have been advanced to solve some of the cruxes as well (e.g., Mays [58] considers the reference to the gate of Jerusalem to be a redactional addition). Even when the text is more or less agreed upon, its meaning is often disputed. (For these reasons there is a relatively large research corpus dealing with this unit; see, e.g., Hillers, *Micah,* 24-30; Wolff, *Micah,* 48-51, 59-64; Shaw, *Speeches,* 32-67; Petrotta, 69-85; van der Woude, "Micha 1 10-16"; Na'aman, "House of No-Shade"). Still, all are likely to agree on two features: the text is shaped around a variety of wordplays (including but not restricted to paronomasia; see Petrotta), and a number of towns from the Shephelah figure prominently both as targets of taunt and as a reason for lament.

Whereas much modern research has focused on the identification of the precise historical circumstances in which the original version of the taunt or lament was likely composed as a work separate from a still nonexistent book of Micah, neither the author/s of Micah 1 nor its intended audience seems concerned with these matters. Unlike prophetic texts that are anchored to particular events and historical circumstances, as the latter are construed from the vantage point of the intended audience, 1:10-15 is clearly unmarked. One may contrast this text with, for instance, Isa 20:1-2; 36:1; Jer 25:1-3. Indeed, it is because Mic 1:10-15 is clearly unmarked in this regard that alternative, scholarly proposals concerning the precise date of the original taunt could have been advanced. Rather than succeeding in demonstrating an unequivocal relation between the text here and certain historical events, such a proliferation seems to attest to the basic "openness" of the text in this matter.

Moreover, given the centrality of Jerusalem in the text and the mocking tone of the language, and especially its emphatic *nomen-omen* perspective, it is even doubtful that the intended audience of the book of Micah would have considered 1:10-15 mainly as an expression of the deep sorrow of a Shephelite (i.e., Micah) who is lamenting the loss of his homeland or is in dread of its imminent loss (so, e.g., Mays, 54). Significantly, the possible association of Micah with one of the towns mentioned in vv. 10-15 that could have contributed to this dimension of the text is not even worked out in these verses; indeed, even the identification of Micah's hometown with one of the towns mentioned here is left equivocal (→ 1:1).

As it stands, the text in vv. 10-15 is closely linked to the rest of ch. 1; in other words, those responsible for ch. 1 wished the intended audience of these verses to approach them as an integral part of this larger unit rather than as a dissociated unit, a pericope by itself. Not only do vv. 10-15 assume a preceding text, but also clear language links are easily recognizable (e.g., the references to "descending," to "gate," to Jerusalem; see vv. 12b and 9b, and vv. 3b and 12b). In addition, the literary trajectory of the term "Israel" cuts across the borders of the subunit. Furthermore, the tendency toward equivocality that leads to multiple rereadings that is well attested elsewhere in this text is also present in vv. 10-15. For instance, in v. 12a ḥālâ, ṭôb, and mar/mārôt all may convey more than one meaning. The first may be related to *yḥl*, "wait" (e.g., R. L. Smith, 19, 20); to *ḥlh*, "grow tired/sick" or perhaps "be anxious," "be in anguish," "long"; or even to *ḥwl*, "shake/dance"; *ṭôb* may have conveyed the meanings of "good" or "sweet" or both; *mar/mārôt* may have evoked an association with "bitter things" but also with "rebellion." V. 11 plays the name *ṣa'ănān* (probably the same town referred to as *ṣĕnān* in Josh 15:37) against *yṣ'*, *ṣō'n*, and probably even *ša'ănān* (von Soden).

Much more significant issues come to the forefront in the equivocal language of v. 15, the conclusion of the lament. Here *hayyōrēš* may refer to "the (rightful) inheritor" or to "the dispossessor," and *kĕbôd yiśrā'ēl* ("the honor [or glory] of Israel") may be interpreted as a reference to Israel's wealth, might, army, or even to YHWH (see, e.g., Num 24:11; Isa 10:3; 66:1 for "wealth"; Isa 8:7; 21:16 for "army"; and Jer 2:11; Ps 106:20 [cf. Deut 10:21; Ps 3:4(NRSV 3)] for "YHWH"; see also Ben Zvi, "Observations"). Thus v. 15, as a whole, could have evoked more than one possible scenario, indeed, even contradictory scenarios. The potential counterclaim that a "salvation" scenario was impossible because the preceding text points to judgment does not hold in the theological and literary world represented by the book of Micah and other prophetic books in which judgment is usually followed by a note of hope and salvation (see, e.g., 2:12-13). Moreover, the potential multivalence of this verse is even enhanced by the probably connoted wordplay between *'ădullām* and *'ad-'ōlām* ("forever") that may communicate a background, secondary message of "the glory of Israel shall come forever." For different proposals regarding "forever" that involve textual emendation, see Elliger, *BHS;* Weiser, 240; Vuilleumier, 19, 23.

The distinctiveness of Jerusalem vis-à-vis the other towns is perhaps conveyed by the general, middle position of the reference to it in vv. 10-15 (Petrotta's count of six place-names before and after Jerusalem is strained; see Petrotta, 85). Much more significant in this regard is the continuous, equivocal language concerning the question of whether Jerusalem itself was affected by YHWH's judgment, which is called here *rā' mē'ēt yhwh* ("evil from YHWH"). Control over the gate most often communicates control over the city (see Gen 22:17; 24:60), and "gate" is actually used as a metonym for "city" on a number of occasions (e.g., Deut 12:12, 15, 21; 17:2, et passim in Deuteronomy; Obad 11). In other words, the fate of Jerusalem remains a central, open issue, claiming the attention of the intended reader. Yet the most revealing item in regard to the theology or ideology reflected and communicated by this text concerns the fact that the towns (and if one follows Na'aman, even the Assyrian Empire) are the object of a direct or indirect mocking based on a wordplay that associates the name of the city with its fate. Thus the fate of the location is tied to an essential and basic feature of the city. In other words, in the horizon of the world conveyed by this language, what will happen to a town is what was supposed to happen to it from the very beginning (or at least since it began to be referred to by the relevant appellative, i.e., *nomen-omen*). Since it is obvious that those responsible for this text were masters of wordplays and that their intended audience was well attuned to them, it is most remarkable that Jerusalem unlike all others was kept aside from this set of wordplays. To be sure, the issue is not likely to be related to any property in the word *yĕrûšālaim* ("Jerusalem"), which could have easily been linked to *yrš* (verbal forms: "take possession," "inherit," or "dispossess"; nominal forms: "inheritor" or "dispossessor"; cf. v. 15), to *šlm* ("repay"; cf. Jer 51:56), or even to *šālôm* ("peace, well-being"), but to the theological concept of Jerusalem: a city *essentially* unlike others. This text reflects and communicates that perspective.

From a structural viewpoint the concluding note of the entire section (v. 16) might seem like nothing more than a short pericope that somewhat formally brings to three the number of proper responses to the circumstances described in the preceding pericopes in the text. But such a viewpoint is misleading. V. 16 contains a call to perform mourning rituals ("make yourself bald . . .") expressed by an imperative, and a final motive clause. The call to mourn provides a corresponding reference to the call to hear at the beginning of 1:2-16, and along with it encapsulates the transformation or trajectory undergone by the world in the text. The motive clause brings along the concluding and heightened reference to the results of YHWH's judgment: "for they have gone from you into exile."

Yet the unequivocal reference to exile is also mixed here with equivocal, potentially polyvalent expressions. Who is "you" (fem. sg.) in this text? Certainly a female figure who is imagined as the mother of the exiles, who is identified with "Israel." Is this mother Zion (cf. Dobbs-Allsopp, 461-62) represented as a sg. distressed female figure, as opposed to the masc. pl. reference to the "peoples" at the beginning of the unit? This is the most likely primary referent — particularly so, given the centrality of Jerusalem in vv. 10-15 — but significantly it is not clearly marked by the text. What does it mean concerning the fate of Jerusalem? Again the text does not allow a clear conclusion, for Mother Zion may mourn the exile of Jerusalemites, but also that of non-Jerusalemite Judahites, including the residents of the other towns mentioned in vv. 10-15 (cf. Allen, 242; Mays, 60; Wolff, *Micah,* 64). The openness of the text is perhaps the most unequivocal feature. The text does not tag the mentioned exile to a particular, precise situation (neither pre– nor post–701 BCE, nor post–586 BCE), and therefore it allows the intended audience of the written text of 1:2-16 to develop multiple readings and understandings of the text.

Genre

The genre of 1:2-16 as a whole is PROPHETIC READING. Given the textually inscribed markers mentioned above, it seems that the text is written so as to suggest to its intended reader that it is to be read as such. It seems reasonable to assume that the intended reader of the text resembles to some extent the actual readers of the text (cf. Kraemer) and, accordingly, that the text is actually reread by the community within which and for which it is so composed in a way that is coherent with the discursive markers mentioned above.

The word *reading* in the aforementioned definition points to the fact that this is a written text to be read and reread as a cohesive unit by a community of readers. The term *prophetic* points to the fact that this reading is a unit within a "prophetic book" and therefore that it claims to carry the authority and legitimacy associated with YHWH, and is most likely understood by the readers as such.

It is also most likely that these rereaders recognize elements of different genres within the literary world of the text. Or, to phrase it differently, the text is likely composed to evoke in its readers an association with literary genres, settings, and scenes that are part of their world of knowledge. For instance, as mentioned above, the text evokes some aspects of a court scene and of a lawsuit in vv. 2-7. It is true that the latter are defamiliarized in the text. Yet defamiliarization implies from the outset an awareness of what is familiar. Another example: vv. 10-15 follow the pattern of a dirge. The readers' understanding of 1:2-16 is dependent on their recognition of such a pattern in these verses, as well as on the recognition of the elements of a taunt embedded in vv. 10-15. Yet the textual cohesiveness that shapes 1:2-16 as a single unit leads them not to read vv. 10-15 separate from 1:2-9, 16. Thus the dirgelike character of vv. 10-15 (and their implied setting) does not lead to a recognition of the presence of a real (or typical) dirge even within the world of the text, but it stands as an important contribution at the service of a literary, written text whose genre is certainly not a dirge but a PROPHETIC READING.

The general tendency in the study of the book of Micah has been to divide the present unit into two main sections, each with its own genre. The first section, vv. 2-7/9*, is generally associated with some kind of lawsuit that is introduced by a summons to court and leads to an announcement of judgment against Samaria (the accused) and within which a theophany is included (e.g., Vargon, 35). Some scholars would separate the two, and much depends on each scholar's view of the redactional history of this section (see above, Structure). Vv. 2-5a have also been categorized as a "prophetic summons of the accused" (so Shoemaker, 112-19). The second main section, vv. 10-16*, is often described as a dirge or lament. It has also been characterized as an announcement of judgment, though one expressed in a very different form than, for instance, the one in vv. 6-7 (cf. Westermann, *Basic Forms,* 203). Both of these sections, or better their original cores, are usually associated with different historical circumstances (see above).

Setting

The wordplays, the many trajectories, and the multiple connoted and denoted readings and the possibilities that they open and close, along with the balance between unequivocal and equivocal statements and descriptions, all point not only to the written character of the text but also to an intended, highly educated audience: the literati. In view of the importance that these literati gave to the texts they read and that they considered them YHWH's word, one may assume that at least in their eyes they were brokers of divine knowledge (i.e., YHWH's word) to those who could not read and understand the text by themselves, that is, the vast majority of Israel. (On these issues and their implications, see also Ben Zvi, *Obadiah;* idem, "Urban Center"; idem, "Observations," and, most recently, idem, "Introduction.")

It is true that here, as in much of biblical literature, the command to the addressees in the world of the text is "hear" rather than "read." Yet it is obvious that in the book of Micah — that is, a written text — the call to attention is aimed not only or even mainly to the mentioned "literary" addressees but to the actual readers of the text. Whereas for the literary addressees (i.e., "peoples, all of them, and earth and all that is in it") *šm'* in v. 2 indicates "hear," for the actual rereaders of the written text of 1:2-16 *šm'* functions as a textually inscribed sign meaning "read," or, even better, "read carefully" (cf., e.g., Deut 6:4).

The numerous references to direct speech and especially the recurrence of oral commands most likely reflect past historical circumstances in monarchic times, or the reconstruction of them accepted by the community of writers and readers within which the book of Micah was written, or both. These texts shape an image of the past in which prophets act as oral speakers and divine communication takes place in oral speech.

Yet this literary setting of the world shaped by the main characters of the book seems undermined by the lack of mimetic correspondence between the speeches reported in the book and actual speeches that may have been given in a real-life setting that is similar to the one suggested by the book. Significantly, the discrepancies between the two are not restricted to those inherent to reported (or better, "constructed") speech (cf. Tannen; Meier), such as compactedness. In addition to these, the discrepancies include the conspicuous fact that the choice of words and the organization of the speeches assigned to each of the speakers in 1:2-16 depends on and reflects other constructed speeches in this unit, whether uttered by the same character to different addressees — and perhaps against different putative settings — or by different characters (e.g., in one case a human voice and in the other, YHWH's). In other words, the speaker is described as keeping an eye on other addressees within the same literary unit in addition to, or even rather than, the purported addressees. Moreover, the blurring of the identity of the divine and human speakers as carried out by the text (and whose purpose within the reading has been discussed above) also does not seem to enhance the mimetic character of the constructed speeches (i.e., their resemblance to real speech), even if the speech is set within a community situated in the past from the vantage point of the community of writers and readers of the book, namely, one that lived in the monarchic period as the later community imagined it.

One should notice also that, at a different level, these texts convey an image of a past that is closer in time to the community of readers and writers within which and for which the book of Micah is composed and redacted. Indeed, this past might even reflect their present too. This image is conveyed by the characterization of the implied author of the book and its intended reader. Both are presented as belonging to a group deeply involved in accessing "YHWH's word" (i.e., divine knowledge, a prophetic book such as the book of Micah) by means of reading and rereading written — and sophisticated — texts.

I must also mention that direct speech and especially oral commands are not only a function of a particular image of the past but also a stylistic feature widely and effectively used to elicit an affective response in readers and rereaders of written texts (e.g., Sanders, passim). The latter observation is most relevant since *direct* access to the particular instance of YHWH's word discussed here (i.e., the *written* text of the book of Micah) is only through reading and rereading, and since the author or authors of the text were certainly aware that such is the case.

Of course, the affective aspect of direct speech would have been at work also if literati were to read the text aloud to a general public, before they proceeded to explain its meaning to that public (see above; cf. Nehemiah 8). It is reasonable to assume that in such cases the presence of direct speech most likely contributes to the enhancement of the identification of the public to whom the text is being read with at least some of the addressees created within the world of the book.

Intention

The intention of 1:2-16 is to express and to shape both a communally accepted — at the very least, interpersonal — theological discourse in general, and to address the issue of exile in particular, from the assumed perspective of YHWH's word. Within the ideological discourse reflected and shaped by the text, issues such as the distinctiveness of Jerusalem, the referent or referents of the term "Israel," and the role of the nations in the divine economy are of central importance and not easily resolved, as the continuous ambiguities around them clearly suggest.

Although it is not the intention of the text, because of its literary characteristics the text contributes to and, at the very least, is consistent with the social and theological role of the literati as brokers of divine knowledge to the general community.

Bibliography

T. K. Beal, "The System and the Speaking Subject in the Hebrew Bible: Reading for Divine Abjection," *BibInt* 2 (1994) 171-89; R. A. de Beaugrande and W. U. Dressler, *Introduction to Text Linguistics* (London/New York: Longman, 1981); J. L. Crenshaw, " 'Wᵉdōrēk ʿal-bāmŏtê ʾāreṣ,' " *CBQ* 34 (1972) 39-53; D. R. Daniels, "Is There a 'Prophetic Lawsuit' Genre?" *ZAW* 99 (1987) 339-60; K. J. Dell, "The Misuse of Forms in Amos," *VT* 45 (1995) 45-61; J. C. de Moor, "Micah 1: A Structural Approach," in W. van der Meer and J. C. de Moor, eds., *The Structural Analysis of Biblical and Canaanite Poetry* (JSOTSup 74; Sheffield: JSOT Press) 172-85; C. J. Dempsey, "The Interplay between Literary Form and Technique and Ethics in Micah 1–3" (Ph.D. diss., Catholic Univ. of America, 1994); F. W. Dobbs-Allsopp, "The Syntagma of *bat* Followed by a Geographical Name in the Hebrew Bible: A Reconsideration of Its Meaning and Grammar," *CBQ* 57 (1995) 451-70; K. Elliger, "Die Heimat des

Propheten Micha," *ZDPV* 57 (1934) 81-152; repr. in *Kleine Schriften zum Alten Testament* (TBü 32; Munich: Kaiser, 1966) 9-71; D. N. Freedman, "Discourse on Prophetic Discourse," in H. B. Huffmon, F. A. Spina, and A. R. W. Green, eds., *The Quest for the Kingdom of God: Studies in Honor of G. E. Mendenhall* (Winona Lake, Ind.: Eisenbrauns, 1983) 142-58; V. Fritz, "Das Wort gegen Samaria," *ZAW* 86 (1974) 316-31; D. E. Gowan, "The Beginings of the Exile-Theology and the Root *glh*," *ZAW* 87 (1975) 204-7; A. J. Heschel, *The Prophets* (New York: Harper & Row, 1962); A. Jepsen, "Kleine Beiträge zum Zwölfprophetenbuch I," *ZAW* 56 (1938) 85-101; D. Kraemer, "The Intended Reader as a Key to Interpreting the Bavli," *Prooftexts* 13 (1993) 125-39; R. Lack, "Le Psaume 1 — Une analyse structurale," *Bib* 57 (1976) 154-67; W. McKane, "Micah 1,2-7," *ZAW* 107 (1995) 420-34; N. Na'aman, "Sennacherib's Campaign to Judah and the Date of *lmlk* Stamps," *VT* 29 (1979) 61-86; idem, "'The House of No-Shade Shall Take Away Its Tax from You' (Micah I 11)," *VT* 45 (1995) 516-27; J. Nogalski, *Literary Precursors to the Book of the Twelve* (BZAW 217; Berlin: de Gruyter, 1993); E. Otto, "Techniken der Rechtssatzredaktion israelitischer Rechtsbücher in der Redaktion des Prophetenbuches Micha," *SJOT* 5 (1991) 119-50; B. Peckham, *History and Prophecy* (ABRL; New York: Doubleday, 1993); J. Renkema, *Discourse Studies* (Amsterdam/Philadelphia: J. Benjamins, 1993); J. Sanders, "Perspective in Narrative Discourse" (Proefschrift Katholieke Universiteit Brabant, Tilburg, 1994); G. Schmitt, "Moreschet Gat und Libna mit einem Anhang zu Micha 1:10-16," *JNSL* 16 (1990) 153-71; D. A. Schneider, "The Unity of the Book of the Twelve" (Ph.D. diss., Yale, 1979); C. S. Shaw, "Micah 1:10-16 Reconsidered," *JBL* 106 (1987) 223-29; W. von Soden, "Zu einigen Ortsbenennungen bei Amos und Micha," *ZAH* 3 (1990) 214-20; F. Stolz, "Zion," in E. Jenni and C. Westermann, eds., *Theological Lexicon of the Old Testament* (tr. M. E. Biddle; 3 vols.; Peabody, Mass.: Hendrickson, 1997) 2:1071-76; D. Tannen, "Introducing Constructed Dialogue in Greek and American Conversational and Literary Narrative," in F. Coulams, ed., *Direct and Indirect Speech* (Trends in Linguistics: Studies and Monographs 31; Berlin: Mouton de Gruyter, 1986) 311-32; J. A. Wagenaar, "The Hillside of Samaria: Interpretation and Meaning of Micah 1:6," *BN* 85 (1996) 26-30; W. G. E. Watson, "Allusion, Irony and Wordplay in Micah 1.7*," *Bib* 65 (1984) 103-5; J. T. Willis, "Some Suggestions on the Interpretation of Micah 1:2," *VT* 18 (1968) 372-79; H. W. Wolff, *Micah the Prophet* (tr. R. D. Gehrke; Philadelphia: Fortress, 1981); A. S. van der Woude, "Micha 1 10-16," in A. Caquot and M. Philonenko, eds., *Hommages à André Dupont-Sommer* (Paris: Adrien-Maisonneuve, 1971) 347-53.

PROPHETIC READING: SOCIAL ETHICS, DIVINE JUDGMENT, AND DIVINE HOPE, 2:1-5

Structure

I. A woe *(hôy)* cry	1-2
A. *Hôy* interjection characterizing the literary unit and	
suggesting the ill fate of the evildoers	1aα_1

*For a possible complementary structure see discussion.

The unit as it stands begins with an exclamation *hôy* ("alas," "woe") followed by a participle. Since the exclamation conveys a summons to attention, it may be considered as a partial equivalent to the call to hear *(šimʿû)* in 1:2 (cf. Isa 1:2-4; and cf. Hillers, *"Hôy,"* esp. 187). However, the exclamation *hôy* asks the rereaders to overhear, as it were, a speech different from the one introduced by *šimʿû* in Mic 1:2. As usual in the prophetic books, there is no introductory narrative to indicate to the readers that the speech in 2:1-5 is set elsewhere within the world of the book than in the one associated with the previous speech. Yet the text suggests not only a new speech, as the opening *hôy* implies, but also a completely different setting, because the speaker is now addressing an audience that is different from the one implied in the previous unit. Moreover, the tone of the constructed speech is unlike the one encountered before, and so are some of its overt, main concerns (e.g., socioeconomic issues).

The exclamation *hôy* may convey more than one meaning, and it may certainly relate in more than one way to the noun or nominal phrase that follows it (see *IBHS,* 40.2.4.a). It seems most likely, however, that the participial clauses point to those whom the textually inscribed speaker is addressing, and accordingly that these participial clauses should be understood as vocatives. That the text is constructed so as to suggest references to this group in the 2nd person in vv. 3 and 5 strongly supports this understanding of the text, and so do similar instances (e.g., Isa 1:4-5). Given the lexical and connotative associations of the participial phrases that follow *hôy* in Mic 2:1 and the frequent use of *hôy* as the opening cry for an accusation — sometimes followed by an announcement of judgment — in prophetic literature (e.g., Isa 5:8-24/25; Jer 22:13-19; Hab 2:6-20; see Westermann, *Basic Forms,* 190-94), it is most reasonable to assume that *hôy* and its participial clauses in Mic 2:1 evoke in the readers not only a negative characterization of the addressees and the perception that some disaster has befallen them or will certainly happen to them, but also the conceptual image of an announcement of judgment against the addressees.

The general characterization of the evildoers opens with two participial clauses. These clauses are linked to the rest of the verse by linguistic and syntactical markers (e.g., the pronominal references). It is significant that this generic characterization is built around relatively common lexical associations, among them *'āwen* ("wickedness," "evil") and *rā'* ("evil," "harm"), which occur in this precise order in Ezek 11:2; Ps 36:5 (NRSV 4); Prov 12:21 (cf. Isa 31:2; 59:7; Ps 141:4; also cf. Ps 28:3); *ḥšb* ("devise") and *'śh* ("do," "make"), which are found tens of times in the HB/OT; *p'l* ("do," "make") and *'śh* (see Isa 41:4; 44:15; Job 21:15; cf. Prov 21:15). The usual expression *pō'ălê 'āwen* ("workers of evil," "workers of wickedness") occurs more than twenty times in the HB/OT (mainly in the Psalms, e.g., Pss 5:6 [NRSV 5]; 6:9 [NRSV 8]; 14:4; 28:3; 36:13 [NRSV 12]; 53:5 [NRSV 4]; but also elsewhere, e.g., Isa 31:2; Hos 6:8; Prov 10:29; 21:15; Job 31:3; 34:8, 22). Here it is split up to suit the parallel structure (cf. Ezek 11:2 and Ps 36:5 [NRSV 4]), and so is *ḥšb rā'/ rā'â* ("devise evil"), another common syntagmatic pair (e.g., Gen 50:20; Jer 18:8; 36:3; Mic 2:3; Nah 1:11; Zech 8:17; Pss 21:12 [NRSV 10]; 35:4; 41:8 [NRSV 7]; Esth 9:25; Neh 6:2). These pairs are also transposed (see below). The sonorous and syntagmatic pair *ḥšb-mškb* (cf. Ps 36:5 [NRSV 4]) is also split up. This feature in this case also creates a kind of envelope encompassing this portion of the characterization. In sum, as in the Psalms, the evildoers are characterized here in a generic form. Moreover, they are characterized in that way by combinations of more or less stock language used in this regard (see examples above).

A few additional observations: First, the verse is often rendered literally as "woe to those who plot iniquity, and work evil on their beds" (e.g., Dearman, 45) or the like. Such translations are misleading, for they fail to recognize the metathetic parallelism in this line, namely, the implied transposition of verbs (see Watson, 16-17, 249-55; cf., e.g., Ps 35:7). In other words, the evildoers do their scheming, not their wrong deeds, while in bed (for a different approach to the text, which leads eventually to "woe to those who plan injustice and crimes on their beds" and similar translations, see Wolff, *Micah*, 67-69). Second, the characterization concludes with a causal phrase, "because it is in their power" (cf. Gen 31:29; also cf. Dearman, 46). Wrongdoing is associated therefore with worldly power.

Within the frame of this text and as the particular characterization of the evildoers points out, such a power is linked to the control of fields and houses, that is, with items that make a most substantial contribution to both the symbolic and actual capital of those who hold them (see Intention). Thus when the text refers to the particular actions of those who plot wickedness and implement what they have devised, the speaker is presented as describing them as those who covet and seize fields and houses or households, and accordingly as those who oppress a householder and his household: a man (i.e., a householder) and his inheritance (i.e., his household). Such a man is thus devoid of economic means and symbolic capital, as he turns into a man without a field and without a household, one who lost his inheritance. In this regard, the connection explicitly emphasized in the text between the semantic fields of *bayit* ("house" or "household") and *geber* ("man"; this term carries a connotation of might and is not used as a designation for the poor — the exception is in Prov

28:3, but the text is doubtful there; see NRSV) is noteworthy, as well as that between *ʾîš* ("man"; this term may be used for a poor person, e.g., Deut 24:12; Ps 109:16, but here is presented as a landowner) and *naḥălâ* ("inheritance"). One may compare this image of the one suffering from the actions of the evildoers with, for instance, that of the typical "free citizen" usually addressed by the speaker in Deuteronomy (i.e., the implied addressee) who is envisaged as a landowner and householder (e.g., Deut 5:14, 18/21 [NRSV 14, 21]; chs. 15–16).

The socioeconomic processes that are in the background of the description of evildoing in Mic 2:2 are certainly not unusual in agrarian societies. They reflect the concentration of property through land foreclosure, which may be accompanied by eviction and similar actions. The evaluation of these actions as akin to robbery and the like, and in general as ungodly, are also a common and recurrent feature in agrarian societies and a common literary and theological topos (see, e.g., Isa 5:8; Neh 5:1-6; cf. Deut 27:17; Prov 23:10-11; 1 Sam 8:14).

As is the case with the general, the particular characterization of the evildoers is also kept together by linguistic and syntactical markers (e.g., the pronominal references). Also as in the case of the general characterization, the text is constructed around semantic pairs found elsewhere. Among these, one may mention *śādeh* ("field") and *bayit* ("house," "household") (e.g., Exod 9:19; Deut 5:21; 2 Kgs 8:3, 5; Isa 5:8); *bayit* and *naḥălâ* ("inheritance") (e.g., Jer 12:7; Lam 5:2); *geber* ("man") and *ʾîš* ("man") (e.g., Jer 23:9; Prov 24:5); *gzl* ("seize," "snatch," "rob") and *ʿšq* ("oppress") (e.g., Lev 5:23; Deut 28:29; Jer 21:12; Ezek 18:18). The reference to "coveting fields" *(wĕḥāmĕdû śādôt)* may be reminiscent of the prohibition in Exod 20:17 and Deut 5:21 (yet see also Isa 32:12), though, significantly, the speaker does not use the topos of "coveting (and taking) wives" to condemn the addressees, nor is this issue raised in the next unit when explicit references to married women are made (v. 9; one may contrast not only with Exod 20:17 and Deut 5:18 [NRSV 21] but also with the imagery developed in texts such as Jer 6:12; 8:10; on the use of *nāśāʾ*, here "take away" or "steal," see below). Perhaps even more significantly, the precise choice of words in Mic 2:2 — the use of the expression *ḥmd śādeh* ("to covet a field") — does not occur in either version of the Decalog, and fields are not even mentioned in Exod 20:17. Thus it is unlikely that the intended reader of this text was unequivocally instructed to approach it from the vantage point of the Decalog (for a different approach, see, e.g., Alfaro, 22-23).

Perhaps the most significant feature of this particular characterization of the evildoers is that in itself it is devoid of unequivocal markers pointing to a specific historical situation. Although a rereading of the text that is informed by Mic 1:1 will situate them in a certain time period, these wrongdoers are presented as a timeless type of "land-grabber," one that could be taken up by different referents depending on the world of the rereaders.

The text as it stands is also clearly linked to the section describing the consequences of the actions of the evildoers. One may mention, for instance, the repeated and contrastive use of *ḥšb* ("devise") in vv. 1 and 3, the pair *rāʿ-*

rā'â (also vv. 1 and 3; notice also the fem. pronominal suffix in *ya'ăśûhā,* "they perform it," v. 1), the semantic pair *nahălâ* ("inheritance")–*hēleq* ("portion"), which is split up between vv. 2 and 4 (cf., among others, Gen 31:4; Num 18:20; Deut 10:9; 12:12; 14:27, 29; 18:1; 32:9; 2 Sam 20:1; 1 Kgs 12:16; Job 20:29; 27:13; for additional instances of splitting semantic pairs in this unit, see above); the split associative pair *nahălâ* ("inheritance")–*mišpāhâ* ("family") in vv. 2 and 3 (found about 20 times in the HB/OT); and the use of *nāśā'* to convey a meaning usually associated with *lāqah* ("take by force," "rob") in v. 2 that in itself is relatively infrequent (see Ezek 38:13; cf. 2 Kgs 7:8) and not used with *bayit* ("house" or "household") as the direct object, but is easily understood once one recognizes the use of *nāśā'* (meaning "lift up") in v. 4.

The description of the future consequences of the behavior of the evildoers opens with a "therefore" *(lākēn)* clause. The presence of *lākēn* in this particular literary setting, and certainly given the preceding textual environment, already creates an expectation of an announcement of judgment (see Genre). The expected announcement begins with the introduction of YHWH's reported speech. The latter consists of what is often called the "prophetic messenger formula," which in reality serves as a citation formula (see Meier, 277-91). The main roles of the latter are (1) to present explicitly the speaker as citing YHWH's word, though the contents of the quotation already characterize it as pertaining to divine — as opposed to human — constructed speech; and (2) to mark the beginning of a new subsection in the text, that of the announcement of judgment.

While the formula sets the quoted speech apart from that attributed directly to the human speaker, as a human reference to a more authoritative, divine speech, the latter is presented in such a way that it not only implies the presence of the former (the "therefore" clause implies an antecedent) but also is constructed so as to echo the human words that precede it (notice, e.g., the use of *hšb* in both, the use of *rā'* and *rā'â,* even the fem. pronominal reference to *rā';* see above). Thus the words of the human voice and those quoted by the human voice but assigned to a divine one blend together, as it were, into a single voice that is characterized by a particular choice of words, tone, and a theological or ideological perspective. Indeed, it is this voice that carries the message of the text. Thus the divine authority of the cited words not only characterizes the quotation itself but spreads over the entire constructed speech assigned by the (implied) author to the human voice both as a citation of YHWH's words and as a nonquoted text (cf. the characterization of the entire prophetic book as YHWH's word; → 1:1). It is worth noting in this regard that the marked beginning of the cited divine words is not paralleled by a clearly signaled conclusion of these words. Indeed, the intended rereader of the text may attribute vv. 4 and 5 to a divine or to a human speaker (or to both, as a case of double meaning; the reference to the "assembly of YHWH" in v. 5 does not necessarily disqualify YHWH as the potential speaker; see Judg 2:22; 6:26; 1 Sam 10:19; 2 Sam 12:9; 1 Kgs 17:14; 2 Kgs 20:5; Isa 49:7; Jer 14:10; 17:5; 23:16; 26:2; 27:16; Zeph 3:12; Mal 1:4; cf. Revell, §27.3). The result is, of course, a potential overlapping of voices as seen in Micah 1 (on this issue and its significance, → 1:2-16 and bibliography there).

Significantly, the occurrence of "this" in the following speech conveys to the readers a sense of distance between the speaker or speakers and the addressees, who have now turned out to be "this family" (namely, "all Israel"; cf. Mays, 64; → Genre; on the issue of distance cf. Shoemaker, 140). An additional instance of the rhetorical use of the demonstrative to express distance or separation in Micah 2 occurs in the concluding remark in v. 11. Moreover, the presence of the unusual pl. form ṣawwĕʾrôt ("neck"), which occurs nowhere else in the HB/OT (though there are another 9 instances of the pl. form of ṣawwāʾr) might be related to the presence of the demonstrative zōʾt in close textual proximity; cf. Deut 32:7; Pss 72:5-6; 77:17-18 [NRSV 16-17]). If this is indeed the case, then the sonorous repetition of -ôt (i.e., the pl. ending) may underscore the message of distance between speaker and addressee, between the pole of the godly and that of those who deserve to be, and will be, punished.

Thus the rereaders of Micah 1–2 are asked to develop an image of the closely related pair YHWH–(true) prophetic speaker as both distant from "Israel" (in its role as proclaimer and carrier of judgment) and close to "Israel" (in its role of lamenter over Israel and eventually proclaimer and carrier of salvation; see 2:12-13 but also v. 5; see Intention). One may note that the image of the mourner quoted in v. 4 is on the one hand unlikely to be associated with the divine/prophetic speaker, because YHWH is an agent of dispossession there. Yet, on the other hand, the wailer's words are quoted by the divine/prophetic speaker, and at least some degree of sympathy with those described as dispossessed people might be implied (see below).

The next section of the constructed speech of the speaker (v. 4) contributes to the affective aspect of the announcement of punishment by introducing the lamentation of a future Israelite who will have suffered the consequences of YHWH's actions instead of directly presenting a description of those actions (cf. Zeph 3:16-17). Significantly, the text allows ambiguity concerning the question of whether the words of the future lamenter are quoted directly by the human speaker or as an embedded citation within the divine speech that the human speaker quotes, or represents another case of blurring the line between the two. Thus there is a lack of determinacy, a degree of openness, concerning the structure of this section. The one outlined at the outset of this discussion may be complemented by one in which v. 4 (and perhaps v. 5 as well; see above) is an integral part of the quoted divine speech. Indeed, given the tendencies found in ch. 1, it seems likely that the structure of this section consists of two different renderings informing each other.

The text is, however, unequivocal with regard to the temporal setting: these words are set in the more-or-less distant future (see bayyôm hahûʾ, "on that day") of the speaker. This sense of temporal distance is emphatically stressed by the presence in close textual proximity of two expressions conveying it, and by their respective place in their textual environment: the first as the concluding element in the announcement of judgment (see ʿēt rāʿâ hîʾ, "that time will be an evil time"), and the other as the opening clause of the description of the aftermath of the judgment. (On the significance of this temporal setting and on redactional approaches see esp. Genre and Intention.)

The constructed speech of the lamenter (who clearly identifies with "Israel"; see the alternation between 1st person common sg. and pl. in the lamenter's words), as well as the conclusion of its introduction (v. 4aβ), is characterized by sound repetition (in addition to repeated consonants notice the pairs *m/n, b/m,* and *š/ś*). Although some aspects of this speech are unclear, the explicit reason for the dirge is unequivocal: the loss of the land. An agent has taken and parceled the inheritance of the wailer's people, "Israel." This agent is surely identifiable on one level with YHWH and on another with an earthly conqueror who carries out YHWH's judgment. In any case the result of the agent's action is that the inheritance of "Israel" is given to an undeserving, negatively characterized inheritor. (The word *šôbēb* in v. 4 may convey a meaning akin to "perverted," "renegade," or "infidel"; see Jer 31:21; 49:4; Isa 57:17; cf. Allen, 285, 291; Hillers, *Micah,* 32; Vargon, 70; Alvarez Barredo, 91; Dempsey, 160; for three alternative approaches see those advanced, among others, by (1) *DBHE* and Zeidel, 16; (2) Elliger, *BHS;* and (3) Barthélemy et al., 3:729-31. Significantly, none of these alternatives substantially alters the aforementioned basic meaning of the taunt.)

This PROPHETIC READING does not end with the description of Israel's dispossession of its inheritance by YHWH. The next "therefore" clause fulfills, on the one hand, the expectation of an announcement of judgment after the accusation and condemnation brought in vv. 1-2 (i.e., of a section roughly parallel to vv. 3-4), though the genre is defamiliarized (see Genre). On the other hand, it provides a clear, albeit implied, image of hope: rather than ending with dispossession, the PROPHETIC READING concludes with the image of a new allotment of territories to future "Israel," who, rather than being a perverse, infidel people or the like, are described as "the assembly of YHWH" (just as in 2 Chr 28:8), an assembly "cleansed" so as not to contain the offspring of the land-grabbers and who will start anew in the land, as in the days of the first allotment (see Intention).

This exclusion of the scions of the transgressors from the assembly of YHWH suggests a transgenerational aspect within the conception of divine punishment expressed in the text, and some indirect form of punishment upon the transgressors themselves because those afflicted will be their descendants; but see 2 Kgs 20:16-19, esp. v. 19.

Genre

It is customary to consider Mic 2:1-5 a prophetic announcement of punishment against a group of individuals (see Sweeney, 529-30; cf. Westermann, *Basic Forms,* 142-61). If so, vv. 1-2 constitute an accusation introduced by "woe" plus participial clause (see Westermann, *Basic Forms,* 192-93; Janzen, 62-63) and vv. 3-5 the announcement of judgment proper, which is introduced by the logical marker "therefore" and the messenger formula (cf. Westermann, *Basic Forms,* 149). For this approach to the text see, e.g., Wolff, *Micah,* 73; Renaud, 69-70, Janzen, 62-63.

But whereas there is no doubt that the text of 2:1-5 is written so as to activate the expectations and general associations that the aforementioned prophetic genre is likely to evoke in the rereading community, it also defamiliarizes this genre because it stands conspicuously in tension with those expectations and associations. Thus in sharp contrast to the expectations, those addressed, described, and condemned in the accusation presented in vv. 1-2 are at the very least not identical with those against whom the judgment is delivered (vv. 3-5), neither temporally nor in regard to attributed social identity and deeds. This becomes clear from the cumulative weight of the following considerations:

1. The likely referent of *hammišpāḥâ hazzō't* ("this family") in v. 3 is "all the people" (cf. Jer 8:3; Am 3:1; for the use of *mišpāḥâ* to carry a meaning akin to *gôy,* "nation," see, e.g., Jer 10:25; Zech 14:18, as pointed out already by Radak). Conversely, it is unlikely that it is used here in reference to a particular subgroup that is from the outset *not* defined by some form of kinship, but rather construed on the grounds of a particularly sinful behavior. In other words, in prophetic literature thieves are less likely to be defined as a "clan" than any group structured around real or constructed kinship (despite Sir 16:4).
2. The reference to *'ammî,* "my people," in v. 4.
3. The temporal perspective informing the description of the judgment, namely, in an indefinite future from the perspective of the speaker (notice the expression *bayyôm hahû'* ["on that day"] in v. 4, *kî 'ēt rā'â hî'* ["for it will be an evil time"] in v. 3).

This lack of correspondence is only heightened by the enhanced expectation for its presence that is created by both the implied image of a disaster (and perhaps even of a funeral; cf. 1 Kgs 13:30 and esp. Jer 22:18) introduced by *hôy* (see below) and by the tit-for-tat (literary and theological) pattern that is so strongly suggested by the language of the pericope (see, e.g., the pun on the participial forms of *ḥšb* ["devise"] in vv. 1 and 3; on these matters see Petrotta, 98-100, and the bibliography there). Moreover, the precise word order in v. 3, with *'al-hammišpāḥâ hazzō't* rather than the direct object immediately following the verb *ḥšb* (for a similar instance see Nah 1:11), seems to channel particular attention to the identity of those against whom *rā'â* ("evil" or "calamity") is devised. (For a different approach, see, e.g., Willi-Plein, 75.)

In fact, scholars such as Wolff, Mays, Renaud, and Alvarez Barredo, to mention a few, have clearly noticed the tension between the text of Mic 2:1-5 and the literary and theological patterns expected from an actual prophetic announcement of judgment against a group of individuals. These scholars have tended to solve these tensions by removing the sections that create them from a proposed original text, on the grounds that they are late additions. Thus Wolff, for instance, maintains that (1) *'al-hammišpāḥâ hazzō't* ("against this family") in v. 3 is a Deuteronomistic addition; (2) *kî 'ēt rā'â hî'* ("for it will be an evil time"), also in v. 3, is the work of an exilic redactor who "interprets the disaster aimed at a particular group of people as an entire epoch of doom"; (3) *bayyôm hahû'* ("on that day") in v. 4 is likely from the hand of an exilic redactor; (4) *nihyâ* ("it has happened," according to Wolff and others) is a result of a dittography that was "understood by the redactor as a confirmation of the loss of the land" (cf. Renaud, 75); (5) *ḥēleq 'ammî yāmîr 'êk yāmîš lî* ("he [YHWH] alters the inheritance of my people; how he removes it from me") is an interpolation, a later expansion that "presents a lament over the entire nation and its loss of land during the Babylonian exile"; and (6) the entire text of v. 5 "supplements the interpolation in v. 4 [see point 5] in a verbose prose style" (Wolff, *Micah,* 67-70, 75-76, 78-80; 87; for similar approaches see Mays, 62, 64-66; Willi-Plein, 75-76; Lescow, "Redaktionsgeschichtliche Analyze," 51-52; Jeremias, 333-34; Alvarez Barredo, 90-92; Renaud, 72-81; etc.).

The text that results from this approach is obviously consistent with the expectations of this literary genre, but it does so because it has been constructed by means of a proposed redactional process so as to be at ease with the mentioned genre expectations. In other words, it surely does not defamiliarize the genre because it has been "familiarized" into it by the reconstruction of a modern scholar. It is possible that the texts mentioned above are additions to an original text; yet one should notice that the proposed additions are considered so on the grounds of a seemingly required coherence between (1) the original text and the expectations created by the genre of the unit, and (2) the reported words of Micah in the world of the book and the actual and reconstructed words of the historical prophet Micah to greedy landowners in 8th-century Judah on a particular but unknown occasion. Significantly, 2:1-5 as a whole (i.e., the mentioned section within the book of Micah, as opposed to any possible yet speculative reconstruction of textual forerunners) stands at odds with this type of coherence and implies an audience that is competent to read a written text lacking such coherence.

But it is not 2:1-5 alone that stands at odds with the aforementioned coherence. Other texts in the book of Micah run counter to the genre expectations that they themselves evoke in their readers (for examples → 1:2-16).

Furthermore, in addition to the defamiliarization of the genre, the speech attributed to Micah in this section is constructed in such a way that it stands in tension with the expectations associated with a mimetic, reported speech. According to these expectations, one is to anticipate that the reported speech be consistent with the intentions attributed to the speaker. But is this the case here? Is the speech in 2:1-5 the most likely speech uttered by an actual speaker addressing in real life and natural language the greedy people of vv. 1-2, either in an attempt to persuade them to change their ways or simply to announce to them their ill fate? The answer is likely to be negative, because of the references to a later time, to all the people as affected by YHWH's judgment, and also because of the several markers of textual cohesion that link the text here to the preceding and subsequent sections in the book (i.e., its textual surroundings). In addition to the general thematic coherence, one may mention among others the use of the word *r'/h* ("evil" or "disaster") in 1:12; 2:1, 3; *'ammî* ("my people") in 1:9; 2:4, 8, 9; the pun on *hbl* ("line" and "destruction") in 2:5, 10; the associative relation between *naḥălâ* ("inheritance," v. 2) and *měnûḥâ* ("resting place," v. 10; cf. Deut 12:9); the sonorous link between *'al* ("not") in the opening word of v. 6 and the *l* sounds that appear in almost every word from the final words of v. 4 to the end of v. 5; the demonstrative *'ēlleh* ("these") in v. 6 that in the world of the text links this verse and the following ones to the preceding unit (vv. 1-5). On these issues, cf. Hagstrom, 48-50; Willis, "Micah 2:6-8"; Renaud, 116-17; and Vargon, 72-73. (Needless to say, none of these observations requires that the mentioned units were written by one hand or at one time. Yet the issue at stake is how the matters are presented to the intended rereader of this section of the book of Micah.)

In sum, it seems that the constructed speech of the speaker in 2:1-5 is phrased so as to serve the intention or intentions of the implied author of the book in regard to its intended audience (about them see below) rather than only or even mainly those of the textually inscribed speaker in 2:1-5 regarding his explicit audience. It is unlikely that the constructed speech attributed to the speaker in 2:1-5 represents a mimetic reflection of an actual speech uttered by the historical prophet in a natural language situation to a living audience, nor is it reasonable to reconstruct this audience mainly on the basis of a reading of 2:1-2 that takes no account of its textual surroundings.

It is preferable thus to consider 2:1-5 as a whole to be a prophetic reading written to recall in its readers the style, theological or ideological associations, and expectations of a prophetic announcement of punishment against a group of individuals, while at the same time it clearly defamiliarizes such type of discourse. The process of defamiliarization occurs not only at the level of the genre and the unit but also at the lower level of forms of speech. Thus the image of a prophetic announcement of punishment against a group of individuals relies on the defamiliarization of yet another type of discourse or form of speech: the "woe cry" (see, e.g., Westermann, *Basic Forms,* 191; Hillers, *"Hôy";* Janzen; Gerstenberger; regarding defamiliarization compare the approach followed by Fohrer and by Dell).

Setting

Micah 2:1-5 is a piece of written literature (as opposed to oral literature and certainly to spontaneous, oral speech; as for orally delivered, ritual readings, see below). The focus should then be on the intended reader and the most likely actual readership of 2:1-5. With regard to both the intended reader and the actual readership, the situation here is similar if not identical to that in 1:2-16. This section of the book of Micah is a written text composed and edited for a primary public that consisted of literati. The literati were fond of sound and wordplays (cf. Dempsey, 146-47), of genre familiarization and defamiliarization, of ambiguity and polysemy.

The text teaches also about some of the central questions and issues that the intended community of readers cared about, some of its theological or ideological viewpoints, and the story they told about their own past. This PROPHETIC READING reflects on the causes of past — from a reader's perspective — national misfortune. This misfortune is presented as (1) the "taking away" of Israel's inheritance, which in turn was most likely epitomized for a post-monarchic group in the fall of monarchic Judah, and (2) as a divine punishment for the wrongdoing of powerful land-grabbers. That these land-grabbers are set in time prior to the fall of Judah does not stand in tension with this understanding; cf. the Deuteronomistic assignment of blame to Manasseh for the fall of Judah and Jerusalem (also cf. 2 Kgs 20:16-19). The text also communicates to the intended rereaders that their own postmonarchic situation is not the end point, that there will be a new beginning of "Israel" in the land, in the future. (On the characteristic focus of postmonarchic discourse on either the monarchic past or the ideal future see Ben Zvi, "Urban Center.")

The text of 2:1-5 neither requires nor suggests that the literati for which it is primarily composed consider themselves (in their own discourse) thieves, oppressors of other owners, or land-grabbers, nor that they have to be persuaded of the idea that "landgrabbing," "stealing," and the like are ungodly practices that eventually lead to divine punishment. Instead, the text is written in such a way that it assumes that the readers take these principles of social ethics for granted. Even if it reinforces these basic positions by assuming them to be self-evident, it is unlikely that the primary intention of the text is to strengthen this message among those competent to read the text (see Intention).

Moreover, it is worth noticing that (1) the text creates a temporal distance of several centuries between the evildoers and the intended readers of 2:1-5 and their contemporaries, and (2) it is unlikely that the literati among whom the book of Micah was composed would identify themselves, within their own discourse, with the land-grabbers and oppressors rather than with the godly voices in the book. Both the latter and the writers and readers of prophetic literature communicate YHWH's knowledge (on their role as brokers see Ben Zvi, "Observations"; also cf. Hos 14:10 [NRSV 9]; Sir 38:34–39:3). Thus whereas the main persuasive appeal of the speech of the godly characters to their literary addressees within the world created in this section of the book of Micah may focus on these issues, the same does not hold true for that of the book toward the community of rereaders within which and for which it is written.

That the setting suggested by the text points to communal rereading and studying activities by the literati does not mean that the text could not have been read to other, "less educated" social groups, or even used in liturgy. The opposite is, indeed, more likely (→ 1:2-16, Setting and Intention, and see esp. the role of these competent readers of prophetic literature as "brokers" of divine knowledge; see also Ben Zvi, "Introduction").

As for the setting of the constructed address of the speaker or speakers to the evildoers at the level of the narrative within the book, perhaps the most significant feature is that the readers of 2:1-5 are not told the where, when, or any of the circumstances surrounding the speech (as opposed, e.g., to Jeremiah 26–29). Since all of the above play significant roles in an actual communication and in any mimetic story of an actual case of communication, one may conclude that it is not written to lead the community of rereaders to a mode of reading aimed at learning about a particular, communicative event in the monarchic past. Rather, the text suggests or even implies a mode of rereading in which the speakers' words are considered of value and an object for interpersonal, communal study or meditation (cf. Hos 14:10 [NRSV 9]) aside from any particular detail concerning context, setting, and verbal exchange. In fact, the readers are not asked to historicize the text (i.e., to integrate it into a historical narrative and understand it in a way that is informed by that narrative), but to contextualize the words that the implied author attributes to the speaker or speakers here in terms of those assigned to godly voices in literary units that stand in textual proximity to 2:1-5, or, in other words, its co-texts (whether the setting evoked in the world of the book for the speakers' speech to the textually inscribed addresses is similar or dissimilar). In other words, the text of 2:1-5 is written to convey to the readers a sense of coherence that covers these verses and the neighboring literary units. This sense of coherence is communicated by means of literary techniques such as wordplays (to mention the obvious, the multiple use of *ḥbl* in vv. 5 and 10, and the pair *tēlĕkû rômâ — qûmû ûlĕkû* in vv. 3 and 10; but see also, e.g., *mišpāḥâ hazzō't* and *hā'ām hazzeh* in vv. 3 and 11; *rā', rā',* and *rā'â* in 1:12; 2:1, 3, respectively; and the back reference of *'ēlleh,* "these," in v. 6) and by content and structure as well (e.g., Hagstrom, 45-57; Shoemaker, 145).

In sum, the text does not ask the readers to contextualize these words in terms of any historical narrative or metanarrative about a singular event that occurred against particular circumstances and in which a prophet said such-and-such to a clearly defined group. Thus the way in which the implied author presents and constructs the words of the speakers in 2:1-5 is strongly consistent with a generalizing approach to YHWH's word (see 1:1) and clearly in tension with a particularizing approach. Yet there is a significant caveat: the readers are required by 1:1 to associate the speech that the implied author placed in the mouth of the godly voice with the monarchic — certainly not with their own postmonarchic — period, and even within the mentioned period, more particularly with the days that preceded Manasseh, and with a time in which other prophets (e.g., Isaiah) prophesied (→ 1:1).

Intention

On the surface level, the text seems to communicate to its readers a position consistent with a widely accepted ideal of social ethics (i.e., one that does not condone unlawful seizure of someone's else land and property) and with a trust in divine retribution against those who violate these ethics. This position, which was neither new nor original to the writers of the book but widely accepted in the ancient Near East as a whole (cf. Weinfeld, passim; Lohfink, esp. 16-23; among others), and expounded many times in the HB/OT, is conveyed to the readers through the voice of a speaker who at a certain point in the past — from the vantage point of the readers — condemned those who violated these ethics in his days and proclaimed that YHWH would repay (notice the repetition of *ḥšb,* "devise," in vv. 1 and 3) them for their deeds in the future, that is, from the vantage point of the speaker and his addressees within the world created in the book.

Yet, as mentioned above, a closer reading shows that those against whom YHWH devises *rā'â* ("disaster" or "evil") consist first of a public much larger than those who "devise wickedness" in v. 1 (cf. Isa 5:8-25, esp. vv. 13, 25), and second of a group that is likely not situated in the time frame shared by the speaker and his addressees.

These observations seem to undermine the claim that the foremost and only intention of the implied author here is to persuade the intended reader of the widely accepted positions mentioned above. What else is at stake here?

Wolff and others are most likely correct in maintaining that, for instance, v. 4 as it stands contains "a lament over the entire nation and its loss of land" after 586 BCE (see Wolff, *Micah,* 80; Mays, 65; notice also the basic meaning of *nihyâ,* "it has happened," which is one of the meanings conveyed by this word in v. 4; on this issue also cf. Renaud, 75; Wolff, *Micah,* 70; Petrotta, 100-102), that the most likely time that the readers of 2:1-5 would have identified as a "time of disaster" (v. 3) is that of the destruction of Jerusalem (see, e.g., Alvarez Barredo, 90; Mays, 65), and that v. 5 is most likely postmonarchic.

As seen above, it is mainly because of their position in this regard that Wolff and other scholars oriented to redaction history tend to remove the relevant references from the text they propose as the original text of Micah and that they closely associate with the historical, as opposed to the literary or the postmonarchic, traditional figure of Micah the prophet (see Genre). Yet their arguments concerning the likely referents of 2:1-5 are cogent. Moreover, it is hardly possible to imagine that from the viewpoint of a postmonarchic community of readers — the likely audience within whom and for whom the book of Micah, as we know it, took shape — these texts were not understood in reference to the fall of Judah and Jerusalem. First, these calamities so central to their image of their own past they could have considered the speaker in the text to foresee; second, the fulfillment in their own past of the image of the future developed in the text legitimizes the text and adds to their persuasive appeal in regard to a different set of images that they cannot see as yet fulfilled. The latter include not only the announcements of salvation in 2:12-13 but also the implicit assertion that there will be a future ideal day of a new beginning in the land, a day in which the land will be reallocated in the assembly of YHWH (see 2:5), as it was in the days of Joshua (also cf. 1 Chr 28:8).

Thus the text functions not only as a common expression of support for a social ethics — which at least in principle was, most likely, widely accepted anyhow — but as (1) an explanation of why YHWH changed "the portion" of the people and divided among others their fields (see v. 4): because of the wrongdoing of a powerful elite (cf. Luther, 221); and as (2) an affirmation of the hope conveyed implicitly in this unit (v. 5) and explicitly in other units in the book by the voice of the speaker. Incidentally, it may well be that the persuasive impact on the readers of the presentation of an image of the future as an obvious matter of fact agreed on by all involved in the discourse, and accordingly as one that needs neither explanation nor particular assertion (namely, that there will be a new allocation of land, a new beginning of "Israel," i.e., YHWH's assembly in the land), far outweighs the impact of explicit announcements of salvation (e.g., 2:12-13).

The interplay in the text between openness to multiple rereadings and determination is noteworthy in this regard. As mentioned above, on the one hand, the speaker in the text was likely understood as first, condemning a group of people who lived during the time frame expressed in 1:1 (i.e., mainly the second half of the 8th century BCE); second, proclaiming future circumstances there that were probably associated with or seen as fulfilled by the calamities linked with the fall of the Judahite kingdom (i.e., more than a century later than the condemnation); and third, pointing to a future still unfulfilled (v. 5). On the other hand, it is clear that the text is fashioned in a way so as to allow additional — but not alternative — identifications of referents through the process of reading and rereading. The sinners are initially described as "those who devise wickedness" and the like, which is hardly a feature that can be associated only with a particular group at a well-defined time. The description then moves to the characteristic actions assigned by the speaker to those who devise wickedness: coveting fields, taking houses, oppressing a householder, and the like. Both the socioeconomic processes that are condemned by this language (the concentration of land property through foreclosure and similar actions) and its evaluation as robbery and the like are a common and recurrent feature in agrarian societies and a common literary and theological topos in the ancient Near East and beyond. Biblical texts explicitly associate such a state of affairs with monarchic Judah as well as with Persian Yehud (see Nehemiah 5). Also the description of the judgment is constructed in general terms that allow for multiple referents, provided that they are situated in the future from the vantage point of the speaker in the text. Not only are "it will be a time of calamity/an evil time" (v. 3) and "we are utterly ruined" (v. 4) clearly generic descriptions, but also "he parcels our fields" (v. 4) is not a completely univocal referent. In other words, in a manner similar to that ubiquitous in the Psalms, descriptions of suffering and causes of suffering are described in most general terms so as to allow different readers to identify themselves with the textually inscribed speaker and the speaker's world. Mic 2:1-5 seems to be written so as to allow for a multiplicity of readings, each depending on the world of knowledge and vantage point from which each community of rereaders approaches the text. This openness facilitates rereading and is consistent with the requirements of a book written to be read and reread, one on which the competent readers meditate (see Ben Zvi, *Obadiah,* passim). Yet once the text moves into v. 5, then the text points unequivocally to an ideal future and a purified Israel. This future is most laconically presented, but still it is referred to in such a way that no circumstances in the past or present of the community of readers can be identified with it. This future is unequivocally still unfulfilled.

One may notice also that on the one hand the text keeps the tension between the generic references to the evildoers and the characterization of those who suffered the divine judgment in the past from the viewpoint of the postmonarchic community of readers (see vv. 1-4); yet on the other hand the text seems unequivocal once it refers to circumstances set in the ideal future of the readers, once it points to the future community consisting of the descendants of those who were worthy of having descendants included in the assembly of YHWH. (In this respect, one may say that the tit-for-tat pattern eventually has the upper hand; cf. Prov 10:7; Job 18:17; and similar texts.)

Micah 2:1-5 serves other, more subtle, persuasive functions. It suggests and constructs a world based on clear oppositions:

- Day versus night.
- YHWH (as just deviser of evil/calamity) and the greedy oppressors (who are devisers of iniquity and doers of evil).
- The evildoers of Israel along with those who will dispossess them (who are also characterized negatively; see *lĕšôbēb* in v. 4) as opposed to the purified assembly of YHWH (most likely "Israel"; cf. 1 Chr 28:8; the term also may connote a sense of sacral assembly in terms akin to those in "P" texts; cf., e.g., Alvarez Barredo, 91-92) among whom the land will eventually be allocated.
- At a higher level of abstraction the world of the past — of sinners, greedy oppressors, rich thieves, and their no-better dispossessors — and the "world that will come," which is associated with the purified assembly of YHWH and with YHWH's correct allocation of the land.

Thus the reading of the text moves the readers from an image of the world that resulted from the last beginning, through violent dispossession, to a new, pure beginning (v. 5). One may compare this trajectory with those included in the pattern of "rebounding violence" proposed by the anthropologist M. Bloch (I am indebted to M. Anderson-McLean for this observation). One should note that nowhere in this text — nor elsewhere in the book — is the character of Micah presented as an advocate of a "millenarian" movement. One of the main features of millenarian movements as generally understood is their refusal to continue with "earthly life" (see Bloch, 85-98, esp. 90-91). Nothing in the text suggests that such a tendency is advocated in the unit; indeed, it seems the issue is nowhere in the horizon of thought implied in the text. For a different approach concerning Micah and millenarianism see Hillers, *Micah,* 4-8.

Bibliography

A. Alt, "Micha 2,1-5: *Gēs anadasmos* in Juda," *NTT* 56 (1955) 13-23; M. Bloch, *Prey into Hunter: The Politics of Religious Experience* (Cambridge: Cambridge Univ. Press, 1992); J. A. Dearman, *Property Rights in the Eighth-Century Prophets* (SBLDS 106; Atlanta: Scholars Press, 1988); K. J. Dell, "The Misuse of Forms in Amos," *VT* 45 (1995) 45-61; C. J. Dempsey, "The Interplay between Literary Form and Technique and Ethics in Micah 1–3" (Ph.D. diss., Catholic Univ. of America, 1994); G. Fohrer, "Remarks on Modern Interpretation of the Prophets," *JBL* 80 (1961) 309-19; E. Gerstenberger, "The Woe Oracles of the Prophets," *JBL* 81 (1962) 249-63; D. R. Hillers, "*Hôy* and *Hôy*-Oracles: A Neglected Syntactic Aspect," in C. L. Meyers and M. O'Connor, eds., *The Word of the Lord Shall Go Forth. FS D. N. Freedman* (Winona Lake, Ind.: Eisenbrauns, 1983) 185-88; W. Janzen, *Mourning Cry and Woe Oracle* (BZAW 125; Berlin: de Gruyter, 1972); J. Jeremias, "Die Deutung der Gerichtsworte Michas in der Exilszeit," *ZAW* 83 (1971) 330-54; N. F. Lohfink, *Option for the Poor*

(Berkeley: Bibal, 1987); M. A. Sweeney, *Isaiah 1–39, with an Introduction to Prophetic Literature* (FOTL XVI; Grand Rapids: Eerdmans, 1996); W. G. E. Watson, *Traditional Techniques in Classical Hebrew Verse* (JSOTSup 170; Sheffield: Sheffield Academic Press, 1994); M. Weinfeld, *Social Justice in Ancient Israel and in the Ancient Near East* (Jerusalem: Magnes; Minneapolis: Fortress, 1995); J. T. Willis, "On the Text of Micah 2,1aα-β," *Bib* 48 (1967) 534-41; idem, "Micah 2:6-8 and the 'People of God' in Micah," *BZ* 14 (1970) 72-87.

PROPHETIC READING: SOCIAL ETHICS, DIVINE CHARACTER AND PATRONSHIP, MISTAKEN THEOLOGICAL POSITIONS, AND JUDGMENT, 2:6-11

Structure

This literary unit is demarcated by the envelope of references indicated by the root *nṭp* in the Hiphil ("to prophesy, preach"). But I should mention again that vv. 6-11 are linked to the preceding unit by cohesive markers (see above) and that the issues addressed here lead, as it were, to those advanced in vv. 12-13 (see below).

One of the first tasks that 2:6-11 presents to its intended reader is to identify the speaker or speakers in the unit. The second main task is to cope with the density of changes in person, the grammatical incongruities, and the presence of some uncommon forms. The difficulty in the first task results from the text's lack of unequivocal discursive markers instructing the community of rereaders about the identity of the speakers in each section, and about the extent of the sections themselves. Thus less than direct indicators, such as the contents of the speeches, come to play a central role. The content of the speeches suggests strongly that the implied author of the text assigned words to more than one character or voice (see below) in this text, either directly or indirectly, that is, as speech embedded in the words of another. Indeed, a kind of dialogue or disputation seems to be described.

Most scholars agree that Micah is one of the speakers and, accordingly that his opponents are either allowed to present their words directly or that Micah includes their words in his own. Micah's opponents are understood, among others, as false prophets (e.g., Edelkoort; van der Woude, "Micah in Dispute," 247; Alonso Schökel and Sicre Díaz, 2:1048-49; cf. de Waard, 511; Vargon, 73), or the land-grabbers, the powerful men denounced in the preceding unit (e.g., Wolff, *Micah,* 73, 80-81; Mays, 68-69), or "the house of Jacob" in relation to the words presented in v. 7 (e.g., Willis, "Micah 2:6-8," 81; Vargon, 74-75), or a combination of the above (e.g., Allen, 294-300). Hillers thinks that "though the rich are in mind, the speakers represent the people." He adds: "Perhaps it is a situation where oppressor and oppressed alike regard prophecy as irreligious" (Hillers, *Micah,* 36). One may also notice that recently Shoemaker (142-43, 306-8) has assigned only v. 6 to Micah, and vv. 7-11 to YHWH, and Dempsey (141) has claimed that vv. 6-11 in their entirety "are Yahweh's words as delivered by Micah." Of course, both maintain that these voices also "quote" others. (For a good summary of the debate and bibliography, see Willis, "Micah 2:6-8.")

It is more difficult to mark unequivocally the limits of the speech attributed to each of these voices. Even if one accepts the model that the opponents' voices are presented as quotations embedded in the language of the main speaker (usually understood as Micah), the precise limits of these quotations seem puzzling. It is generally agreed, for instance, that most of v. 6 consists of such a quotation with the exception of *yaṭṭîpûn,* "they preach," which is generally understood as a discursive marker indicating that the speaker is presenting what he claims to be someone's else words. Notice also the unusual postpositive position of the marker introducing the quotation, a position that makes sense in terms of the speaker's speech (cf. Shoemaker, 303); this speaker is usually understood as Micah (but see Dempsey, 140-43). There is much debate, however, concerning the extent of the citation in v. 7. Some consider v. 7 in its entirety to be a "quotation" (e.g., Allen, 292-96; Mays, 66-70; Alvarez Barredo, 94; also, though not for the same reasons, Dempsey, 166-69); others claim that the citation consists of most if not all of the first half of the verse (i.e., from the beginning until *ma'ălālāyw,* "his doings"; e.g., Wolff, *Micah,* 68, 70, 81-82; de Waard, 511); and others remain undecided (e.g., van der Woude, "Micah in Dispute," 248). There is also considerable debate concerning the first verset of v. 7. On the surface the outcome of the discussion seems to depend on text-critical considerations (i.e., on whether one emends the text of v. 7 and, if so, which emendation one chooses). For instance, should one read *dĕbāray* ("my words"; see MT, Pesh., Vg., Tg.; and, e.g., Wolff, *Micah,* 70) or *dĕbārāyw,* "his words," as suggested by the LXX (see, e.g., Hillers, *Micah,* 35; Vargon, 75)? Should one read with the MT, *he'āmûr bêt-ya'ăqōb* ("should/can it be said, O house of Jacob?" or perhaps "the house of Jacob is the one saying" (for the first option along with a summary of research, see Renaud, 91-92; for the second, Vargon, 74-75) or "cela est-il décreté, maison de Jacob?" or "est-il vraie que l'on dit dans la maison de Jacob"? (see Barthélemy et al.,

3:732). Or should it be emended to *he'ārûr bêt-ya'ăqōb* ("Is the house of Jacob cursed?" e.g., Mays, 66; Elliger, *BHS*) or to *he'āmîr bêt-ya'ăqōb,* which is understood as meaning: "The house of Jacob affirmed (what has been undertaken by Yahweh)" (e.g., van der Woude, "Micha II.7a"; idem, "Micah in Dispute," 247-48; Allen, 292, 295; and Alvarez Barredo, 93)?

Yet an analysis of the argument in favor of the mentioned emendations shows that their starting point is, in most cases, that the MT does not make sense, which means that the text as it stands violates the emendator's expectations of this text regarding matters of coherence of meaning, style, structure, or type of discourse. For the same reasons, grammatical "incoherence" is sometimes "corrected." Since 2:6-11 violates many of these expectations, Mays's claim (p. 68) that "the MT of these verses is in poor condition" and that "it *cannot* be understood without emendations and reconstructions" (emphasis mine) is quite typical. The categorical, universal aspect of Mays's claim is worth stressing. Mays is not saying that he cannot understand this text, nor that his and similar approaches fail to elucidate the meaning of the present text; instead he says that it is the text that cannot be understood (implicitly by anyone, at any time). Moreover, given the number of violations to his expectations, the issue is clearly not one of a particular word here or there, but of the text as a whole.

But is it likely that the community of writers and rereaders for which and within which the book of Micah was composed or reached its final form shared Mays's and similar expectations for textual coherence? Is it reasonable to assume that a text that is composed or redacted within a group of readers and writers who were proficient in Hebrew, and which was accepted by them, and then read and reread by them, could not be understood by them? Moreover, if, as is most likely, the intended reader of the book resembled the actual community of readers, should one characterize the intended reader as unable to understand the text?

Of course, the answer to the preceding questions is negative. To be fair to Mays and other scholars who follow his path, one should take into consideration that their main interest rests not in the book of Micah per se but in a metanarrative, which they consider to be historically reliable, about a prophet who lived in the 8th century and who addressed orally different groups and social circumstances. Thus abrupt changes of person, grammatical incongruities, and unclear speakers and referents tend to be seen more as a barrier to be overcome than as features of a highly literate, written text characterized by a high density of meanings per sentence or semantic unit, because the aforementioned features are not well suited for a short oral communication. They are, however, consistent with a highly literate text written first to be read and reread by a community of literati, and second to be explained by the literati to other social groups with less than high literacy. (Cf. Ben Zvi, *Obadiah,* 211, et passim.)

If the critical approach focuses from the outset on the *written* book of Micah, then perhaps the first observation is that the blurring of speakers and addressees that was found in the previous units is even more noticeable here. Thus, at the beginning of v. 6, *'al-taṭṭipû yaṭṭîpûn,* " 'Do not preach,' thus they preach," suggests strongly that the speaker is human, likely Micah; that he is constructing the speech of his opponents and presenting it as a direct quotation; and that the quotation is shaped to create an image of them opposing a group of rightful preachers or prophets or both (notice the ambiguity in the root *ntp* in the Hiphil, "prophesy" and also "preach") that includes Micah and others. Yet by the end of v. 7 the words *hălô' dĕbāray yêṭîbû*, "do not my words do good?" suggest that the speaker is YHWH (even if one follows Dempsey and claims that here YHWH expresses the discourse of the evildoers); by the end of v. 9, the reference to *hădārî*, "my glory" (another word often emended), makes this identification self-evident. Thus, as before, the reader is confronted with a fluid identification of the speaker who carries the godly teachings. Sometimes this character seems identified with the prophet, sometimes with YHWH, sometimes it is unclear whether one or the other or both. In any case, the text attributed by the implied author to each one is deeply interrelated to that attributed to the other. Indeed, the "godly" voice and message shaped by the implied author consists of both, the voice and words assigned to the prophet and to YHWH. (On the importance of the association between prophet and YHWH → 1:2-16 and bibliography there.)

A similar fluidity is observed in the characterization of those who opposed the godly voice. They are presented first as prophets or preachers or perhaps both (see above). The speaker then characterizes them as people who are on the surface knowledgeable of the theological tradition of Israel about divine traits and their liturgical expressions, yet come to make an absolutely mistaken conclusion when they apply that knowledge to their own circumstances. Notice the key terms in their speech: (1) *qāṣar rûaḥ*, "hasty temper," and contrast the attribution of its opposite, *'erek 'appayim*, "slow to anger" (Prov 14:29), to YHWH (e.g., Exod 34:1; Num 14:18; Joel 2:13; Jonah 4:2; Neh 9:17; Pss 86:15; 103:8; 145:8); and (2) *ma'ălālāyw*, meaning "YHWH's deeds" here; cf. the use of the term in Pss 77:12 (NRSV 11); 78:7 (cf. also the characterization of Jonah in Jonah 2). Later in the text (v. 8) the opponents are referred to as "my people" (YHWH's people) and characterized by YHWH — as a speaker — as those who have risen up (against YHWH). The reference to them as "my people" there strongly emphasizes the rebellion of the people, who despite their being YHWH's people (i.e., those who are supposed to honor YHWH, their "patron") have become an enemy. Then the general description of being an enemy is explained from a particular angle: they are depicted as greedy, shameful thieves who are even more disgraceful than the evildoers of vv. 1-5. Such an increased degree of shamefulness is strongly suggested by the transition from the image of stealing and oppressing male owners in vv. 1-5 to that of similar actions against women and children in v. 9, especially when this transition is read against the background of the traditional, honor-shame society within which and for which the text was written. V. 8 seems to provide a transition between the two images and in any case takes away from the evildoers any symbolic capital or honor that they may have claimed (on v. 8 see Vargon, 76-77; for text-critical issues in particular see Williamson, 360-64; and Barthélemy et al., 3:735-36). Significantly, within this unit the heightening of the negative characterization of the opponents does not reach its conclusion with their description as thieves without any honor, nor even as those who undermine YHWH's honor as patron of women and children of YHWH's people (see v. 9 and notice the language of divine honor), a description that is surely consistent with the general characterization of evildoers as YHWH's enemy (v. 8), but with the mockery of their theological wisdom. If v. 7 attributes to them at least some degree of mastery of the accepted theological language and discourse, by the end of the unit the speaker characterizes and hyperbolically caricatures (cf. Shoemaker, 291-92) them as a community within which one who utters wind and lies and preaches or prophesies or both (see above) about the virtues of wine and strong drink (v. 11) is accepted as a prophet or preacher or both. Incidentally, the text suggests an awareness of the type of feedback processes between prophet and community that allow the former to fulfill his or her role (cf. Overholt, "End of Prophecy"; idem, *Channels of Prophecy,* 21-25). Since the community is supposed to receive divine instruction and messages from YHWH through the prophets (or preachers who communicate YHWH's word), this choice of prophet (notice that the implied author does not wish the speaker to call such a person "prophet"; he uses the word אִישׁ, "man") denies such a possibility, and what counts as knowledge of YHWH in their eyes is only lies, wind, wine, and strong drink.

Another comment concerning the characterization of the opponents of the godly voice or voices: Although the actions attributed to them by this voice depict them as only a group within "Israel," the speaker or speakers explicitly associate them with "the house of Jacob" (v. 7), with "my people" (YHWH's people, v. 8), and with "this people" (v. 11). In other words, "Israel," more precisely "monarchic Israel," is identified with the evildoers. This identification creates an expectation for divine judgment against "Jacob," as opposed to judgment against a particular group within "Jacob" (cf. the similar situation in vv. 1-5). Significantly, the next unit in the text (vv. 12-13) implies that this expectation was fulfilled in the past — from the perspective of the community of readers.

If we turn to the issue of multiple meanings within this unit (→ 1:2-16), a reexamination of the first verset in v. 7 provides an apt illustration. As mentioned above, the verbal expression there occurs nowhere else in the HB/OT. Some scholars have claimed that the verset makes no sense, and several proposals for emendation have been advanced. Yet the precise form there, *he'āmûr,* shapes the text in such a way that it allows for the following interpretations: (1) "the house of Jacob is the one saying" (the passive participle may convey a meaning akin to that of the active participle; see Vargon, 74-75, and bibliography; see also JM, §50e), and (2) "should (or can) [this] be said, O house of Jacob?" (see Wolfe, *IB,* 6:913; Renaud, 91-92; R. L. Smith, 25, 27; and cf. KJV, RSV, NRSV), or perhaps "Is it being said, O house of Jacob?" (e.g., NASB). Moreover, it is possible that the choice of words in this verset might even connote a sense akin to "is the house of Jacob cursed?" It is not only that the word *'āmûr,* usually "be said," may occasionally convey the meaning of "be cursed" (see Job 3:3; cf. Ehrman) but also that, given the literary context of this text, which is full of significant sonorous combinations, one should not disregard out of hand the similarity of sounds between *'ārûr,* "cursed," and *'āmûr,* "said."

Another case of multiple meanings, this time at the structural level, occurs in v. 10. This verse serves as an announcement of dispossession of the land (see the outline above). Yet it serves a second duty as well: to describe the behavior of the evildoers as dispossessors of land. Thus the text is able to convey a direct connection between the evildoers' wrongful dispossession of the land and their being dispossessed in the future, due to YHWH's actions against them (cf. 2:1-5).

The structure of the literary text as it stands seems relatively clear. The text deals, at least at the surface level (see Intention), with the description and judgment of evildoers, who are identified at different points with "Israel," and in particular with monarchic Israel. This is done first by mentioning their rejection of the godly message of the speaker and of similar messages (cf. vv. 1-5). The text moves then to the presentation of their way of understanding YHWH as one who would not act against them. Their interpretation is rejected on the grounds that they have risen up as an enemy (against YHWH). The implicit notion is that such a rebellion will and should be matched with divine judgment. Then the text explains what kind of behavior led them to be considered in such a way by YHWH: breach of social ethics, shameful thievery, and oppression of the powerless. The consequence of their behavior is that they will lose their control over the land (v. 10; for the language cf. Ps 95:11; 1 Kgs 8:56; notice also the split reference to the pair *naḥălâ*, "inheritance," and *mĕnûḥâ*, "place of rest," in vv. 2 and 10; cf. also Deut 12:9; in other regards cf. Lev. 18:25; Num 35:34). I must stress that v. 10 is written so as to suggest a secondary reading of the text, namely, as the words of the evildoers as they dispossess the women and children of YHWH's people. Thus the text connotes the message that one action is intrinsically interrelated with the other: wrongfully dispossessing others leads to divine dispossession of the dispossessor.

One may notice that the position advanced here regarding the double meaning, or at least double connotation, of the text in v. 10 stands in tension with a widespread tendency toward univocality (i.e., to prefer either-or alternatives over both-and). Thus, for instance, Allen (298) and Vargon (79) consider this verse to be the verdict against the evildoers, whereas Hillers (*Micah,* 34, 36) and others prefer the second reading. For a recognition that the verse may be read both ways, see Alonso Schökel and Sicre Díaz, 2:1050. For redaction-critical solutions that point to one meaning at one time, see, for instance, Jeremias, 339-40; Wolff, *Micah,* 84; Mays, 71-72; Alvarez Barredo, 93-94.

Finally, after the verdict is given in v. 10, an additional characterization of the evildoers ("this people") is included, this time in terms of their access to the divine and to divine knowledge. On the one hand, this characterization creates a loop that brings the reader back to the literary slot of accusation in the pattern accusation-verdict and therefore creates an expectation of a second announcement of punishment. (On "loops" see Ben Zvi, *Zephaniah,* 335-36; idem, *Obadiah,* 73, 144-45.) Since vv. 12-13 assume a postjudgment viewpoint, one may think of an implied, elliptical reference to judgment filling the gap between v. 11 and v. 12 (cf., e.g., Westermann, *Prophetic Oracles,* 106). On the other hand, the reference to preaching or prophesying is not completely unexpected because it closes the envelope opened in v. 7 and because of the theological message it conveys in this case (see Intention).

Genre

Micah 2:6-11 is a PROPHETIC READING, a text written so as to be read and re-read and that lays claim to the legitimacy and authority of a prophetic text, of YHWH's word. Not only its *Sitz im Buch* but the links binding 2:6-11 to the preceding and following units suggest that the implied author wished the intended readers of this unit to approach it in a way informed by the others.

This unit likely evoked in the community of readers within which and for which it was written an image of a disputation. As is common in the book of Micah, it also defamiliarizes this image and clearly indicates to the intended readers that the text should not be taken mimetically. One may mention in this regard the cumulative effect of, among others, abrupt changes of address, grammatical incongruities, the presence of expressions carrying a double or even triple meaning, the fluidity of speakers and addressees, and a wording that clearly links this unit to other units in the book of Micah (see Structure above and cf. previous discussions of Genre). Moreover, unlike an actual disputation involving two speakers, here only one type of speaker, the one carrying the godly message, is allowed a voice in the text. The opponents' words are presented only as embedded within the discourse of the godly speakers and as a rhetorical counterfoil that contributes to the communication of the godly message of the speaker. The presentation of their words in the form of citations is above all a stylistic choice that contributes to the affective power of the text. Neither the opponents' speech as reported by the godly speaker nor the speech of the latter as reported by the authorial voice of the book — within which the former is included — represents natural, spontaneous, spoken speech. Both are instances of a written, literary, and above all constructed speech that is well integrated into a larger literary unit. (For literature on reported or, better, constructed speech as present in written communication vis-à-vis spoken speech in oral communication, see, e.g., Coulmas; Tannen.)

One may notice that the characterization of the unit as disputation — as widely proposed — might suggest a situation in which each side aims at showing its superiority and, accordingly, at affecting in some way the behavior and beliefs of the other. If this is so, then this characterization of 2:6-11 runs the risk of obscuring that the point of reading the text in postmonarchic communities is, of course, not to convince characters in the book (which according to 1:1 are set in 8th-century monarchic Judah) nor even to preempt the fall of Judah (understood as dispossession from the land), for, from the perspective of the reading community, the land has already fallen. (For the position that this unit should be considered a disputation see, e.g., Westermann, *Basic Forms,* 201; van der Woude, "Micah in Dispute," esp. 247-48; Wolff, *Micah,* 73-74.)

Setting

The setting of the reading and rereading for which the text of 2:6-11 is written is the same as the setting of the previous units. The text as it stands indicates a vantage point situated after the fall of monarchic Judah and a repertoire of language and ideas that seem consistent with Deuteronomistic and Priestly literature, and is reminiscent of some Jeremianic material. Scholars working within redaction-critical models have usually been aware that such is the case, but they have tended to explain the relevant features in a different manner. For instance, the mention of the dispossession of the land; the choice of words such as *ṭomâ,* "uncleanness," and *měnûḥâ,* "resting place," in v. 10; the identification of the evil-doers as the house of Jacob (i.e., "Israel" as a theological concept as opposed to the northern kingdom of Israel; → 1:2-16, Structure) and as the entire people; the reference to *rûaḥ* ("wind," but also "spirit") and *šeqer* ("lies"), among other features, are often explained in terms of an exilic, or exilic and postexilic, redactional process. This process is usually imagined as beginning with a possible but surely hypothetical text or texts that are reconstructed by these scholars and dated by them to the monarchic period, eventually reaching the present text after several reconstructed redactional stages. These texts claimed to be monarchic closely resemble the present text except that they are devoid of features that, according to the scholar advancing the textual reconstruction, indicate a period later than the monarchic, or that she or he considers inconsistent with Micah's proclamation (Micah here meaning an 8th-century prophet reconstructed in the main from the literary character Micah present in the book of Micah). See, among others, Renaud, 97-100; Jeremias; Mays, 71-72; Wolff, *Micah,* 76-76, 84; and esp. Alvarez Barredo, 92-95.

As for the setting of the speaker's speech in the world of the book, the readers are not told when precisely the speakers spoke, nor where, nor against which historical events — however reconstructed — they did so. Indeed, nothing can be said about the setting of the speech in the world of the book, except that it is set somewhere in the large span of time indicated in 1:1. It seems that in the case of 2:1-6, for instance, the implied author neither requires nor suggests that the intended reader approach this text from a perspective informed by a historical narrative or metanarrative. It is true that the text is written so as activate in the community of readers the image of a disputation, but as mentioned above the same text also defamiliarizes that image and undermines a mimetic understanding. (For examples of historical metanarratives against which some modern scholars have interpreted this text, see, among others, Shaw, 78-96; Shoemaker, 289-91.)

Intention

The intention of the text as it was likely reread by the postmonarchic communities for which it was written is to address the fall of monarchic Judah from a theological or ideological perspective. The end of monarchic Judah — conceived as usual in terms of dispossession of the land — is grounded, as in vv. 1-5, on shameful and decisive transgressions in the socioethical realm. Although from a perspective based on social reality the actual Judahite transgressors could not have included all the people, within the text's world of meaning "the house of Jacob," namely, all "Israel" (= YHWH's people), are those accused, condemned, and upon whom the divine judgment will fall, or (from the perspective of the community of rereaders of the present text) has already fallen. Yet if this were the only point of the text, this unit would have served a theological or ideological role very similar to vv. 1-5. But this is not the case. For one, vv. 6-11 address the issue of how to square the divine judgment against "Israel" (in reality, monarchic Judah; on this issue → 1:2-16; see Ben Zvi, "Inclusion") with the attributes and recounted actions that the community of readers associated with YHWH and with YHWH's particular relation with "Israel" (namely, patronage in its many possible metaphors, such as king, father, shield). This YHWH was characterized as slow to anger, forgiving, a savior of "Israel," and the like.

Significantly, but not unexpectedly, the claim advanced in the text is that this characterization of YHWH is correct (cf. the words that the implied author of the book attributes to the godly speaker in 7:18). Although this depiction of YHWH is put in the mouth of the evildoers, the godly speaker in 2:7-8 does not deny its truthfulness. Rather, the opposite is true. The implied author constructs the speech of this speaker as beginning with an adversative *waw* ("but") and with an explicit reference to *'etmûl* ("recently"). Accordingly, this speaker is then presented as one implicitly affirming the general validity of this image of YHWH and its coherence with events in the past until recently — from the perspective of that textually inscribed speaker. Thus the speaker introduces a particular limitation to the manifestation of the "nature" of YHWH: monarchic "Israel" (i.e., the house of Jacob) has sinned so heavily by acting as a dispossessor that YHWH has to dispossess them. Yet, significantly, even at that time, "Israel" is described as YHWH's people, both to enhance its shame and rebellion when "Israel" is associated with the seemingly powerful and surely shameful dispossessors (see v. 8), and to express the particular closeness between YHWH and Israel when the latter is associated with the powerless and the dispossessed, those from whom the "glory of YHWH" was taken, as it were (see v. 9). The postmonarchic community of readers within which and for which the present text is written are naturally more likely to consider themselves in terms similar to the dispossessed than to the dispossessors.

Verses 6-11 address another issue. The text links the behavior of the evildoers with their wrong understanding of YHWH's relationship with them, that is, with "Israel." This wrong understanding is not presented as the result of their lack of knowledge or awareness of a communally accepted, trusted description of YHWH's attributes and doings, but of their rejection of the message of prophetic voices that interpret those accepted descriptions from a viewpoint informed by the particular circumstances of their time. The heightened conclusion of the unit points precisely to a community that accepts hyperbolically ridiculed preachers or prophets, or both, and rejects the godly ones. Thus the text conveys to the readers that the future fate of the community, and its behavior in the present, depends strongly on their acceptance of the correct prophets or preachers as those who carry YHWH's word. Of course, the community of readers of the book of Micah have access to YHWH's word through their reading of the book, and those who are unable to read by themselves (the immense majority of the population) require the help of those able to do so, the literati, who read for them and explain to them the text, and accordingly act as brokers of divine knowledge to the public. (On these issues → 1:2-16 and bibliography there.)

Bibliography

A. Alt, "Micha 2,1-5: *Gēs anadasmos* in Judah," *NTT* 56 (1955) 13-23; F. Coulmas, ed., *Direct and Indirect Speech* (Berlin: Mouton de Gruyter, 1986); J. A. Dearman, *Property Rights in the Eighth-Century Prophets* (SBLDS 106; Atlanta: Scholars Press, 1988); C. J. Dempsey, "The Interplay Between Literary Form and Technique and Ethics in Micah 1–3" (Ph.D. diss., Catholic Univ. of America, 1994); H. Donat, "Micha 2,6-9," *BZ* 9 (1911) 351-66; A. H. Edelkoort, "Prophet and Prophet," *OTS* 5 (1948) 178-89; A. Ehrman, "A Note on Micah II 7," *VT* 20 (1970) 86-87; J. Jeremias, "Die Deutung der Gerichtsworte Michas in der Exilszeit," *ZAW* 83 (1971) 330-54; E. A. Neiderhiser, "Micah 2:6-11: Considerations on the Nature of the Discourse," *BTB* 11 (1981) 104-7; T. W. Overholt, "The End of Prophecy: No Players without a Program," *JSOT* 42 (1988) 103-15; idem, *Channels of Prophecy* (Minneapolis: Fortress, 1989); D. Tannen, ed., *Spoken and Written Language: Exploring Orality and Literacy* (Norwood, N.J.: Ablex, 1982); J. T. Willis, "On the Text of Micah 2, 1aα-β," *Bib* 48 (1967) 534-41; idem, "Micah 2:6-8 and the 'People of God' in Micah," *BZ* 14 (1970) 72-87; A. S. van der Woude, "Micha 2,7a und der Bund Jahwes mit Israel," *VT* 18 (1968) 388-91.

CONCLUDING READING:
ANNOUNCEMENT OF FUTURE SALVATION, 2:12-13

Structure

I. The shepherd-flock metaphor	12
II. The breach maker–king metaphor	13

This short concluding reading wraps up the first macrosection of the book of Micah (1:2–2:13) with a message of hope for the readers of the book. (On 1:2–2:13 as the first of three macrosections, see esp. Willis, "Structure.") At the same time, it functions in a similar manner at a lower structural level, for it also takes up the threat of dispossession and exile developed in the preceding reading (vv. 6-11), and not only implies that it has already happened but announces a future in which YHWH will surely gather Jacob, who at this stage is identified with *šĕ'ērît yiśrā'ēl*, "the remnant of Israel." Moreover, it claims that Jacob will be empowered by YHWH, who will act as their king and leader rather than as their agent of punishment. In this regard, despite their differences, one may compare the role of vv. 12-13 here with that of v. 5 in 2:1-5. (Notice also the background of a "new beginning" that influences both; cf. v. 13 with, e.g., Isa 52:11-12; cf. Wolff, *Micah*, 85-86.)

Many of the stylistic features that were found in the previous units occur in vv. 12-13. For instance, vv. 12-13 include a double-duty, connotative expression, *ṣō'n boṣrâ,* that plays on the meanings "flock of Bozrah" and "flock in a fenced place." When this expression is read pointing to the former, it may refer to the quality or quantity of the flock (cf. Isa 60:7; Am 4:1; also cf. the connotation of "plenty" in Ezek 36:37-38; Ps 107:41). A reference to abundance of population in v. 12 is also carried by *tĕhîmenâ mē'ādām,* "there will be a tumult of people" (Wolff, *Micah,* 68), or "they shall resound with people" (Dempsey, 126); yet notice the pun on *'ādām,* "people" or "person," and *'ĕdôm,* "Edom." One should not ignore the possibility that Edom could have been associated with Babylon in the worldview of the intended readers of this postmonarchic text. Other texts from the postmonarchic period point to such an association (e.g., Ps 137:7-8). If the community of readers was aware of such a view, then their reading of the text was likely informed by it (cf. Wolff, *Micah,* 85). When the expression *ṣō'n boṣrâ* is read as pointing to "flock in a fenced place," it completes the metaphor of the good shepherd (YHWH) who leads the flock to safety. Notice the associations with the semantic area of "fortify" and "fortified" that are carried by the root *bṣr.* All these networks of connotations contribute to the density of meaning in the text.

Verses 12-13 also show fluidity in regard to the identity of the godly speaker. The words that the implied author put in the mouth of the speaker in v. 12 indicate that the readers are supposed to understand the speaker as YHWH, but as the text flows into v. 13, the reference to YHWH in the 3rd person gives the impression (though not the necessity; → 2:1-5) that the speaker is likely to be other than YHWH, that is, the human, prophetic voice. Yet the words of these two speakers are intertwined, for both together — or if one wishes, the godly voice as a whole consisting of two elements — carry the note of hope and salvation.

There are also sharp changes of grammatical person, and *kullāk,* "all of you," in v. 12 (where the intended readers anticipate *kullô,* "all of it") appears as an inverted image of the textual situation in 1:2. In v. 12 there is no doubt that *kullāk* points to "Jacob," but who constitutes this "Jacob"? The implied addressees of the speaker? The rereaders of the text (and notice the affective function of a 2nd-person address)? Both? (For text-critical proposals that lay aside the MT *kullāk,* "all of you," see, e.g., Watson, 306-7; Elliger, *BHS;* Mays, 73; but see Renaud, 104; sharp changes of person for rhetorical purposes are not uncommon in the book of Micah. See, e.g., 1:2 at the beginning of the book and 7:18-20 at its conclusion.)

One may mention that this unit also includes puns on the structure of the parallel clauses (cf. the metathetic parallelism in 2:1), in this case, a staged, sequential set of ellipses that involve almost all the key words, for *pārĕṣû wayya'ăbōrû ša'ar wayyēṣĕ'û bô* stands for:

wayya'ăbōrû (bô)	*pārĕṣû (ša'ar)*
they have passed (through it)	they have broken through (the gate)
wayyēṣ'û bô	*(pārĕṣû) ša'ar*
they have gone out through it	(they have broken through) the gate

(see Vargon, 85; and as most Eng. translations suggest).

Just as the godly speakers flow into one another, so does the main metaphor for the savior. The savior, YHWH, is depicted first in terms of a shepherd (and "Israel," accordingly, as "flock"; see v. 12). Then the pastoral image of a shepherd recedes to the background and the associated image of a king as a powerful, commanding, and victorious leader of peoples and armies (notice the military connotations of *prs*, "break forth"; cf. 2 Sam 5:20) comes to the forefront. Kings are often described as shepherds of their people in ancient Near Eastern texts (cf. 5:1-5; notice also the reference to YHWH's shepherding in 7:14; and see discussion in Renaud, 114). It is worth noting also that the intertwining of the images of the shepherd and king results in two metaphors that are clearly interwoven, yet still somewhat distinct so that the rereaders of the text may ponder the relation between the two. Is the text claiming that YHWH will breach "the gate" that keeps "Jacob" (which here stands for the remnant of "Israel") in exile and bring it back to "its pasture"? Or that YHWH will bring "Jacob" back to "its pasture" (v. 12) and then (i.e., once "Israel" is empowered) will march before them and breach someone else's (i.e., "Israel's" enemies') gate so "Israel" may pass through it, that is, to conquer (v. 13; cf. 4:13; 5:7; see Kaufmann, 3:272-73)? Or perhaps both? This ambiguity, or even lasting indeterminacy, not only allows this announcement of salvation to be reread in several ways — all of which are consistent with other images of salvation in Micah and elsewhere in the prophetic corpus — but also is likely to draw the attention of the reading community to itself, because ambiguities often function to get attention in addition to facilitating the communication of a complex multilayered message in the most economical way. (See Ben Zvi, *Obadiah*, 146; idem, *Zephaniah*, 86, 185-87, 220-23, 227-30, and bibliography there.)

Scholars have, of course, advanced alternative interpretations of this text. For instance, since medieval times, some have argued that the speakers in the text are the false prophets (e.g., Ibn Ezra; van der Woude, "Micah in Dispute"; idem, "Three Classical Prophets"; de Waard, 511). It is unlikely that the intended readers of the text were asked to adopt this reading strategy. For one, the implied author provides some clues about these false prophets and their theological argument. Their argument is not consistent, to say the least, with an image of these prophets and their associates, the land-grabbers, as freely admitting that "Israel" will be sent into exile and only a "remnant of Israel" left, and then musing about how YHWH will restore the fortunes of that remnant in the future. (Cf. Tanhum HaYerushalmi [Shy, 158-59]; J. M. P. Smith, 66-67; Margolis, 11-12; Hillers, *Micah*, 40.)

Brin is one the most recent representatives of a long tradition of an alternative interpretation of this text as an announcement of judgment rather than of salvation. (See, e.g., Radak [who identifies the king in v. 13 not with YHWH but with Zedekiah]; Calvin, *Commentary*, 212-14; and for a list of scholars from different times and backgrounds who adopted this approach, see J. M. P. Smith, 66-67.) Yet the strength of this interpretation depends on an ironic approach to the image of YHWH as the king of Israel who victoriously leads them to exile. Although theoretically possible (cf. Ps 80:13 [NRSV 12]), this approach has not commanded widespread support, and with good reason.

In its present context it suggests a reversal rather than an affirmation of images such as that in Ps 80:13 (NRSV 12) (cf. the use of *ša'ar,* "gate," in Mic 1:9), and perhaps an intertextual pun on the image of kings and gods marching into the exile such as those in Am 1:15; Jer 48:7; 49:3 (see Vargon, 85-86). Moreover, the general sense of salvation communicated by vv. 12-13 is enhanced by the choice of words and images that clearly associate it with other announcements of salvation in the book of Micah, especially with 4:6-7 (notice also the references to *šě'ērît,* "remnant," in 5:6-7 [NRSV 7-8], and see 7:18). One may also compare the main aspects of the language and imagery of 2:12-13 with that present in other texts of salvation elsewhere in the prophetic books (e.g., Isa 11:12; 52:12; Jer 23:3; Ezek 11:17; 34:12; cf. Westermann, *Prophetic Oracles,* 131).

Indeed, one wonders if the ad hoc interpretation of this text as an announcement of judgment would have been proposed at all had not those who have advanced it thought from the outset that an announcement of salvation is out of place at this particular point in the book; in other words, whether the proposal is not meant to bridge the gap between the expectations held beforehand by those who propose this interpretation and the presence of vv. 12-13 just after vv. 6-11, and before ch. 3.

The same problem of bridging the gap between what one thinks the text should be and what is written there is solved in a different way by another group of scholars. They also maintain that an announcement of salvation is out of place in this section of the book and so propose that the text has been transposed from its original place in ch. 4. (For a summary of the proposals and bibliography see Willis, "Note," 53 and esp. n. 37 there; cf. J. M. P. Smith, 670). It is worth mentioning that for Willis and others who maintain that the book of Micah is structured in three main macrosections marked by similar calls to attention (imperatives from *šm',* "hear"), an announcement of salvation is precisely what is expected at this point in the book. Willis's position is supported by textually inscribed discursive markers, and in any case v. 5 already suggests that an implicit or explicit announcement of salvation is surely not out of place after vv. 6-11, but indeed is likely to occur. See also, from a different perspective, Otto, esp. 144-45, 150. (For a recent redaction-critical proposal that relates 2:12aα to 4:6-7 in an earlier text, see Lescow, "Komposition," 218-19.)

Genre

This text has been referred to above as an "announcement of salvation." Yet I must stress first that those to be saved are not the individual addressees of the textually inscribed speakers. The announcement points to a future that will be manifested only after the fall of monarchic Judah, far beyond the temporal limits mentioned in 1:1. This future is likely to be imagined as still unfulfilled even from the perspective of the reading community. Second, this community learns this notice of hope and transmits it to those who are unable to read it directly not by listening to a living prophet but by reading and rereading the note as a literary text in a way informed by their rereadings of the preceding units in the book (notice the mentioned cross-references and the coherence of the unit). Third, the text of the notice neither resembles oral speech nor asks the readers to understand it as a self-contained oral communication that took place in a set of specific circumstances within the narrative world of the book. Fourth, the speakers in vv. 12-13 do not focus their attention only on those hearing the words they utter on this occasion in the world of the text, but seem to look over the words of other godly speakers in the book and toward the community of readers of the book.

Setting

The actual setting of the reading of this unit is not different from those of the other units discussed above. One may mention only the presence of probable references and allusions to images and expressions that were likely to be within the repertoire of postmonarchic communities (for examples, see above). Such references and allusions seem to point to the world of knowledge of the intended reader.

There is no information about the particular setting of the speech in the world of the book, nor is there any sign to the readers to approach the speech from the vantage point of any reconstruction of a particular, historical event in the 8th century BCE (such as Sennacherib's invasion [cf. Allen, 302-3] or Menahem's coup against Shallum [Shaw, esp. 95-96]). In fact, no historical event is associated with the proclamation of the speech by the speakers in the book. The only historical circumstances that are referred to are clearly put in the future of the speakers, and they point to an exilic situation that, from the vantage point of the postmonarchic community of readers and postmonarchic discourse in general, was most likely associated with the fall of monarchic Judah. Whether the references to the gathering of the remnant and the empowering of "Israel" were seen as fulfilled in the Achaemenid period is very doubtful. To a large extent, "Israel" — within its own discourse — considered itself to be composed of "the exiles." (On these issues see Ben Zvi, "Inclusion"; idem, "Primary (Hi)story.")

Intention

The intention of this unit is to conclude the reading of the macrosection (1:2–2:13) and the preceding unit (2:6-11) with a note of salvation, to provide a bridge between the idea of the expected status of "Israel" because of their relation to YHWH (their king, leader, patron) and the fate of monarchic "Israel" on the one hand, and the status of the postmonarchic community of readers themselves. (See Ben Zvi, "Understanding"; idem, *Zephaniah*, 325-46.) The lengthy depiction of the appalling sins of monarchic "Israel" serves a similar bridging role, only this time between the image of YHWH as slow to anger and the like (e.g., 7:18) and the conviction that YHWH brought about the fall of monarchic Judah and Jerusalem, of "Israel" as conceived in their own discourse.

One may mention again that the movement from powerlessness, dispossession, almost death (notice the "remnant" language) to strength, positive association with YHWH (who is described as leading Israel), and the expression of this movement by language showing clearly military or violent overtones in v. 13 is coherent with Bloch's anthropological model of "rebounding violence." Significantly, the aforementioned overtones exist even if one maintains that this verse refers only to the process of "gathering Jacob," and obviously if one understands the military actions referred to there as pointing to a later time and not directly related to that process. If the basic logic of Bloch's model is followed, then the announcement of salvation is not only expected but is the heightening point of the narrative, the beginning of a new life empowered by the numinous. (→ 4:1-5, Intention.)

Bibliography

M. Bloch, *Prey into Hunter: The Politics of Religious Experience* (Cambridge: Cambridge Univ. Press, 1992); G. Brin, "Micah 2,12-13: A Textual and Ideological Study," *ZAW* 101 (1989) 118-24; C. J. Dempsey, "The Interplay between Literary Form and Technique and Ethics in Micah 1–3" (Ph.D. diss., Catholic Univ. of America, 1994); Y. Kaufmann, *Toledot Ha'emunah Hayisra'it* (8 vols.; Tel Aviv: Bialik, 1937-56); E. Otto, "Techniken der Rechtssatzredaktion israelitischer Rechtsbücher in der Redaktion des Prophetenbuches Micha," *SJOT* 5 (1991) 119-50; W. G. E. Watson, *Traditional Techniques in Classical Hebrew Verse* (JSOTSup 170; Sheffield: Sheffield Academic Press, 1994); J. T. Willis, "A Note on ויאמר in Micah 3₁," *ZAW* 80 (1969) 50-54.

PROPHETIC READING EXPLAINING THE FALL OF JERUSALEM/ZION IN TERMS OF WRONG LEADERSHIP, 3:1-12

Structure

I. Self-citation marker — 1aα₁
II. First announcement of judgment against individuals — 1aα₂-4
  A. Introduction to speech that includes identification of the individuals (by means of a call to hear) — 1aα₂
  B. General accusation — 1b-2a
  C. Development of the accusation — 2b-3
  D. Description of the corresponding judgment — 4
III. Second announcement of judgment against individuals — 5-7
  A. Introduction to speech that includes identification of the individuals (by means of a divine citation formula) — 5aα
  B. General accusation — 5aβ
  C. Development of the accusation — 5b
  D. Description of the corresponding judgment — 6-7

The most conspicuous feature of this READING is the abundance of literary items conveying to the intended readers a sense of textual cohesiveness. The three announcements of judgment share a common theme, and their structure is very similar. Moreover, the first and last of them begin in an almost identical manner (cf. vv. 1 and 9), with a call to hear addressed to the same public. Both of the two "odd" sections (see below) turn the reader's attention from the outset to the textually inscribed speaker — to the "I" in the text — characterizing that speaker as a powerful and authoritative personage separate from and in opposition to the wrongful, monarchic leadership depicted in the book. Furthermore, a ubiquitous network of repeated vocabulary and of puns extends over the entire text. For instance, *rāʾšê* ("heads") appears in vv. 9, 11 (also cf. 2:13; cf. Luker); *mišpāṭ* ("justice") in vv. 1, 8, 9, and cf. *yišpōṭû* ("give judgment") in v. 11 and *hipšîṭû* ("tear [skin] off") in v. 3; *hălôʾ* ("is it not?") in vv. 1 and 11; *ʿammî* ("my people") in vv. 3 and 5; the pair Jacob-Israel in vv. 1, 8, and 9; *lōʾ yaʿăneh* ("he will not answer") in v. 4 and *ʾên maʿănēh* ("there is no answer") in v. 7; *qsm* ("divining") in v. 6, *qōsĕmîm* ("diviners") in v. 7 and *yiqsōmû* ("they divine") in v. 11; *hammatʿîm* ("who lead astray") in v. 5 and *hamătaʿăbîm* ("who abhor") in v. 9. (Cf. Hagstrom, 39-43; Vargon, 87-88; Dempsey, 200-203.)

As in the other units of the book of Micah previously discussed, ch. 3 shows not only puns on words and sound repetitions but also sharp grammatical shifts in person, "unexpected" (or "ungrammatical") pronominal references, split up word pairs, double meanings, and at least a connoted blurring of speakers.

Instances of puns on words are mentioned above. One may add to them also the different meanings conveyed by the six occurrences of *ʿal* in vv. 5-7 (cf. Petrotta, 93-94; Dempsey, 201). Sound repetition is evident, for instance, in the sibilants in v. 3b (see Dempsey, 201; cf. Luker). For grammatical shifts in person, see, for instance, the shift from the 2nd person to the 3rd in relation to those condemned in vv. 1-3, and the one from the 3rd to the 2nd and then the 3rd person again in relation to those condemned in vv. 5-6. For unexpected pronominal references see the emphatic and repeated reference to *"their"* skin, *"their"* flesh, and *"their"* bones (*ʿôrām, šĕʾērām, ʿaṣmôtām*, respectively) and "from *them*" *(mēʿălêhem)*, which occur in v. 2b, and note that none of them points to a textually inscribed antecedent, though context suggests that the reference is to "Israel." *Laylâ* ("night") and *yôm* ("day") in v. 6 provide a good example of a split word pair. Additional semantic word pairs occur in v. 5: *šālôm* ("peace") (cf. 5:4 [NRSV 5]) and *milḥāmâ* ("war"), and *šinnêhem* ("their teeth") and *pîhem* ("their mouth"). The last pair serves in this context to evoke an animal imagery that may be compared with imagery in v. 3. On a different level, note also the reference to "his face" in v. 4. (On these issues cf. Petrotta, 93-94.) The connotations evoked by the use of *nšk* ("to bite"), whose typical subject is a snake (e.g., Gen 49:17; Am 5:19), associated here with "teeth," are also evident once one recognizes that *nšk* may also mean "to lend on interest" (e.g., Deut 23:20 [NRSV 19]; and notice the wordplay in Hab 2:7; see, e.g., Luker, 240).

A clear instance of a significant clause that allows more than one meaning is *'et-rûaḥ yhwh* in v. 8. The expression may be understood as a heightening item in a series of two, or an equivalent to or an explanation of the word immediately preceding the expression in the text, *kōaḥ*, "power" or strength." Any of these understandings leads to an English text such as "I am full of power, of YHWH's spirit." These readings of the text are all consonant with an understanding of the *'et* that introduces the expression as either marking the following text as the definite accusative of "substance" of an intransitive *ml'* in the Qal, "be full of" (e.g., Jer 6:11), or as a resumptive/emphatic or explanatory *'et* (e.g., Ezek 4:1). It may also be understood as clarifying the text in this way: "I am full of power with [the help of, or through the agency of] YHWH's spirit." Significantly, the reference to the "spirit *(rûaḥ)* of YHWH" in Mic 3:8 suggests to the readers an obvious link between the text here and that in ch. 2, where according to 2:7 the sinful leaders claim to understand "YHWH's spirit" but surely fail at that, and the text there clearly communicates (notice also the opposition between YHWH's spirit [*rûaḥ*] there and "walking wind [*rûaḥ*] and falsehood" in 2:11). This is, in fact, only one of several links binding ch. 3 to ch. 2 (see Luker, esp. 289-90; cf. Hagstrom, 57-59).

Incidentally, the expression *'et-rûaḥ yhwh* is often excised from the proposed original text (see, e.g., Alvarez Barredo, 100; Renaud, 135-37; Willi-Plein, 81; Wolff, *Micah,* 91-92; for a different approach see Hillers, *Micah,* 45). This expression in the context of prophetic literature seems to suggest a date later than the 8th century BCE, and it serves many purposes in the book of Micah.

As for an at least connoted blurring of the godly voices (i.e., those of the prophetic speaker and YHWH), the text is unclear about when the quoted divine speech begins (v. 5? v. 6?) as well as about the point at which the human voice citing YHWH's speech completes the quotation (also cf. Meier, 116-17, 213).

Finally, the presence of literary links connecting ch. 3 to ch. 1 and to chs. 4–5 is noteworthy. I discuss these links, particularly those between ch. 3 and 4:1-5, in more detail later in this chapter. At this stage, it may suffice to mention the play on the terms *bāmôt yā'ar* ("a height of forest") and *bahămôt ya'ar* ("animals of [the] forest"). The first term occurs only in 3:12 (//Jer 26:18); the second appears in Mic 5:7 and nowhere else in the HB/OT. Given this pattern of occurrences and the obvious assonance, it is likely that the presence of these two terms is not the result of blind chance. Moreover, the trajectory from one term to the other conveys and encapsulates the transformation of "defeated, razed Jerusalem" (i.e., *bāmôt yā'ar*) to "victorious Israel" (i.e., even stronger than *bahămôt ya'ar*); from "forest" as the undesirable opposite of the "cultural world" (i.e., Jerusalem, the city), to "forest" as pointing to the desirable — in the world of the text — unrestrained character of the lion, who is even more unrestrained than the "animals of (the) forest." For the use of identical or similar terms to communicate significant differences in Micah, see, for instance, the use of *qbṣ* ("gather") in 4:6, 12, and the similar case of the forms from the root *nṣl* ("save, deliver") in 4:10; 5:7 (NRSV 8). (For a discussion of *bāmôt* and *bahămôt* from a different perspective, see Hillers, *Treaty-Curses*, 53-54.)

As for the presence of literary links connecting ch. 3 to ch. 1, one may mention the reference to *ʿiyîn* ("heaps of ruins") in 3:12 (see the text in 1:6; cf. Ps 79:6; notice also the reference to *śādeh*, "field") and to the pair *pešaʿ–ḥaṭṭāʾt* ("transgression–sin") in Mic 1:5 and 3:8; all of these associate the destruction of Jerusalem with that of Samaria and, accordingly, continue the line of thought developed in ch. 1. In addition, references to the pair Jacob–Israel also appear in both chs. 1 and 3, and the same holds true for the pair *ṭôb–rāʿâ* ("good"–"evil, calamity").

There are also in Micah 3 turns of language and expressions that evoke concepts similar to those communicated by other texts in the HB/OT (not necessarily in the book of Micah) and some that are particular to this text. For instance, one may compare the reference to the lack of divine response by means of the syntagmatic pair *zʿq* ("cry") and *ʿnh* ("answer") in v. 4a with the relevant text in 1 Sam 8:18 and Prov 21:13. The "hiding of YHWH" in v. 4b is not referred to elsewhere in Micah, but appears numerous times in the HB/OT (e.g., Deut 31:17-18; Isa 8:17; 54:8; on the hiding of the face of YHWH, see Balentine, 1-79). Most of the expressions in Mic 3:6 appear nowhere else in the HB/OT, nor is there a very close parallel to the imagery in vv. 2b-3 (Vargon [93] compares this metaphor with Ezek 11:2-11; 24:1-14).

There is widespread agreement about the identification of the three largest subunits, namely, the three announcements of judgment against individuals. Each of them has a clear discursive marker indicating its beginning. All of them are structurally shaped mainly around the pattern of announcements of judgment as constructed in prophetic literature. Each of them shows a number of formal links (e.g., grammatical links) as well as stylistic and thematic connections. The latter include imagery and particular features that serve to present the three larger subunits to the intended community of readers as distinct subunits within the larger unit (cf. Miller, *Sin and Judgment*, 31-35; Hagstrom, 29-39; Petrotta, 93-95; Freedman, 145-46; among others). What about subunits I and IV?

Subunit I, *wāʾōmar* ("And I said:" or "But I said:"), tends to be explained (and at times explained away) as (1) the sole remnant of a developed prophetic narrative that was removed from the text (see, among others, Budde, 222-23; Weiser, 254; Allen, 305; Shaw, 97; Vargon, 89); (2) a redactional link between 3:1-4 and 2:1-11 in a proposed text that did not include 2:12-13 (cf. Mays, 77-78; Wolff, *Micah*, 96; but cf. also Peckham, 295, 368); or (3) as the beginning of the response of Micah to the speech of the pseudoprophets in 2:12-13 (e.g., Ehrlich, 433; van der Woude, "Micah in Dispute," esp. 257). In addition, one may mention that several scholars have proposed that the original Hebrew text here likely read *wayyōʾmer* ("and he said" or "but he said") instead of *wāʾōmar* (e.g., Hillers, *Micah,* 41; cf. LXX); Lescow ("Redaktionsgeschichtliche Analyze," esp. 47-49) has suggested that *wā'ōmar* originally stood before not only the text in vv. 1-4 but also that in vv. 5-8* and 9-12.* (For good surveys of the entire debate, including additional positions and variants, see Willis, "Note"; Renaud, 119-21; for Renaud's conclusion see 148.)

The first option (above) is definitely unverifiable. As discussed before, it is very unlikely that 2:12-13 contains the words of the pseudoprophets or, in general, Micah's opponents; accordingly, the third option falters too. The second option provides an explanation for the process that led to the present text, but the likelihood of this explanation cannot be greater than that of the redactional history of the text that it presupposes and on which it stands. In any case, this option does not shed light on the way in which the text of ch. 3 — as opposed to any of its possible but still hypothetical forerunners — was reread by its intended, postmonarchic rereadership, unless one assumes that the latter were fully aware of the history of composition of the text, as reconstructed by modern scholars, and that their mode of rereading the text was strongly governed by their knowledge of the proposed redactional history of the text. Significantly, whereas ch. 3 is abundant in textually and contextually inscribed markers conveying a sense of textual coherence, nowhere in this text is there a request (either explicit or implicit) or even a hint to the effect that readers should approach the text in a way that is informed by a redactional history of the text. Indeed, it is unlikely that the ancient readers of ch. 3 approached that text as many modern scholars do, that is, that they first divided it into redactional layers, and then interpreted each of these layers in its own terms. Thus for the purpose of this work the question is, what was *wā'ōmar* in v. 1 signaling to the intended rereaders of the book of Micah?

To begin with the obvious, it certainly suggested to them that a new, distinct literary unit — a self-citation, to be more precise — was being introduced. At the same time it signaled to them that this new unit was not to be approached as if it were unconnected to the preceding section in the book, likely the entire macrosection of 1:2–2:13, though some may argue that it binds together only 2:12-13 to 3:1-5.

Although *wā'ōmar* creates the clear expectation among the readers of the text that the following literary unit in the book consists of a self-quotation of the speaker, it is obvious that by itself *wā'ōmar* cannot determine the extent of the self-quotation or the related matter of the possible position, or the hierarchical level, of this unit in relation to other units in the book. Thus *wā'ōmar* brings these issues or questions to the audience of the book. They now have to read and reread the following citation, interpret its discursive markers, and then ponder where it concludes. The last task is surely not easy when the speaker's speech may include citations of other speakers within its own. Only after the extent and, accordingly, the contents of the self-quotation are clarified is it possible to begin to address the question of whether the citation serves the role that one would associate with the macrounit within the book. Given the presence of cohesive links that bind sequential macrounits in the book (see 5:14 [NRSV 15] and 6:1; cf. Willis, "Structure of Micah 3–5," esp. 197; idem, "Note"), there is no reason to consider the loose connection that *wā'ōmar* creates with the preceding text as necessarily precluding its possible role as marker of a new macrounit within the book, or of a unit within a macrounit, or even of a subunit within a unit. Moreover, *wā'ōmar* may serve more than one of these roles, in which case it will be instrumental in the shaping of a multiplicity of possible rereadings. (Cf. Willis, "Note"; Hagstrom, 57-58.)

In addition to those already mentioned, *wā'ōmar* fulfills three other significant functions. First, it creates a literary world in which the quoted words are presented by the speaker to an implied audience as "my recollection of the words that I said in the past," since any "faithful" report of past actions or events looks back on them and therefore must be understood as being later than the described actions or events. If so, then the audience of the reporting speaker is constructed as later than that of the reported speaker. Significantly, the text provides no reason to believe that the two audiences are even similar. Indeed, within the context of the book it is more reasonable to assume that the audience of the reporting speaker is implicitly characterized as being receptive to the speaker; the same surely does not hold true for that of the reported speaker. Significantly, the relation between the reporting and the reported speaker here (and their respective audiences) is analogous to that of the implied author and the reporting speaker (and their respective audiences), except that all those who are constructed as receivers of the godly report of the speech (i.e., the audience of the reporting speaker and that of the implied author) are certainly not characterized negatively. Their characterization in the text stands in sharp contrast with that of the addressees of the speech itself.

The gap between the proclamation and the retelling of a proclamation created by *wā'ōmar* has led to its excision from the "original words of Micah" by those scholars who are convinced that the speeches assigned to the prophetic speaker in ch. 3 directly reflect the oral proclamation of the historical prophet in monarchic times. According to these scholars, *wā'ōmar* is a later editorial addition that was written either by Micah (on the basis of an identification of the character referred to in the text by the 1st person sg. with the actual author) or by a later redactor (cf. Wolff, *Micah,* 95; Alvarez Barredo, 95-96).

Second, *wā'ōmar* brings to the forefront the character of the speaker. Rather than being a self-effacing figure, the speaker is presented as calling attention to "my persona," to "my words." Third, these words do characterize this persona as one who has been speaking with a godly voice, as one who has cited YHWH's words (in a way analogous to that in which this speaker cites "my words"), as one with the authority and socioreligious legitimacy to summon, address, and condemn the leaders of Judah and Jerusalem, and to proclaim correctly the future razing of Jerusalem/Zion. Significantly, the proclamation of the latter in 3:12 is assigned by the reporting speaker to the realm of "my words," whereas in Jer 26:18 it is presented as Micah's citation of divine speech.

Unit IV is most often included within unit III (e.g., Margolis, 37-39; Allen, 309-15; Wolff, *Micah,* 93-94; Mays, 80-86; Weiser, 256-59; Alonso Schökel and Sicre Díaz, 2:1052; Vargon, 88). On the one hand, there seem to be good reasons for their inclusion there. First, v. 8 can hardly be part of the third announcement of judgment, which begins with the call to hear in v. 9. Thus two options remain: either v. 8 is a unit by itself or it is included in the second announcement of judgment. Second, the latter option is enhanced by the presence of the connective *wĕ'ûlām 'ānōkî* ("but I"), by the irregular size and structure of a unit consisting only of v. 8 within this literary context, and by the claim that v. 8 reflects the speaker's self-understanding as a true prophet who stands in opposition to the "prophets who lead my people astray" (v. 5). On the other hand, connective markers are present also between units and even macrounits (see above). Moreover, if regularity is the norm, then a unit consisting of vv. 5-8 would present an irregular structure, for if this is the case only here a fifth element will be added after (1) the introduction to the speech that includes identification of the individuals, (2) general accusation, (3) development of the accusation, and (4) description of the corresponding judgment. Further, regularity of structure and size are not reliable grounds for a decision, one way or another, because sharp shifts in structure or size may, for instance, be used as stylistic devices to channel the readers' attention. The self-identification of the speaker in general is set in the main by the polar opposition between the godly speaker and *all* the wrongful leaders (cf. v. 1) as they are characterized in the speakers' speech, not only or even mainly the misleading prophets or diviners. Notice also the identity of the "you" in the heightened conclusion of the unit, "because of you Zion shall be plowed as a field." Moreover, the speaker does not use the word "prophet" in self-reference, as one might expect if the main thrust of the unit would be to emphasize the opposition between true prophet or diviner (see vv. 5-6) and false prophets or diviners. In addition, if the intended readership of the text was unequivocally asked to approach v. 8 as an integral part of vv. 5-7, then why does the choice of words in v. 8 point to links elsewhere in ch. 3 and not to vv. 5-7? For instance, *mišpāṭ* ("justice") occurs in v. 8 and vv. 1, 9 (and cf. *yišpōṭû,* "give judgment," in v. 11 and also *hipšîṭû,* "tear skin off," in v. 3) but nowhere in vv. 5-7; *'ammî* ("my people") appears in vv. 3 and 5 but not in v. 8; and the pair Jacob–Israel occurs in vv. 1, 8, and 9 but nowhere in vv. 5-7. The simple fact is that not a single term is shared between vv. 5-7 and v. 8, a striking feature given the tendency toward repeated words or allusions to words in ch. 3 as a whole and in each of its subunits. At the word level, only two words appear in both vv. 5-7 and v. 8, the particle *'et* and *yhwh,* but notice that YHWH in v. 8 appears as part of the expression "YHWH's spirit," not as a self-standing noun as in v. 5. As for the possible connotations of *mišpāṭ ûgĕbûrâ* ("justice and might") see Isa 28:6; and for those of YHWH's spirit, see Isa 11:2; 40:7, 13; 59:9; 63:14. It occurs nowhere else in the so-called Minor Prophets except in Hos 3:15, but there it points more to "mighty wind" than to YHWH's spirit.

Thus it seems reasonable to favor an interpretation of v. 8 as a unit by itself — separate from vv. 5-7 — and within the general frame of Micah 3 (cf. Alvarez Barredo, 100; Dempsey, 198-200; this division is adopted also by Willis [e.g., "Structure of Micah 3–5"] and Miller [32-34], among others). If so, it is reasonable to understand its middle position within the text and its structural and thematic distinctiveness as features calling attention to the unit itself. Thus Dempsey is likely to be correct when she claims that this unit is at the heart of the text and plays a pivotal role, looking back to vv. 1-7 and forward to vv. 9-12 (Dempsey, 200). The more central this unit is considered the more is likely to be at stake in the message it conveys to the readers of the text. I discuss this issue below under Intention, but it suffices to note here that the only other unit in this text that is not part of the main system of three announcements of judgment also brings the speaker's persona to the forefront.

I may mention at this point that various scholars have considered the following among the units, or subunits, mentioned in the outline as editorial additions to a proposed original text:

1. Unit I, *wā'ōmar,* "and I said," in v. 1 (see above)
2. Most of II.2: *hălô' lākem lāda'at 'et-hammišpāṭ,* "should you not know justice," in v. 1 (on the grounds of being a Deuteronomistic addition, e.g., Alvarez Barredo, 96)
3. Unit IV, i.e., v. 8 (e.g., Alvarez Barredo, 100).

Those who maintain that these units were not part of what they claim to be, an original text, will of course not include them in any discussion about the structure of that text.

Genre

Micah 3:1-12 is a PROPHETIC READING, that is, a text written to be read and re-read and that makes claims to the legitimacy and authority of a prophetic text, claims of being YHWH's word. Already at the beginning of the unit, *wā'ōmar* signals to the readers that 3:1-12 is not a free-floating unit in the sea of the book but one that is linked to the preceding macrounit (1:2–2:13; or at very least, but less likely, to 2:12-13). As will be shown later, there are also links between ch. 3 and ch. 4 (cf. Willis, "Structure of Micah 3–5"; Luker).

The reading consists of a monologue, or, better, a section of a monologue (on the links between chs. 3 and 4 see below), in which there is much emphasis on the persona and authority of the textually inscribed speaker. There is far less emphasis (and a degree of ambiguity) concerning the identity of the literary addressees of the monologue. They are not mentioned in 3:1. The "heads of Jacob and rulers of the house of Israel" are the addressees of a previous announcement that is being quoted for the purpose of the monologue by the speaker of the monologue. It is plausible that, within the context of the monologue, the reference to "Jacob" and "Israel" in v. 8b may hint at (though certainly not unequivocally decide the question of) the identity of the interlocutors of the speaker in the world created in the text. If this is the case, then the monologue is addressed to "Israel." This "Israel" is a theological and trans-generational concept that includes both the likely interlocutors of the godly speaker set in the monarchic period and the intended readers of a book written, read, and reread in the postmonarchic period. On this concept of "Israel" see the discussion on 1:2-16 and bibliography there; it suffices here to mention that this concept is consistently and repeatedly conveyed to the intended readers of ch. 3; see vv. 1, 8, 9, and cf. 6:2 and see detailed discussion on ch. 1. One may also mention that the word pair *pešaʿ–ḥaṭṭāʾt* ("transgression"–"sin") appears also in 1:5 in relation to Jacob–Israel, in 1:13 to "Israel–Daughter Zion" (where Daughter Zion symbolically stands for Israel or, at the very least, for its "heart"; cf. 3:9-12), and 6:7 to the individual Israelite, that is, a worshiper of YHWH.

In any case it is worth noticing that v. 8, which is the only section of any length in the monologue that is not presented as a recollection of announcements of judgment, shows the only reference to the "sin" of all the people in the monologue in ch. 3, in contrast to the numerous characterizations of the "sin" of groups of individuals — though in leadership positions — in the self-quoted, past announcements of the speaker. (Some scholars have interpreted this piece of evidence as supporting the idea that v. 8 is an exilic, Deuteronomistic gloss added to an original, monarchic period text, e.g., Alvarez Barredo, 100.)

Most of the speaker's monologue consists of three self-citations, each of which activates the expectations and general associations conveyed by prophetic announcements of judgment against individuals. As usual in prophetic literature, these are not simply individuals but members of a social group in a position of leadership. This being the case, the expectation is for punishment that befalls either (a) the group itself — and likely in a way that befits their sin (cf. 3:1-4 with Prov 21:13; concerning Mic 3:5-7 and 3:9-12 see Miller, 32-35, esp. his categories of correspondence I-E1, I-E2, III-C on pp. 113-19); or (b) given the leadership and representative role of the sinners' group, the larger entity that it leads and represents, which in the case of 3:9-12 is certainly the entity identified as Zion, Jerusalem, Jacob, "Israel," and whose referent is monarchic Judah and its capital as understood within the discourse of the community within which and for which the text of ch. 3 was written.

For the relation of this type of correspondence with those mentioned in (a) see Miller's understanding of Micah in terms of his categories I-E3, I-E4, II-B (pp. 114-16); for the rhetorical and ideological identification of represented and representative see Ben-Zvi, "Inclusion," esp. 120-25 and bibliography there. Since Israel is the one about to be punished (though it is not mentioned as the culprit), Westermann and others include the type of discourse reflected in alternative (b) in their category "announcement of judgment against Israel." (Westermann thinks that 3:1-2, 4, and 2:1-4 also belong to this genre; see *Basic Forms,* 174-75). When option (b) is followed there is a degree of defamiliarization in the genre, for those who have been oppressed are then depicted as about to be punished too (see 2:1-4 and 3:1-4, the latter, of course, if "they" in v. 4 is understood as pointing to the entire people rather than only the leaders of Israel).

I must stress that, as in the case of previous announcements of judgment in Micah, the constructed speech is, on the one hand, presented to the readership of the book (at least at face value) as a mimetic representation of an oral, real-life, direct announcement of judgment against a certain group; accordingly, it brings along the expectations and circumstances associated with this type of discourse. But, on the other hand, it is written in such a way that it stands at odds with its own face-value claim. For instance, the text of each of these supposedly direct speeches is phrased and structured in relation to that present in the other texts that stand in its immediate textual vicinity in ch. 3 (and beyond), a feature that leads to the textual cohesion mentioned above under Structure. This is so despite the claim in the world of the text that the three announcements were not given at the same time or to the same audience. In other words, the written, literary character of ch. 3 (and beyond) is well reflected in the choice of words present in these supposedly independent speeches.

In this regard, one may stress the interesting case concerning the identity of the addressees in the concluding announcement of judgment (3:9-12). They are initially identified with those of the first announcement. As a result a literary envelope is shaped, binding together ch. 3. Then the identity of these addressees shifts to encompass all of those mentioned in ch. 3 and the priests, the only other main leadership group with which divine knowledge is usually associated that was missing in the text. By doing so, the text brings together and complements all the converging lines of sin and transgression in the leadership present in 3:1-7 so as to lead to the climax of the text: the divine judgment against Zion/Jerusalem and, by implication, Jacob/Israel, in the concluding verse, v. 12. Of course, the shift in the identity of the addressees makes perfect sense within the literary world of ch. 3, but is less coherent with a proposed, orally delivered, independent announcement of judgment against a particular public. Consequently, several scholars working within redaction-critical models have proposed to excise the relevant section of v. 11 (i.e., the one that carries out the shift of addressees) from their reconstructed original text (cf. Lescow, "Redaktionsgeschichtliche Analyze," 49-50; idem, "Komposition," 202-8; Alvarez Barredo, 101-2).

In addition, the first announcement explicitly and repeatedly constructs the divine punishment as something that will take place in an indefinite future far from the perspective of those directly addressed by the reported speaker proclaiming judgment. By implication the announcement assumes a discourse shared by accuser and accused in which no harm will come to those condemned in vv. 1-3 in any near future, or perhaps during their entire lives. Of course, such a temporal delay in judgment makes sense in a theologico-literary discourse informed by, or even focused on, the fall of monarchic Judah and Jerusalem (cf. the final and heightening conclusion of this unit in 3:12) or the exile (cf. the final and heightening point in 1:16; and cf. 2:4, 10), but surely weakens the rhetorical strength of a supposedly sharp oral proclamation actually delivered to and against the leaders of monarchic Judah in the 8th century, more than a century before the mentioned "fall" and "exile." Redaction-critical scholars whose goal it is to reconstruct the oral speech of the historical Micah tend to be well aware of this tension, and solve it by excising the unequivocal *bāʿēt hahî'*, "at that time," from their proposed original text (e.g., Wolff, *Micah*, 91; → 2:1-5, Genre). One should note that *bāʿēt hahî'* strongly reduces the ambiguity regarding the temporal reference conveyed by *ʾāz*, "then," slightly earlier in the text (cf. Hillers, *Micah*, 42).

Moreover, even within the world of the book these announcements are explicitly taken out of their supposedly original setting and presented as part of a monologue addressed to another public, in a different setting. All these considerations, in addition to the always present differences between literary, constructed speech that purports to reflect direct speech and actual natural speech, and the unverifiable and speculative character of redactional reconstructions render questionable all attempts to abstract the actual proclamation of an 8th-century prophet Micah. Furthermore, from the perspective of the intended readers of the book of Micah (the subject of the present commentary), the words of the character Micah — or, better, YHWH's word, as the book of Micah calls itself in 1:1 — are those of importance. There is no reason to assume that these readers were aware of a scholarly reconstructed ipsissima verba of a historical prophet, nor is there any indication in the text that they were asked to reread it in a way informed by "historical" considerations.

Setting

Wolff expresses a quite common position, at least in its general approach:

> The ancient prophecies in this chapter [i.e., ch. 3] were sayings proclaimed in Jerusalem itself. This is sufficiently clear from vv. 10 and 12. . . . We may suppose that the locality [of the proclamation] was the outer court of the temple. . . . If Micah had been a member of the elders of Judah, it is certainly intelligible that precisely in this place he would have stood to proclaim his message. . . . The date of this scene cannot be precisely determined. The Assyrian crisis . . . need not be pushed forward to the time around 701, when Sennacherib besieged Jerusalem. If Micah already saw the siege of Samaria as a threat also to Jerusalem . . . , and if he already at that time referred to the Judaic authorities as "Israel" . . . , then we cannot with certainty exclude . . . the sayings in chap. 3 from the decade between the Syro-Ephraimite war (733) and the conquest of Samaria (722).
>
> (Wolff, *Micah*, 96-97, under Setting)

One may question Wolff's approach to the setting of ch. 3 in terms of, first, the likelihood of any reconstruction of the actual addressees, in natural language, of a historical prophet (i.e., "the ancient prophecies") on the basis of the constructed speech that the implied author put in the mouth of a literary character in a book, which at the very least is not necessarily dominated by concerns about mimesis and historical accuracy; second, the logical strength of the argument that it "is *sufficiently clear* from vv. 10 and 12" that the "sayings [were] proclaimed in Jerusalem itself" (emphasis mine). Yet the most revealing feature of the approach characterized by the quotation from Wolff is the lack of discussion about both the setting of the writing and reading of the text of ch. 3, and the setting against which the words of the textually inscribed speaker are placed in the world suggested by the text and against which — one would assume — the intended readers of ch. 3 were supposed to understand them.

In this regard, I want to stress that ch. 3 neither mentions the outer court of the temple nor identifies the place of the proclamation of the monologue attributed to the speaker or of the cited, previous addressees that are embedded in that monologue. Moreover, ch. 3 mentions neither the Assyrian crisis nor any particular event in the life of the community to which the speaker and his addressees belonged. The only crisis referred to in ch. 3 is an internal, sociotheological crisis due to faulty leadership. The text presents the life of the monarchic society as shaped by the "heads" and rulers of "Israel," its priests and prophets, rather than by the words (and teaching) of a speaker who characterizes this leadership as utterly corrupted, and himself as "full of YHWH's spirit." Significantly, this speaker is, in turn, characterized by the implied author as an authoritative, "godly" speaker whose voice tends to blur with YHWH's. Thus the speaker's words about, perspective on, and evaluation of the monarchic society as suffering from a sociotheological crisis are fully validated.

Whereas the approach to setting exemplified by Wolff's work focuses on a reconstructed historical metanarrative and a reconstructed set of original addresses of the historical prophet Micah, the text (i.e., the explicit approach to setting that ch. 3 suggests to its intended readers to follow) clearly avoids unequivocal associations with any precise set of geographical and temporal circumstances. The only temporal setting that ch. 3 conveys to its readers is that of the monarchic period (as opposed to that of the postmonarchic), specifically, within a reading informed by 1:1, during the reigns of Jotham, Ahaz, and Hezekiah (i.e., for the most part, 8th-century Judah, as understood by the intended rereaders of ch. 3). In ch. 3 the destruction of Jerusalem is still in the future (i.e., from the vantage point of the speaker in the world of the text), and the references to the leaders of the people and their behavior are consistent with other images of the monarchic period in prophetic literature (e.g., Isa 1:23; Jer 22:13-17; cf. Lam 2:14). Significantly, the text does not claim that the announced punishment of "Israel," and of Jerusalem, has to be fulfilled within the time limits set by Mic 1:1.

In relation to the last statement, however, one should mention that the text in Jer 26:16-19 seems to imply that the judgment was supposed to take place during Hezekiah's days; yet the reference to Micaiah's (Micah's) words there serves the rhetorical purposes of the unit in Jeremiah (see the stressed conclusions of Jer 26:13, 19). Significantly, the precedent of Micaiah has to be understood as an announcement of a destruction that was supposed to be fulfilled but did not come to pass in Hezekiah's own time, if it is to support the argument advanced there concerning YHWH's possible relenting. In sharp contrast to Jeremiah 26, there is no reference in Micah 3 to Hezekiah, or to "all Judah," or to their repentance, or to YHWH's relenting; in fact, even the addressees of the speech are characterized differently (cf. Jer 26:18 and Mic 3:9). The texts are different.

In sum, Micah 3 shows a clear tendency to avoid any specific anchoring in a too narrowly defined set of historical circumstances. Budde, among others, was well aware that such is the case in ch. 3, as in other prophetic texts. He explained this feature of the text, however, in terms of a redaction that stripped an original — and hypothetical — text of all its historical references. Such a tendency is consistent with a text written so as to allow multiple readings, each informing the other, and each within the theological matrix and world of knowledge of the community, or communities, of literati within which and for which the text was written, read, and reread. (This feature is, of course, not limited to Micah 3; cf., e.g., Sweeney's position that the lack of specific references to historical background "enables [Isa] 1:4-9 to be read in relation to various historical settings" [Sweeney, 77].)

In other words, the lack of precise setting in the world of the text is consistent with the actual setting of the writing and reading of the text: this is an activity taken up by postmonarchic literati who can be characterized among others as bearers of high literacy and as those (1) who shared a theological or ideological view centered in Zion/Jerusalem, (2) whose discourse deeply associated their concept of "Israel" (/Jacob) with Zion/Jerusalem, (3) for whom these concepts pointed directly to monarchic Judah, as they thought it to be in their own story of the past (→ 1:2-16; see Ben Zvi, "Inclusion"), and (4) who likely acted as brokers of divine knowledge to those unable to read, reread, and study by themselves texts that require high literacy.

Intention

The intention of the literary unit consisting of 3:1-12 as it was likely read by the postmonarchic community for which and within which it was written is to address the destruction of Jerusalem/Zion and to abstract a theological lesson from it (cf. Jer 9:11). The end of the monarchic period, approached this time from the perspective of the razing of Zion (for a complementary perspective, that of the dispossession of "Israel," see ch. 2; cf. the heightened reference to the "exile" at the end of ch. 1) is here explained in terms of the wrongdoing of the monarchic elite (for the lack of reference to "king" see below). From the perspective of a reading informed by 1:1, this elite is associated with a particular period in monarchic "Israel" (which signified the kingdom of Judah within the discourse of these postmonarchic communities), when its members may be seen as paradigmatic of false prophets, corrupt judges, and the like.

Within this basic frame, some more specific features are also noticeable and contribute substantially to the understanding of the likely intention of this text against the background of the aforementioned postmonarchic communities. First, it is worth stressing the presence of an underlying, unifying theme throughout the unit: that of communication (or the breakdown thereof), both in the sense of the process of interaction (i.e., involved in communication) and in the sense of what is communicated through the process (i.e., a certain set of messages, knowledge, or the like). Thus, and given the character of those described as involved in communication (or its breakdown) in ch. 3 and the character of the text itself, ch. 3 further addresses concerns about the reliability of what is presented as authoritative knowledge (see, e.g., 2:6-7, 11; see below).

On the one hand, the speaker in ch. 3 repeatedly characterizes the leaders as those who willfully pervert the messages and basic lore whose source is in

YHWH, that is, the contents of "divine, authoritative communication or instruction." Thus their prophecies and revelations are false; their priestly teachings, unreliable. In addition, they are described as those who have absolutely disregarded the basic socioethical principles of justice in general and of the administration of justice in particular. Since the latter are surely conceived in the discourse of the time as anchored in YHWH and YHWH's will, the described actions of the leaders point to a rejection of a divine justice whose categorical validity they are supposed to know (i.e., a rejection of godly knowledge), and an implied, misleading message that this is YHWH's justice (cf. v. 11b, and notice the emphasis on "us" [see below] and the explicit opening verset). On the other hand, the announced actions of YHWH that correspond to the activities that the speaker associates with the sinful leadership explicitly involve the halt of YHWH's communication with these leaders in the first two announcements (see 3:4, 6-7; on v. 12 see below).

Significantly, the concluding proclamation of punishment in the first announcement, the one about "YHWH causing YHWH's face to hide," not only suits the logic of the announcement in which it is included, but its potential range of evoked meanings is developed in two different ways: in the second announcement of judgment, which surely deals with separation and breakdown of communication as decided and fulfilled by YHWH as a punishment, and in the third announcement (cf. Isa 54:7; Ezek 39:23; and esp. Jer 33:5; see below). Finally, I must stress that just as the language of punishment in (→) Mic 2:5 implies restoration and salvation, that of "*hiding* the face" also conveys an implicit hope or even promise of salvation (see Balentine, esp. 65-76).

The third announcement, which concludes with the destruction of Jerusalem/Zion, is not dissimilar to the previous announcements; to the contrary it further develops their main themes. Given the salient role of this announcement, a more detailed study is in order. To begin with, whereas the first announcement of judgment focuses on a particular group of the elite and the second on another, and neither of the two explicitly relates the condemned groups to Zion/Jerusalem, the third announcement shows a text constructed so as to bring together the aforementioned groups, and to convey an image of a Jerusalemite elite — rather than a set of disparate social groups — and to associate it firmly with the place whose razing is about to be announced. In this way v. 11 serves as a fitting preamble to the dramatic announcement in v. 12 that concludes ch. 3.

On the surface, as in the previous units, each group in v. 11a is described separately and in terms of their particular "contribution" to society, the only difference being that the priests are mentioned for the first time. Yet all three groups are connected now by the triple reference to the city (notice the three identical pronominal suffixes: "*her* heads," "*her* prophets," and "*her* priests"); by the thematically identical, and formally similar, explanation of their wrongdoing in terms of their willingness to accept bribes, payment, or silver; and by the similar structure of the three lines carrying this characterization that itself also conveys cohesiveness. Yet, even more significantly, once the text moves from v. 11a to 11b and stands immediately before the announcement in v. 12, the three groups coalesce into one that is characterized by a theological position. This position is encapsulated in their words, "YHWH is surely in our midst, no harm shall come upon us." First, one may notice the ironical emphasis on *"our"* rather than *"her"* (contrast with, e.g., Isa 12:6; Zeph 3:15, 17; also cf. Obad 17) that the implied author put in the mouth of the sinful leaders — of course, through the mediation of the authoritative speaker within whose speech the leaders' constructed speech is embedded. This choice of words is also likely related to the issues raised above, and in particular brings to the forefront the claim about the connection between themselves and YHWH that the condemned leaders have advanced (see above). Second, it is obvious that the text asks the readers to place them all in a common mental category based on a single attribute: they all share a wrong knowledge of the character of YHWH (cf. 2:7). The corresponding action of YHWH (notice the *biglalĕkem*, "because of you," which immediately follows v. 11b and relates the action to the opponents as a unified group) is presented now as being the destruction of Zion/Jerusalem.

It is true that at first sight one may deem the announced deed as being essentially different from the previously mentioned interruptions of divine-human communication. One has to admit, however, that the announcement is meant to have a strong affective impact on all its audiences: the interlocutors of the speakers, those of the speaker responsible for the monologue, those addressed by the implied author, and the intended and actual communities of rereaders of the book. In any case, it is significant that the text that stands next to 3:12 in the book of Micah, namely, 4:1-4/5, refers explicitly and emphatically to Zion/Jerusalem as the place of divine instruction. Within a reading of ch. 3 that is informed by 4:1-4, the removal of the place in v. 12 is presented in the context of the book as tantamount to the removal of the possibility of learning YHWH's ways.

Is the text written to suggest to its readers an understanding of 3:12 from the vantage point of 4:1-4? It seems so, for this understanding is not only consistent with the previously mentioned interruptions of divine-human communication, but strongly supported by the various cohesive links that bind 4:1-4 to 3:9-12 and that suggest to the readers of these adjacent units within the book of Micah that the two are indeed related. These links include not only that one unit talks about the destruction of Jerusalem/Zion and the immediately following unit deals with the status of rebuilt Zion/Jerusalem in the future, but also that YHWH is depicted in 4:1-4 as taking the role previously fulfilled by the wrongful leadership. Thus YHWH will "judge" (*špṭ;* cf. 4:3 with 2:11), and YHWH will teach (*yrh;* cf. 4:2 and 3:11). Moreover, YHWH's word — that is, the divine knowledge associated with prophecy within a perspective akin to that reflected, for instance, in 1:1 — is not only present but will come forth from Zion/Jerusalem. In addition, one may notice (1) the repetition of the terms *har,* "mountain," and *bayit,* "house," in 3:12 and 4:1 (the former occurring twice in 4:1); (2) the opposition between *śādeh,* "field," and *har,* "mountain," that binds 3:12 and 4:1 and encapsulates the changing fate of Jerusalem/Zion (i.e., it is now a "mountain," will turn into a "field," but eventually will be "the highest mountain"); (3) the sound repetition in *ʿiyîn,* "heap of ruins," in 3:12 and *yāmîm,* "days," in 4:1; and (4) the probable relation between the expressions *rāš'ê bêt ya'ăqōb,* "the leaders of the house of Jacob" (3:9), and *bêt 'ĕlōhê ya'ăqōb,* "the house of the God of Jacob" (4:2). The last two expressions share two out of the three words, and the third shows a shift from sinful leaders to YHWH. The first expression occurs nowhere else in the HB/OT except in Mic 3:9, and the second appears only in Mic 4:2 and in its parallel text in Isa 2:3. In sum, it seems that the text was composed to convey a connection between Mic 3:12 and 4:1-4, and accordingly to suggest also here that the divine response concerns itself with the interruption of communication and the lack of access to YHWH's word *(dĕbar-yhwh)* or instruction *(tôrâ).* (For lack of communication with YHWH, and the lack of access to YHWH's word [*dĕbar-yhwh*] as the end result of YHWH's punishment, see also Am 8:11-12; cf. Alfaro, 35.)

It is in the context of this underlying and encompassing theme of reliable communication with and knowledge of the divine, and the associated theme of its truthful transmission to other members of the community (cf. 2:6-7, 11) that one of the main intentions of the monologue of the speaker in ch. 3 becomes clear. The two units that do not consist of announcements of judgment emphasize the persona and authoritative character of the speaker and the differentiation between the speaker and the sinful leaders, which are set rhetorically at opposite poles (see v. 1 and esp. v. 8). Significantly, in ch. 3 no personage in any position associated with authority except the speaker and YHWH (and their two voices tend to be blurred; see above) is presented in a positive light. Moreover, the intended readership is asked to accept as valid and authoritative a self-presentation of the speaker according to which YHWH's and the speaker's words converge. It is the speaker's self-evaluation and evaluation of all the others that is presented as authoritative to these readers.

This strong stress on the authority and legitimacy of the speaker alone within human society is remarkable. What function could this emphasis serve within the discourse of the literati within whom books such as Micah were written? It seems that the key for understanding the function within the social frame of the community of postmonarchic rereaders of these texts resides in the somewhat analogous situation existing between themselves and the speaker in the text. The speaker constructs an authoritative place for himself within the world of the text to the exclusion of all other elite groups. It is only his voice that carries the truly divine knowledge. Yet even in the world inscribed in the book, it is the implied author who constructs the speech of the speaker and all his words (as well as YHWH's). In the world outside the book, those who are empowered to shape and transmit the divine knowledge are within a social group that includes both the actual authors of the book and its rereaders, that is, the literati in postmonarchic communities. As the speaker in the world of the text claims authority to transmit a godly message to his interlocutors, so do these literati when they claim to learn YHWH's word by reading this book (→ 1:1) and to transmit it reliably to those who are unable to read the book directly, that is, most of "Israel." When the speaker claims to be the only legitimate broker of the divine word and teaching to monarchic Israel, this group of literati is most likely to see a reflection of their own story about themselves, and their own claims for superiority over contemporaneous alternative groups (→ 1:1; see Ben Zvi, *Zephaniah*, esp. 350-56; idem, *Obadiah*, 260-62, et passim; idem, "Micah 1:2-16"; cf. idem, "Prophets"). It is only to be expected that within this group the razing of Jerusalem/Zion is mentioned at the concluding climax of the unit and that it is directly related to the upholding of a wrong theological position (v. 11b). In this regard, it is worth noting that also in ch. 2 wrongdoing is explicitly associated with upholding a wrong theological position (see 2:7), there, one in relation to "YHWH's spirit," which in fact is not too different from the one expressed in 3:11.

Although this is not the overt intention of ch. 3, the text certainly communicates and reflects the Jerusalem-centered theology (by the use of the term "Israel" or "Jacob" in reference to monarchic Judah, and Zion/Jerusalem) that characterized the work of this literati (→ 1:2-16 and bibliography there). This postmonarchic, Zion/Jerusalem-centered theology cannot accept the idea that Jerusalem/Zion cannot and will not be destroyed (a position associated in the text with sinful leaders), but has to address the issue of its destruction and explain it. Ch. 3 reflects and communicates also a conception of socioethics anchored in YHWH, as well as a construction of history as being led, at least in part, by the behavior of the ruling strata, and a particular reconstruction of monarchic history.

A final observation in this regard: the text projects an image of the corrupted monarchic elite in which there is no explicit reference to sages or scribes, or to mighty warriors or the commanding officers of the army. The main function associated with those depicted as "heads of *(rā'šê)* the house of Jacob" and "rulers of *(qĕṣînê)* the house of Israel" in vv. 1 and 9 is to administer justice. Yet, at least on the surface, it is even more striking that there is no reference to the king himself (cf. Ben Zvi, *Zephaniah*, 280-81). Is he not the one responsible for justice (e.g., 2 Sam 15:4; 1 Kgs 3:8-11; Ps 72:1-2; cf. Ps 99:4)?

The lack of reference to the army commanders might be explained from a theological or ideological perspective within which a national disaster does not result from, or is not actually grounded on, their lack of ability to run an efficient army. In fact, within this perspective, lack of military power is never the decisive and most fundamental cause of a national calamity, but such will surely come if judges will not administer justice. Similarly, the lack of reference to wise men or scribes may be explained partially in terms of their political or worldly aspects (cf. Isa 19:11-12), but above all in terms of a postmonarchic construction of the monarchic period of Judah as one in which the words spoken by the prophets are of much more importance and authority than those crafted by the pen of the scribes (cf. the relative status of Jeremiah and Baruch). But in the postmonarchic period, it is the contemporaneous pen of the scribes that controls what the mouth of the literary characters in a written book may utter. Thus, even in a book in which the scribes or sages are occasionally mentioned as opponents of the message of the prophet (see Jer 8:8), they are never allocated a major opposing role (see the book of Jeremiah, where "false prophets" and "political leaders" are much more significant).

So why is the king not mentioned in Micah 3? First, the lack of reference to the king in this kind of text is part of a well-attested pattern in prophetic literature (the king is not mentioned, e.g., in Zeph 3:3-4; cf. Isa 1:21-26; 5:8-11,

20-23; Zeph 1:8-9; Am 5:7, 11-13, 6:3-6; 8:4-6; see also Lam 4:13; on Zeph 3:3-4, including the issue of its relations to Ezek 22:25-28, see Ben Zvi, *Zephaniah,* 190-206). In fact, within this pattern, the culprits for the calamity are those who administered injustice for their own benefit (numerous times), and wrongful prophets and priests (Micah 3; Zeph 3:3-4; Lam 4:13). Thus the question is unlikely to be resolved only on the basis of any particular consideration applicable solely to the text of Micah. Although arguments grounded on silence are doubtful, one may ponder whether an image of the monarchic period in which Hezekiah and Josiah are both good characters (see ch. 3, as informed by 1:1, and Zeph 1:8; 3:3-4) had no influence in the shaping of these texts. In addition, one may wonder whether the social and political realities of postmonarchic communities had nothing to do with the selection of culprits in these texts.

Incidentally, if one would accept some degree of influence from the mentioned realities, then the lack of reference to writers (and readers) of authoritative literature may be seen in a different light, but still one has to remember that no written work of the postmonarchic period claims that prophetic books were written and read and reread in the monarchic period. Moreover, the strong tendency in prophetic literature is to render both the actual and the implied authors as "invisible" as possible, so as to empower their words with the legitimacy and authority of textually inscribed, godly voices such as YHWH and the truthful prophet.

If the focus shifts from the intention of ch. 3 to that of the monologue in ch. 3 within the world of the book, then it seems that it serves to legitimize and characterize the speaker in the sight of those to whom the monologue is addressed. Previous words of the speaker on different occasions and the direct message of vv. 1 and 8 serve this purpose.

The explicit intention of the texts included in the embedded self-citations in ch. 3, by themselves and within the world of the book, is to condemn the addressees who are described in positions of leadership and to announce the divine judgment that their actions have led to, including the destruction of Zion/Jerusalem. To be sure, from the vantage point of the speaker and his interlocutors the *fulfillment* of the judgment is in the future, yet the judgment itself is not; in other words, YHWH has already decided how to respond to the leaders' actions. It is possible that such announcements might have carried an implicit call for repentance, but this perspective is not advanced in the text.

Bibliography

S. E. Balentine, *The Hidden God: The Hiding of the Face of God in the Old Testament* (Oxford: Oxford Univ. Press, 1983); J. R. Bartlett, "The Use of the Word ראש as a Title in the Old Testament," *VT* 19 (1969) 1-10; K. Budde, "Eine folgenschwere Redaktion des Zwölfprophetenbuchs," *ZAW* 39 (1922) 218-29; M. B. Crook, "Did Amos and Micah Know Isaiah 9_{2-7} and 11_{1-9}?" *JBL* 73 (1954) 144-51; C. J. Dempsey, "The Interplay between Literary Form and Technique and Ethics in Micah 1–3" (Ph.D. diss., Catholic

Univ. of America, 1994); A. B. Ehrlich, *Miqra kePeshuto,* vol. 3 (1901; repr. New York: Ktav, 1969); D. N. Freedman, "Discourse on Prophetic Discourse," in H. B. Huffmon, F. A. Spina, and A. R. W. Green, eds., *The Quest for the Kingdom of God: Studies in Honor of G. E. Mendenhall* (Winona Lake, Ind.: Eisenbrauns, 1983) 142-45; I. Himbaza, "'Se couvriront-ils la moustache' (Michée 3:7)," *BN* 88 (1997) 27-30; B. Peckham, *History and Prophecy* (ABRL; New York: Doubleday, 1993); M. A. Sweeney, *Isaiah 1–39, with an Introduction to Prophetic Literature* (FOTL XVI; Grand Rapids: Eerdmans, 1996); J. A. Wagenaar, "The Hillside of Samaria: Interpretation and Meaning of Micah 1:6," *BN* 85 (1996) 26-30; J. T. Willis, "A Note on וַאֹמַר in Micah 3₁," *ZAW* 80 (1969) 50-54; idem, "The Structure of Micah 3–5 and the Function of Micah 5₉₋₁₄ in the Book," *ZAW* 81 (1969) 191-214.

A SET OF PROPHETIC READINGS CHARACTERIZING THE FUTURE TO COME, 4:1–5:14 (NRSV 5:15)

Structure

I.	First Reading	4:1-5
II.	Second Reading	4:6-8
III.	Third Reading	4:8–5:1
IV.	Fourth Reading	5:1-5
V.	Fifth Reading	5:6-8
VI.	Sixth Reading	5:9-14

This SET OF PROPHETIC READINGS evokes an image of the future by means of a series of particular characterizations and snapshots of the circumstances that will obtain in the future. A horizon of the imagined future is thus constructed through the interweaving of a number of different, though not unrelated, images that inform one another. Each of these particular images or described facets of the imagined future is shaped by a PROPHETIC READING; the converging horizon of the ideal future is communicated by the set as a whole.

Images of an ideal future are significant indicators of the horizon of thoughts, dreams, desires, fears, and self-understanding of the community in which they develop. It is true that images of the past are shaped, at least partially, by the present; but even more so are images of the future. One may open a most significant window into the world of the community whose future is addressed, as well as their understanding of themselves, when one examines, for instance, the way in which people approach the issue of describing the future; the matters that they choose to mention or to omit, to resolve or to leave unresolved; the scenes that figure prominently when the community develops snapshots of its future; and the relation between these images of the future and those through which the community understands, or shapes its understanding of, its past and present. In this sense, this SET OF PROPHETIC READINGS represents an important testimony regarding the shared world of the implied authorship and the intended and actual primary rereadership of the book of Micah.

The descriptions of a hoped or dreamed future are therefore among the most important sources for the historical-critical study of the book of Micah.

The particular READINGS in this SET OF READINGS (i.e., 4:1–5:14) are set apart from the others by (1) markers of textual coherence such as lexical cohesion and reference to elements within the literary unit itself (e.g., the references to *bat-ṣîyôn*, "Daughter Zion," in 4:8–5:15; the series of pronominal suffixes and multiple instances of repetition and word pairing in 4:1-5); (2) thematic discontinuities; (3) either a concluding note (e.g., *lĕ'ôlām wā'ed*, 4:5; cf. 4:7) or markers of a new unit (e.g., *bayyôm hahû'*, 4:6), or both; and, (4) in one case, a very clear instance of *inclusio* (see 4:8 and 5:1).

At the same time, it is important to stress that these readings convey to the intended readers of chs. 4–5 a sense of interrelatedness among the particular READINGS included in the set, and among each of the partial images conveyed by these READINGS. This is achieved by an array of literary features that include the following:

1. The presence of encompassing themes that unify the set such as (a) the relation between "Israel" and the nations, (b) the relation of each of them to Jerusalem/Zion, (c) the issue of their leadership, and (d) the focus on Zion/Jerusalem and the temple.
2. The explicit orientation toward the future of all the panels in this paratactically organized unit.
3. Clear, textually inscribed markers, among which one may mention the following:
   a. Similar openings and endings: readings I and V open in a similar manner (*wĕhāyâ* followed by an abstract noun formed with the suffix *-ît* and in the construct form); readings II and VI begin in the same manner; and readings III and IV begin with *wĕ'attâ* followed by a reference to a geographical location. Moreover, this feature is present at the level of the subunits within readings; thus two subunits in the third reading are marked by their shared beginning with *wĕ'attâ;* and the fifth reading is subdivided by means of a repetition of the opening clause (i.e., . . . *wĕhāyâ šĕ'ērît ya'ăqōb*, 5:6, 7).
   b. Repetition of key words and terms: "Zion" occurs not only in 4:2, which links the new unit with the previous unit (see 3:12), but also in 4:7, 8, 9, 10, 11, 13 (i.e., in readings I, II, and III); the word *gôy* in 4:2, 3, 7, 11; 5:7, 14 (i.e., readings I, II, III, V, and VI) and the expressions *gôyîm rabbîm* in 4:2, 11 (cf. *'ammîm rabbîm* in 4:3; 5:7) and *gôyîm 'ăṣumîm/gôy 'āṣum* in 4:3, 7. The presence of *yôlēdâ* in 4:9, 10, and 5:2 is also noteworthy, and so too the term *'ôlām* in 4:5, 7 (cf. 2:9), that is, at the conclusion of reading I and the first conclusion of reading II where it means "forever and ever" (i.e., "everlasting"), and its inverted role at the conclusion of reading III and at the beginning of reading IV (see 5:1) where it points to "from everlasting" (see KJV). One may mention also the presence of two double-duty verses (4:8 and 5:1) that are to be associated with and bind together the two readings (see below).

c. Similar opening of the two double-duty verses in the unit: 4:8, which belongs to both the second and the third readings (see below), and 5:1, which belongs to the third and fourth readings; both begin with "*wĕ'attâ* X" ("and you X"), where "X" stands for a place.

The above features in chs. 4–5 develop a sense of textual coherence within the readings. In other words, these readings are not presented to the readers as a haphazard aggregate of separate readings, but as part of a literary unit to be read and reread as such. (For studies of the "unifying features" within chs. 4–5, see Luker; Hagstrom, 68-72; also cf. Willis, "Structure," esp. 38-39; and Nielsen, 85-92; regarding proposals of a chiastic structure in chs. 4–5 see Renaud, esp. 276-82; and the critique in Willis, "Structure of Micah 3–5," 198-202; Hagstrom, 74-77.)

Moreover, chs. 4–5 are not a floating, independent unit within the book of Micah. Indeed, they are presented to the intended readers as an integral part of this book. This section of the book (i.e., chs. 4–5) is bound to the preceding and following texts (see Luker; and regarding ch. 7, which is not covered in Luker's paper, see, e.g., the references to Assyria [5:5; 7:12], to *yĕmê 'ôlām* [5:1; 7:14; cf. 7:15, 20], and cf. *šĕ'ērît ya'ăqōb* and *šĕ'ērît naḥălātô* [5:6; 7:18]).

The most salient of these links, and the most significant in terms of conveyed message, closely associates 3:9-12 (particularly 3:12) and 4:1-5 (esp. 4:1). The relationship between the two units goes far beyond the genre observation that announcements of future salvation or descriptions of an ideal future in the prophetic books appear in a literary context that includes implicit or explicit references to Israel's disaster (e.g., descriptions or announcements of judgment); or, in other words, within the world of the prophetic books these units are not fully independent but are always contextualized. The intertwining of the two relevant units is emphasized here (cf. 4:8–5:1). The conveyed textual coherence between 3:9-12 and 4:1-5 is underlined by thematic links, particularly in adjacent sections of the text. In 3:12 it is announced that the mount of the house of the Lord (and Jerusalem/Zion) will be destroyed, and in the next verse in the book (4:1) that the same mount will be established above all others, and nations will stream to it. Moreover, the verse next to 4:1 claims explicitly that Zion/Jerusalem will serve as a source of divine instruction that will be a magnet for the nations. It is also unmistakably communicated by repeated leading words such as *har* ("mountain," "mount," "hill," or "hill country"), *bêt* ("house" or "temple"), *yĕrûšālaim* ("Jerusalem"), *ṣîyôn* ("Zion"), and by the opposition between *śādeh* ("field," "open field or country," "arable land") and *har*. One may also notice the suggestive repeated occurrence of the words *ya'ăqōb* ("Jacob") in 3:9 and 4:2; of *rō'š* in 3:9 and 4:1; and of words from the root *yrh* and *špṭ* (3:11; 4:2-3). The unit that follows 4:1-5 (i.e., 4:6-8) begins in a way that resembles the opening of the note of salvation in 2:11. (On these issues cf. Luker; Mays, 94; Nielsen, 91-92; it is worth noting that Willis has proposed that the literary unit consists of 3:9–4:5, due — at least in part — to the mentioned, conspicuous textual coherence between 3:9-12 and 4:1-5.) Furthermore, these links have been the primary reason that led some scholars to posit that 4:1-5 belongs to a structural subunit that includes 3:1-12 or 3:9-12 rather than 4:6–5:14 (see Allen, 257-61; Willis, "Structure of Micah 3–5"). Although this position is understandable, it is often the case in Micah and other prophetic books (e.g., Obadiah; see Ben Zvi, *Obadiah,* passim) that structural subunits are bound to one another by language and by a line of thought. These linkages strongly communicate a multi-unit sense of textual coherence and suggest that the intended readers were to read one structural unit in the light of the other. (On the relation between Micah 2 and particularly 3:12 and 4:1-5, see Intention below.)

There is a long scholarly tradition, dating even earlier than the famous work of Stade in 1881 (cf. Marti, 94, and see J. M. P. Smith, 8-12, 16) and including many redaction-critical scholars today that argues that Micah 3 and 4:1-5 are the products of at least two different periods (e.g., Wellhausen, *Skizzen,* 139-40; Wolff, *Micah,* 117-18; Mays, 93-96). The first, for the most part, is associated with the proclamation of the historical 8th-century-BCE prophet, and the second usually with late, postexilic communities. One basic argument advanced in support of this position is that a prophet would not pronounce Jerusalem's destruction and at the same time pronounce that the city will be rebuilt and serve as a magnet for the nations.

First, a person may pronounce both, provided that the two events are associated with different points in the future. The argument stands on a construction of the historical prophet that requires that he consistently proclaims only judgment and doom, but as Scheffler (53) stated: "If one decides *a priori* that Micah was solely a prophet of doom then the argument of denying a salvation oracle to him is actually a *petitio principii*" (see also his critique of Mays's and other approaches; the claim that the reference to Mic 3:12 in Jer 26:18 proves that Micah pronounced only doom goes not only beyond the evidence but also does not take into consideration the context of Jer 26:17-19).

Second, the best starting point for a study of the book of Micah is *not* what a historical prophet may or may not have said according to one's reconstruction of the redactional history of the book. Nor is the best approach one that is based on the acceptance of some words that the authorial voice puts in the mouth of the textually inscribed speaker as faithful representations of the actual speech of the historical prophet — while rejecting others' words similarly placed by the authorial voice — on the basis of (1) one's assumptions about the role and rhetorical style (e.g., fiery and gloomy preaching or proclamation) of prophets in the late monarchic society, or (2) one's dating of some of the material in the book of Jeremiah, and one's assumption about its mode of production, the historicity of some of the claims advanced there (see Jer 26:18), and one's interpretation of them (see Wolff, *Micah,* passim). The best starting point for a historical-critical study of the book of Micah is the book itself (i.e., a postmonarchic rather than monarchic work) and the claims that it presents to its rereaders. In this regard, the text of the book of Micah clearly requires its intended readers to address the two sections as related. The requirement is communicated by means of the markers of textual coherence that the authorial voice has placed in the mouth of the speaker in both sections. To be sure, this does not mean that one should rule out the possibility of multiple or sequential authorship of these units, because a good writer could have added the second text in a way that creates this sense of coherence with the first one. Significantly, the same holds true for every ancient author who may use and reshape preexisting sources for the purpose of a new composition. (For approaches different from the one outlined here, see, e.g., Wolff, *Micah,* 12-14, 17-27; cf. Hillers, *Micah,* 2-4, 52-53. Van der Woude ["Micah IV 1-5"] claims that 4:1-5 represent the words of the pseudoprophets who here are quoting Isaiah. On the relation of 4:1-5 to Isa 2:2-5 see below; and for a survey and critique of the position that the text of Micah 4–5 is the result of accidents in the textual transmission, see Willis, "Micah IV 14–V 5," esp. 529-31.)

Whereas there is today a relatively widespread agreement that Micah 4–5 is one of the main literary subunits of the book of Micah, there is little agreement concerning its subdivision into particular units. The questions of to which subunit one is to assign 4:8 and whether 4:14 and 5:1-3/5 belong to the same subunit are particularly debated. The proposal advanced here is that there are *two* similarly introduced double-duty verses, 4:8 and 5:1 (on double-duty verses, → 1:5). These double-duty verses not only belong to both subunits but also convey to the intended reader that the relevant subunits are not worlds apart but rather inform one another. In this way they provide a guide for the rereading of the text, according to the intentions of the implied author. For the argument in favor of the integrity of 4:8 in the second reading (4:6-8) see there under Structure. As for its integrity in the third reading (4:8–5:1), one may mention the following: (1) that 4:9 is not to be read apart from its preceding verse (4:8) as clear from the references to the 2nd person in 4:9; (2) that 4:8 and 5:1 are the delimiting markers of a subunit is indicated, among other factors, by the *inclusio* created by these verses; and (3) that 5:2 is not independent, but rather is supposed to be read in the light of the text in 5:1, becomes clear already by its beginning *lākēn,* "therefore." (On these issues see the following discussions under Structure.) The position advanced here is consistent with the traditional division of the text in closed and open sections, except for the double-duty verses that such a system cannot allow from the outset. (For a helpful chart of many of the different proposals, see Hagstrom, 82-83; for an additional, alternative view see Shaw, 97-127; see also Kaiser, *Grundriss der Einleitung,* 131; Vargon, 108-64.)

Genre

Each of the texts included in this unit is a PROPHETIC READING about the future (see Genre in the analysis of the respective READINGS). The genre of the unit as a whole is a SET OF READINGS about the future.

Setting

Within the world of the text, and as in 2:1-5 and other READINGS in Micah, the setting of the speaker's words is left as open as possible. That is, the readers of chs. 4–5 are not told where, when, or any of the circumstances surrounding the speeches reported there. As mentioned above (→ 2:1-5, Setting), these features suggest a text that is *not* written so as to lead the community of rereaders to a mode of reading aimed at learning about a particular, communicative event or events in the monarchic past, such as Micah's proclamation of this or that speech under this or that historical circumstance. Rather the text suggests or even implies a mode of reading in which the speaker's words are considered of value and an object for interpersonal, communal study and meditation aside from any particular detail concerning context, setting, and verbal exchange. Whereas the rereaders are neither required nor asked to historicize the text, that is, to integrate it into a historical narrative and understand it in a way that is informed by that narrative (except for what is implied in the very general note in 1:1), they are asked to contextualize each of these subunits or READINGS within a SET OF READINGS. The numerous and ubiquitous markers of coherence mentioned above are tantamount to a request from the readership to contextualize each of these READINGS, to understand each one in the light of the other rather than against a historical narrative or metanarrative. The text clearly constructs the words that it attributes to the speakers in one READING so as to intertwine them with those it attributes to the speaker or speakers in another READING within this set, and to some extent elsewhere in the book of Micah.

The actual setting of the reading of this SET OF READINGS is the same as that of the READINGS themselves. Mic 4:1–5:15 is a written product aimed primarily to those able to read and reread it, to bearers of high literacy.

Intention

The intention of the set as a whole is to suggest an image of the future through interweaving a number of different though not unrelated images that inform one another. These constructions of the future are not shaped for their own sake, but to communicate a reaffirmation of the basic tenet of the Jerusalem-centered theology shared by the authorship and the intended readership of the book of Micah, and to provide hope that the world will eventually reflect the circumstances that this community holds as consonant with the true will of YHWH and with YHWH's divine economy.

The converging horizon of the ideal future is communicated through the interaction of the different images advanced in the particular readings in this set (regarding which see Intention in the following analyses). It suffices to say at this moment that although the readings provide a potpourri of images of the ideal future, one can easily discern certain common features. Among them one may mention the following:

1. The future of Israel tends to be described in relational terms, that is, it tends to involve a future and godly (in the sense that it is claimed that it reflects the will of YHWH) interaction between "the nations" and Israel. Although the precise type of interaction varies, in all cases Israel is imagined as being in a higher status.
2. The godly future will be substantially different from the present, which

is tantamount to claiming that the present does not reflect even in its broadest outline the divine order desired by YHWH.

3. There is a pervading "underdog" perspective informing these images (cf. Greenspahn, 109-10, et passim). The texts not only assume a community that sees itself as powerless, but they also refer explicitly to exile in general, to exile to Babylon, and to humiliation. This perspective is most consistent with the postmonarchic period.

4. A theological position is omnipresent: the intended and primary readership and the society that they represent (i.e., postmonarchic Judah/ Yehud) are Jacob (i.e., Israel). (On this particular issue see Ben Zvi, "Inclusion.")

Bibliography

F. E. Greenspahn, *When Brothers Dwell Together* (Oxford: Oxford Univ. Press, 1994); O. Kaiser, *Grundriß der Einleitung in die kanonischen und deutero-kanonischen Schriften des Altes Testaments* (Band 2, Die prophetischen Werke; Gütersloh: Gütersloher Verlagshaus, 1994); K. Marti, *Das Dodekapropheton* (Tübingen: Mohr, 1904); E. Nielsen, *Oral Tradition* (SBT 1/11; London: SCM, 1961); E. Otto, "Techniken der Rechtssatzredaktion israelitischer Rechtsbücher in der Redaktion des Prophetenbuches Micha," *SJOT* 5 (1991) 119-50; B. Renaud, *Structure et attaches littéraires de Michée IV–V* (CahRB 2; Paris: Gabalda, 1964); E. H. Scheffler, "Micah 4:1-5: An Impasse in Exegesis?" *OTE* 3 (1985) 46-61; B. Stade, "Bemerkungen über das Buch Micah," *ZAW* 1 (1881) 161-72; J. T. Willis, "The Structure of Micah 3–5 and the Function of Micah $5_{9\text{-}14}$ in the Book," *ZAW* 81 (1969) 191-214; idem, "Micah IV 14–V 5 — A Unit," *VT* 18 (1968) 529-47; A. S. van der Woude, "Micah IV 1-5: An Instance of the Pseudo-Prophets Quoting Isaiah," in M. A Beek, A. A. Kampman, C. Nijlands, and J. Ryckmans, eds., *Symbolae Biblicae et Mesopotamicae. FS F. M. T. de Liagre Böhl* (Leiden: Brill, 1973) 396-402.

FIRST READING, 4:1-5

Structure

I. The world as a truthful manifestation of the divine order — 1-4
  A. The speaker's own voice: introduction — $1\text{-}2a\alpha$
    1. Temporal sphere — $1a\alpha_1$
    2. Spatial sphere — $1a\alpha_2\text{-}\beta$
    3. Human sphere: the spatial response of the nations — $1b\text{-}2a\alpha$
  B. Speaker's citation of the speech of the nations: — $2a\beta\text{-}b$
    1. Citation marker — $2a\beta_1$
    2. The verbal response of the nations: characterization of the temple, Zion/Jerusalem, and implicitly of Jacob/Israel — $2a\beta_2\text{-}b$

The first READING is one of the most widely known texts in the HB/OT. Thus it is justifiable to address it with more detail than other READINGS in this set. The reading may be divided into five main subunits. The first one (4:1-2aα₁) introduces the text (and the world that it evokes) in several ways. First, it clearly links the reading to the previous one in the book and particularly to its last verse (3:12). By doing so it serves communicative and affirmative structural roles that are discussed under Intention below; it also suggests that the two readings are related and provides an interpretive key for the intended rereaders: they are supposed to read one subunit in a way informed by the other subunit. In this regard, it is worth noting that from the perspective of the postmonarchic readership, for which the present book of Micah was primarily intended, there was no contradiction between an announcement that monarchic Jerusalem will be destroyed (as in 3:12) and an assurance that in the future Jerusalem will serve as a magnet to all peoples. To the contrary, it is the fulfillment of the former that strengthens the latter. For this reason, and others to be discussed under Intention, announcements of salvation tend to follow those of judgment in the prophetic books.

The introduction also sets the basic characteristics of the world evoked in this subunit. First, this is a future world. The expression *bĕ'aḥărît hayyāmîm* points clearly to an indefinite future that may be expressed in English by "in the days to come." One should not translate *bĕ'aḥărît hayyāmîm* as "in the end of the days," because it is not an eschatological term (see Gen 49:1). Yet the future imagined in vv. 1-4 is obviously not simply a continuation of the present but a golden age. The evoked future implies the removal of the personal, political, and religious circumstances of the present and of history as experienced and understood by the readership. Indeed, it is this distance between imagination and present reality that provides the READING with rhetorical power.

The first section already points to two central and closely related dimensions in which this future will differ from the present: one concerns the realm of the spatial, physical world, the other that of the human world. Significantly, both are presented as related manifestations of the same divine will or as two sides of one theological coin. In this imagined future, the temple mountain, Zion, and the "house of the God of Jacob" (as in v. 2), or the abode of YHWH, will be established above other mountains. Thus the physical world will reflect the preeminence of that mountain, and of YHWH as understood in the Jerusalem-centered theology that characterizes both the authorship and intended readership of this book. The text communicates an unequivocal and unique association between Mt. Zion and the rightful temple of YHWH (cf. Ben Zvi, "Inclusion"). In other words, this future world will be a faithful manifestation of the divine economy and of Jerusalem's role in that economy.

(On mountains as the abode of gods in the ancient Near East see, e.g., Clifford; cf. the Gudea Cylinders [Jacobsen, 386-444; and see, e.g., 424-25,

444]. On the image of a future Zion/Jerusalem/temple standing very high see also Ezek 40:2 and cf. Zech 14:10; on elevation or height as a most positive characterizing feature see, e.g., Ps 36:7 [NRSV 6]; Isa 57:15. On the future replacement of the present geography of Jerusalem by a different one with a stronger degree of consistency between Jerusalem's role in the divine economy and its actual geography along with its connoted meanings see also Joel 4:18 [NRSV 3:18]; Zech 14:8, 10; and Ezek 47:1-12. On the contrast between this divine action and the one in Mic 1:4 see Luker.)

The phrase "the God of Jacob" is relatively common in the Psalms (see Pss 20:2 [NRSV 1]; 46:8, 12 [NRSV 7, 11]; 75:10 [NRSV 9]; 76:7 [NRSV 6]; 81:2, 5 [NRSV 1, 4]; 84:9 [NRSV 8]; 94:7), but elsewhere occurs only in 2 Sam 23:1; Isa 2:3//Mic 4:2; and in the stereotypical references to the God of the ancestors in Exod 3:6, 15; 4:5. The phrase "the house of the God of Jacob" in Mic 4:2, which appears here and in the parallel text in Isa 2:3 but nowhere else in the HB/OT, is set in a literary context in which the reference to the "heads of the house of Jacob" in 3:9 (an expression that occurs only in 3:9) and the reference to "head" in 4:1 resonate. Beyond that, the use of the phrase is consistent with the use of the term "Jacob" for the theological concept of "Israel" (→ 1:2-16) and on a different plane for the postmonarchic community that held a Jerusalem-centered theology, and that identified its past — including their story about their own exile — in the main with that of monarchic Judah (cf. Ben Zvi, "Inclusion"), and within which one is to find the primary readership of the book of Micah.

The reassuring message for the readership of the book of Micah is that, from their perspective, the past destruction of monarchic Jerusalem announced by the speaker in the previous unit (see 3:12), a matter of fact known to them, has certainly not abrogated YHWH's choice of Jerusalem. Moreover, it explains the actual "height" of Mt. Zion — and themselves — in their world. On the one hand the reading assumes a direct relation between the physical and metaphorical height of the temple mount (Jerusalem and Israel) and YHWH's "stature," and on the other it maintains that the present "height" of the temple, Zion, and Jerusalem (and indirectly Israel) are anything but a misleading reflection of the divine economy that is to disappear in the future. This position is consistent with the theology of the implied authorship and intended readership, and provides them a way to withstand the tension between an accepted vision of the divine economy and the actual world. Their low "height" in the present is therefore interpreted as a marker that a glorious future is coming. Significantly the text here also implies an intended readership that accepts the claim of the written text (or book) considered to be YHWH's word over the testimony of any present circumstances.

The truthful manifestation of YHWH's will in the natural world is not, however, the main focus of this READING. The text quickly moves its focus from (1) a world that, once it has reached its true manifestation, turns into a stable state (notice the two parallel participial phrases and that the first of them begins with *nākôn*, "established," i.e., "unmovable"; one might argue that *nś*' is a *qtl* form, but even in this case, the verb would be stative, not fientive) to (2) the dynamic world of crowds, peoples, and voices (expressed by active *w*-

qtl forms, *wĕnāhărû,* "they shall stream," *wĕhālĕkû,* here, "they shall come," and *wĕ'āmĕrû,* "they shall say"). This human world is also to become a true expression of the divine order as the peoples (i.e., all the peoples of the world) will habitually "stream" to YHWH's mountain, to YHWH's house, in the future described in this unit. This peaceful and godly pilgrimage of the nations stands in contrast with other images of the future in which the nations are described as coming to Jerusalem to wage war against it; see 4:11, which is an integral part of the third reading in this SET OF READINGS.

It is worth noting that the word translated as "stream" (*nāhărû,* v. 1) may carry an additional connoted meaning, "be radiant, shine" (see Jer 31:12). Thus the nations may be described as streaming to the mountain of the house of YHWH, but also "glowing (in joy)" because of the mountain of the house of YHWH (cf. Jer 31:12). This stylistic device of plays on connotations of words and double meanings occurs elsewhere in the book (see, e.g., ch. 1).

The general image of the nations' pilgrimage to Jerusalem appears elsewhere in the prophetic corpus. Significantly, in the world that 4:2 (//Isa 2:3) describes, the peoples are not the depleted survivors of a divine judgment (e.g., Zech 14:16). They are explicitly and repeatedly characterized as mighty (see *rabbîm,* which serves as a double-duty term pointing to "many" and "powerful," and *'ăṣumîm*). Moreover, the focus of this pilgrimage note is not the riches that the nations may bring to the temple (cf. Isa 60:3-7; Hag 2:7), or their bringing Israel back (cf. Isa 66:20), or temple worship and offerings (cf. Isa 66:20; Zech 14:16). In a manner similar to Zech 8:22-23, the peoples' reason for their pilgrimage to Zion is explained to the rereaders of the book through a quotation of the future speech of the nations as they go up to Jerusalem. (Notice also the general resemblance between Mic 4:2-3 [//Isa 2:2-3] and Zech 8:21-22.) First, the particular construction of the direct speech (Mic 2:2) characterizes the nations as eager to come to YHWH's mountain (notice the volitional verbal forms). Second, it presents them as recognizing (a) the status of YHWH and of YHWH's abode, which is set now above all mountains, and toward which they are ascending, and (b) the particular relation between YHWH and Jacob/Israel. Indeed, the nations call YHWH the God of Jacob. Both points (a) and (b) are fully consistent with the self-understanding of the authorship and readership of the book of Micah and their Jerusalem-centered worldview, but in the image of the future that is advanced in this text, it is the many and mighty nations — not Israel — that are depicted as fully convinced and as proclaiming this viewpoint. Thus the text evokes a positive characterization of Israel and of the nations in the future, and at the same time serves to reaffirm the readership's understanding of itself. The rhetorical ploy of presenting the other as affirming one's own position is relatively common (see, e.g., Deut 4:6). On the surface this presupposes granting some authority to the other, but this "other" is constructed completely by the self, and its voice in the text is controlled by the implied author (cf. Ben Zvi, "When the Foreign Monarch Speaks").

In addition, the text describes the reason that the nations are ascending to Jerusalem, from their perspective (as constructed in the text). They come to Jerusalem to receive, and implicitly to follow, YHWH's teachings, which in the language of the text are referred to as "torah" and "YHWH's word." It is most significant that the latter term is nothing less than the title of the book of Micah (and similar prophetic books). Significantly, Jerusalem is, in the words of the text, the place where the nations go to receive YHWH's word, and in the historical world it is the most likely location of those who composed, read, and reread the book of Micah (i.e., YHWH's word). Although the image in v. 2 is set in the future, the presence of an analogy to the present circumstances of those able to read and reread prophetic literature is hard to ignore and unlikely to be the result of chance. The construction of the future is somewhat related to the present.

The subtle shift in the concept evoked by the term "torah" in relation to that in the previous units in the book is also worth mentioning. Whereas in 3:11 torah is associated with the priests (cf. Jer 18:18; Ezek 44:23; Hag 2:11-13) and is not directly related to the establishment and administration of justice (see Mic 3:7, 11, in which justice is associated with the "heads" of the people and its qĕṣînîm, "leaders"), there is nothing in 4:2 that points to priestly issues such as holiness, purity, or the like (see Ezek 44:23; Hag 2:11-13). Both the parallel structure and the subsequent clauses in Micah point to a more general concept of "torah" as "divine instruction" and associate it with peace and justice (cf. Isa 42:4; 51:4; Jer 31:33).

The ancient authors, rereaders, and interpreters who shaped the texts that, from their own perspective, express divine instruction and whose works they considered to be YHWH's words were self-effacing. From their viewpoint, their own role is merely one of brokers of the divine instruction. Thus YHWH's torah or word (and laws, statutes, etc.) and YHWH tend to stand at the center of their works. In the Writings, where such an assertion is in tension with the genre of the works, the authorship is more than once associated with ideal figures of the past (e.g., David, Solomon). It is not unexpected, therefore, that in v. 3a the text shifts from a focus on torah or word from Zion to YHWH and YHWH's actions in the evoked future. Still, the text is written so as to allow, and perhaps even to suggest, the possibility that YHWH's word will judge the people. (Cf. Tanhum HaYerushalmi; a hypostatization of YHWH's word is certainly possible within the works of the literati responsible for the writing and reading and rereading of prophetic literature; cf. Isa 55:6-11; also cf. Pss 33:6; 147:15; see W. H. Schmidt, *TDOT,* 3:120-25; of course, this hypostatization may be more of a linguistic and stylistic feature than a reference to a belief about the ultimate reality of YHWH's word as something more than a character or activity of YHWH. On these issues see Barr.) The connotation is clear: YHWH and YHWH's word are constructed as deeply related.

Verses 3b-4a move the description of the future further by shifting the attention to the transformed realm of the life of human beings. Significantly, the mighty and many nations who will be going up to Jerusalem to receive the divine instruction continue to be the speaker who describes the ideal future. Yet it is noteworthy that the text is written to allow the possibility that the main prophetic speaker has completed the citation of the nations' words by the end of v. 3b, and if so vv. 3b-4a (or perhaps 3b-4b) are to be attributed to this prophetic speaker. Ambiguities regarding the identity of the speakers have been noted several times before in the book of Micah. They serve to convey an overlap or deep association between different voices. Even if for the sake of argument one would assume that the speaker here is only the prophetic voice, then still that voice is dependent grammatically and thematically on the constructed voice of the nations — v. 3 has no independent standing — and accordingly, the two voices remain deeply interwoven. In addition, as the conclusion of v. 4 indicates, these two voices also overlap a third voice, the divine voice. Thus YHWH, mighty and numerous nations in the ideal future, and the prophetic speaker, as well as the voice of the implied author that controls all the above in the text, all converge into one godly voice. Similar instances of this feature obtain in other chapters of the book of Micah, as demonstrated several times in this study.

The world that is imagined in vv. 3b-4a to represent divine rulership is characterized in relation to polities and individuals. Thus the nations will live in eternal peace; war will be forgotten. YHWH as a just ruler and judge (cf. Ps 99:4, among many others) will fulfill one of the sovereign's main responsibilities, namely, to bring peace, tranquillity, or rest to the kingdom (cf. 1 Kgs 5:5; Isa 9:6 [NRSV 7]; 11:1-9; Jer 23:5-6; 33:15-16; see also Isa 16:5; 32:16-18). The motif of peace among the nations is then interwoven with a snapshot of the life of a person at that time (see 1 Kgs 5:5; cf. Zech 3:10). The text brings an agrarian image of security and stability: people will be able to sit and enjoy the produce of their vines and fig trees without anyone making them afraid. The reference to vines and fig trees, as opposed to grain crops, for instance, points to long-term stability and peace. It conveys also a sense of prosperity (cf. 1 Kgs 5:5 and notice its context). Additionally, it implies an image of "a person" (*'îš*) as one who "owns" a vine and a fig tree (→ 2:2; see 1 Kgs 5:5; cf. also Zech 3:10). The image of lack of fear is reinforced by the conclusion of v. 4a: *'ên maḥărîd* ("no one shall make them afraid"; cf. Jer 30:10; 46:27; Ezek 34:28; Zeph 3:13).

Everything that is to obtain in the ideal future is precisely what is lacking in the present as experienced by the community of readers. Mt. Zion is not the highest of the mountains, numerous and mighty people do not stream to it, they do not learn the divine instruction that comes from Zion, there is not universal peace, no people beat their swords into plowshares. In other words, the text plays on the aspect of difference by emphasizing the lack. But if this is so, it suggests strongly that there were those who could make the community of readers afraid and that they did not consider themselves to be in a secure, stable, and well-established position. They longed for circumstances in which such a position could obtain.

Verse 4b consists of the formula *kî-pî yhwh ṣĕbā'ôt dibbēr* ("for the mouth of YHWH of hosts has spoken"). This formula, with or without *kî* ("for") and usually without *ṣĕbā'ôt* ("hosts"), appears twelve times in the prophetic literature (Isa 1:2, 20; 21:17; 22:25; 24:3; 25:8; 40:5; 58:14; Jer 13:15; Joel 4:8 [NRSV 3:8]; Obad 18; Mic 4:4; cf. the almost identical formula in, e.g., Ezek 5:13; 17:21; 21:37; 26:14; the exact formula occurs also in 1 Kgs 14:11; significantly, despite its relative popularity in the book of Isaiah, this formula does not occur in Isa 2:2-4). The formula may be considered an integral part of the quoted speech or it may stand outside the speech as a narrator's concluding comment (on the potential multiple readings allowed by this feature, see below). The formula may be understood as "for (the mouth of) YHWH (of hosts) has spoken," or, in a paraphrase, "(for) these are the words of YHWH," which would be tantamount to a request to the readers to understand the text as either a direct quotation of YHWH's speech or as unequivocally reflecting what YHWH has said or promised or prophesied. In either case these readers are asked to understand the text as directly related to the voice of YHWH. This type of concluding remark draws the attention of the rereaders to the preceding text while legitimizing it with divine authority.

The combined effect of the ambiguity regarding the speaker's identity and the potential polyvalence of the formula merits close examination. If the readers consider the formula an integral part of the speech of the nations, then the nations are described as knowing a most significant statement or oracle of YHWH, for they will be saying: "for YHWH has said [or prophesied] so." Since the "so" refers to preceding words, and since the nations are depicted as reliable speakers in this section, then the presence of the formula fulfills two functions: (1) it draws the readers' attention to the preceding text and marks it as representing YHWH's true position in general and, at least at some level, also YHWH's voice (see the presence of the verb *dbr*); and (2) it depicts the nations in the future as a group that (a) has true knowledge of YHWH's word, (b) acknowledges its value (and indirectly that of YHWH), and (c) proclaims and rejoices in YHWH's word. All these attributes are clearly consistent with the depiction of the nations in the time to come as advanced elsewhere in the unit. The text as a whole clarifies that divine instruction and YHWH's word originate from Zion, the temple mount, which is on the one hand the "abode of YHWH," and on the other the most likely geographical and social location of the literati among whom one finds both the authorship and the primary readership of the book of Micah as we know it.

If the rereaders did not consider the formula an integral part of the speech of the nations, but a closing comment of the "narrator" or the "main prophetic voice," then they may have understood it as "for YHWH has spoken [or prophesied] so," or "for it was the LORD of Hosts who spoke" (NJPSV), or, in a less literal way, "these are the 'words' of YHWH." Given that the entire book of Micah is considered YHWH's word, and that it certainly contains numerous citations of other voices, it is not impossible that the formula reaffirms that in this sense the preceding text is referred to as YHWH's word or words (cf. the use of "thus says the Lord YHWH" in Obad 1; see Ben Zvi, *Obadiah*, 25-29). If the formula is interpreted as "for YHWH has said [or prophesied] so," then the entire description of the future, including the speech of the nations, is attributed to YHWH, though in a slightly different form. If one takes this path of rereading the text, the following becomes a salient question: Where did YHWH say or prophesy so? It is possible to answer this question by claiming that this is a (veiled) reference to Isa 2:2-4 (cf. Meier, 157-58, 213; Fishbane, 477-78); or to a written text that acted as a shared source for Isa 2:2-4 and Mic 4:1-5 (on the relation between Isa 2:2-4 and Mic 4:1-5 see below); or that this is an open statement pointing to legitimization with no particular referent (see Rashi, for whom it points to Lev. 26:6). Yet given that the formula directly follows and refers to a text that is considered to be part and parcel of YHWH's word (Mic 4:1-4a; see 1:1), one may wonder whether at some level the question could not have been answered, "right here" in 4:1-4a. Nonetheless, whichever of these answers or combinations of answers was accepted, the message of the text remains the same; the text is legitimized and associated directly with YHWH.

Moreover, the same phenomenon occurs on a larger level, for all the possible rereadings examined in the last two paragraphs point to a very similar message. Thus the text shows both (1) a clear openness that draws attention to the issues at stake and allows multiple readings informing each other, and (2) a stressed and unequivocal claim on the main issues at stake, namely, (a) the preceding is to be associated with YHWH, (b) this is clearly a truthful statement, and (c) the events and circumstances described there will take place: (i) there will be time a of universal and stable peace; (ii) the nations will know and acknowledge (and joyfully proclaim) YHWH, (iii) the nations will know and acknowledge YHWH's word or instruction and the role of Zion/temple mount as the place from which this divine word/instruction comes; (iv) there will be prosperity and tranquillity in all lands when YHWH takes the roles associated with present earthly rulers.

This combination of indeterminacy and determinacy appears elsewhere in the previous chapters in Micah and elsewhere in prophetic literature (see also Ben Zvi, *Obadiah*, 37-43). This combination is understandable in terms of the requirements of a text written to be reread many times (cf. Ben Zvi, *Obadiah*, 3-4, et passim; idem, "Observations"; idem, "Wrongdoers"). It is also a powerful stylistic device that serves to channel the attention of the readers to the main unequivocal issues advanced by the text.

The notorious ambiguity regarding the identity of the speakers in the previous verses seems resolved in v. 5. The speaker there is the inclusive "we," that is, the "we" that includes the "I" of the speaker and the "you" of the audience (cf. Shoemaker, 268). Of course, the readership of the book is likely to identify itself with the textually inscribed audience, and therefore the text contributes to a blurring of the differences between speaker, audience, and actual readership; all are "Israel," which "walks in the name of YHWH, *our* God."

The text of the verse itself is centered on the pair "we–YHWH, our God" and "they–each its own god." That is, two identities, "Israel" and "(all) the nations," are constructed in terms of association with either YHWH or other gods. This position represents a worldview for which there is ample testimony in the literature of postmonarchic Israel. The issue here is, however, which of the following the text suggests to the readers:

1. The distinction between Israel and the nations will remain in the ideal future described in vv. 1-4 because, although the nations will accept YHWH's rule and teachings, each nation will keep its own god; or, in other words, the text suggests an ideal model for each nation (including Israel), its own god (only Israel's is YHWH; cf. Deut 32:8-9 LXX [see Tov, 269] and with the characterization of the pious sailors in the book of Jonah).

2. The distinction refers to the present of the textually inscribed speaker

and audience, and to that of the readership of the book of Micah, but not to the ideal future described in vv. 1-4 (see J. M. P. Smith, 88; Allen, 327-28; Mays, 99; Hillers, *Micah,* 51; cf. Tg.). In other words, in the ideal future all nations will worship only YHWH.

The text raises the question but allows more than one answer. Indeed, there is no grammatical, syntactic, or even contextual reason within 4:1-5 to prefer one option over the other. In other words, the future and the ideal world evoked by the unit are constructed in unequivocal terms but contain more than one possible image. Significantly, chs. 4–5 as a unit convey many and diverse images of the ideal future. The horizon of thought suggested by the unit in this regard is consistent with a system of different images informing and balancing each other. The lack of a univocal and categorically defined image of the ideal future is rather an expected feature, as this is most often the case when social groups address the nature of their ideal future.

Some have claimed that v. 5 represents a later liturgical response to vv. 1-4 (e.g., Wolff, *Micah,* 118; Hillers, *Micah,* 51). But a liturgical response assumes the existence of a liturgy to respond to. There is no solid evidence that either the text of vv. 1-4 or of v. 5 was uttered in or composed for a liturgy. Moreover, if the starting point is the present text of 4:1-5 (rather than possible but speculative proto-texts and the theologies and intentions attributed to them), then it becomes clear that the language of v. 5 conveys a sense of textual coherence with vv. 1-4 (notice the references to *hālak,* "walk," *îš,* "a person," *'ammîm,* "peoples"), which suggests that the readers of the book of Micah were asked (and expected) to read 4:1-4 and 4:5 as unit, "a READING." This observation does not rule out a possible redactional history in which 4:1-4 preceded 4:5, but the burden of proof is on those who claim that there was such a redactional history and that the readers of the book of Micah were asked to and did read the book in a way that was informed by this textual history.

A vast corpus of literature has addressed the issue of the relation between 4:1-4/5 and Isa 2:2-4/5. Much attention has been paid to the question of who borrowed from whom. All possible alternatives (that Isaiah took from Micah, Micah from Isaiah, both from a common source, or that a common redactor included this note into both books) have been advanced. In addition it has been proposed that the pseudoprophets mentioned in Micah took the text from Isaiah. Still others have expressed agnosticism regarding the possibility of reaching any clear conclusion on this matter. (For different positions see, e.g., Wildberger, 81-87; Cannawurf; Hillers, *Micah,* 51-53; Nielsen, 91-93 [also cf. 81-83]; Mays, 94-96; Gosse; van der Woude, "Micah IV.1-5"; Strydorm.) Given that this study is about the book of Micah itself, the most relevant observations are that, first, the intended readership of the book of Micah is not asked to read 4:1-5 as a non-Mican, or Isaianic, passage; second, 4:1-5 is certainly a "Mican" text in the sense that it is integral to the book, that it fits its immediate (broader) textual environment, and that it clearly communicates a sense of coherence within the larger set of readings in chs. 4–5 and with its preceding unit (see above). This situation is most often the case in other instances of "double texts" (see Ben Zvi, *Zephaniah,* 190-205; idem, *Obadiah,* 99-114). As a trend, it points to the effort made by the literati responsible for these books to provide each of them with a particular character even if they worked with sources. (On these issues see Ben Zvi, "Urban.")

Genre

Some have claimed that 4:1-4/5 reflects (postmonarchic) temple liturgies, and particularly those associated with the dedication of the (second) temple (see, e.g., Wolff, *Micah,* 118; Lescow, "Redaktionsgeschichtliche Analyze," 76). Allen maintains that 4:1-5 is a poem "closely connected with the cultic traditions attested in the hymnbook" but associates it with times earlier than the historical Micah (see Allen, 323; see also Kapelrud, 395-96). Others have claimed that 4:1-4 is to be understood as an older oracle (e.g., Nielsen, 91; according to Nielsen, this oracle is older than the period of time mentioned in Isa 1:1 and Mic 1:1) or that this was an orally transmitted saying that "was characterized as a divine oracle by the secondary addition of v. 4b," and "as such it was proclaimed within the worship service" (Wolff, *Micah,* 177).

One may speculate such things about a hypothetical precursor of either the text in 4:1-5 or of a source used by the writer of the book of Micah responsible for 4:1-5. As an integral part of the book, 4:1-5 is clearly a PROPHETIC READING about the ideal future. Indeed, it belongs to a SET OF PROPHETIC READINGS that delineates a horizon of an ideal future by suggesting a kind of dialogue among different and yet related images of that future. This READING, in accordance with its (→) intention, activates motifs that are common in oracles of salvation, as they are depicted in the world of the prophetic books (e.g., "Pilgrimage and Peace among the Nations," Westermann, *Prophetic Oracles,* 90-94, 125-26, 135-36). Moreover, the text seems to have been written so as to evoke in its intended readers the image of an oracle, because it associates important sections with YHWH's direct voice.

Setting

As mentioned above, some scholars have advanced a liturgical setting for 4:1-4 or 4:1-5, or for both but at different times. For instance, Wolff claims that 4:1-4 was used liturgically at the dedication of the second temple and that the commentary in v. 5 was made on the occasion of a later liturgical reading of vv. 1-4 (*Micah,* 118; cf. Lescow, "Redaktionsgeschichtliche Analyze," 76). Hillers considers v. 5 to be "a congregational response to the prophetic vision, . . . a liturgical addition to a prophetic word, of undetermined date" (*Micah,* 51).

A few observations follow. The text does not indicate to its readers that the speaker or speakers of 4:1-5 proclaimed these words in the temple or in a liturgical setting of any kind. The words themselves are not attached in the world of the book to any particular setting or audience (except that it implies that it identifies with Israel — not the northern kingdom but the theological concept of Israel). Significantly, as in other READINGS in the book, the activity of the speaker is not associated with any historical or claimed-to-be-historical circumstances or dates (except perhaps for the reference in 1:1). The text is clearly open in this regard, and most likely intentionally open. One may also mention that the lack of reference to sacrifices and to holiness requirements from the pilgrims suggests that the image of the actual temple and its service is not the most salient in the background of the implied author. (Gerstenberger [88] associates comparable texts, e.g., Psalm 15, with congregational worship.)

As its reference already suggests, 4:1-5 is an integral part of the book. Indeed, it is deeply connected with its co-texts in the book as mentioned above. Moreover, the intended readers are asked to read this section of the book in a way particularly informed by the preceding unit, especially 3:12. Whether it or a precursor had an earlier life independent of the book of Micah — or of a historical Micah — is unverifiable and hardly central for the readership of the book, who are asked to associate the text with the character of Micah as described in 1:1.

As a READING included in a work to be read and reread, 4:1-5 represents a product aimed primarily to those bearers of high literacy who were able to read prophetic books. Moreover, all the marks of texts that are supposed to be read many times by the literati (e.g., equivocality, overlapping speakers, and the like) that we found elsewhere in the book of Micah are present in 4:1-5 as well. As in all other instances, one is to assume that the literati found a way to transmit the message of this literature, as they understood it, to those who did not possess high literacy and who were the vast majority of the population. In this sense, these literati most likely took the role of brokers of divine knowledge.

Intention

The main intention of the piece becomes clear from its *Sitz im Buch*. It follows 3:12, in which the destruction of Jerusalem and temple are announced. Such an action introduces in the world of the text, and evokes in the readers, a sense of breakdown or chaos because the announcement itself and certainly its fulfillment from the perspective of the readers represent a serious threat to the way in which the Jerusalem-centered world is structured both in the world of the text and in the worldview of the readers. Moreover, the behavior that brings chaos is — and must be — assigned to YHWH, who is supposed to stand for the structured world believed to be true. As cross-cultural studies suggest, when "chaos," or the dissolution of structure, or the possibility of them is confronted a common response is to domesticate the chaos-creating behavior or action; and societies develop social instruments for reaffirming order, if not reestablishing it, in the face of chaos or the specter of it (cf. the affirming of God's justice and just dominion over all the universe in a funeral, in the face of a death that may seem to undermine any structure and meaning).

In the book of Micah, the destruction of Jerusalem is domesticated by explaining it in terms of the incredible sins of the monarchic elite (see ch. 3; cf. chs. 1–2), and by characterizing it as an action of temporal — and in the long run, fleeting — importance. Mic 4:1-5 communicates a sense of reestablishing structure and order because, among other things: (1) it reaffirms the role of Zion in the divine economy and provides the audience of the speaker in the text and the readership of the book the assurance of YHWH's word that this role will be manifested in the "real world" in the future; and (2) it reassures the audience and above all the readers that (a) YHWH will eventually establish a world fitting YHWH's rule (i.e., one in which the subjects of YHWH's [real] will suffer from no lack [see 4:3-4]); (b) YHWH is and will be the God of Jacob/Israel (i.e., their god; see 4:2), and will provide for them and their city a most significant role in the future; and (c) YHWH is validating the Jerusalem-centered worldview of the readership through the godly voices in 4:1-5. (For the general issues raised in this paragraph see Hoffman.)

If one uses models for the understanding of religious thought and behavior such as those developed by Bainbridge, one may consider 4:1-5 as a most general compensator, that is, as a compensator that substitutes for rewards of great scope and value that are not achievable in the world of both the textually inscribed audience of the speaker in the book that is associated with the circumstances in monarchic Judah, and that of the postmonarchic community of readers of the book of Micah. The explicit reference to such a major, general compensator here is due to the immediate mention of the loss in 3:12, which calls for a reaffirmation of structure and meaning, that is, for a significant compensator. (On the general issues involved here, see, e.g., Bainbridge, 7-12.)

Scholars have usually said, or even stressed, that vv. 1-4 convey an image of universalism, and that, significantly, they "have absolutely nothing particular to say about Israel" (Wolff, *Micah*, 118). If these statements are correct, then they have to be taken into account as central elements in the discussion about the intention of these verses. But these claims should at the very least be strongly qualified. Not only do these verses mention Israel (Jacob), but they are aimed at an Israelite readership. We know that this is the case because they were written for them not only because of their language but also because of the worldview that they imply. Is it likely that they would have nothing particular to say to their readership about themselves?

First, the implied author of these verses claims that YHWH, that is, the God whose ruling the nations will abide, is understood by the same nations as "the God of Jacob [Israel]." This certainly says something regarding Israel/Jacob from (1) the perspective of the nations in the world of the text, (2) the authorial point of view, and (3) the standpoint of those who identify with it, including the rereaders of the text.

Second, the so-called universalism of these verses is an essential element in the dream of a universal theological empire that is advanced in this text. This empire is described as grounded on and reflecting the worldview of Israel. This universal empire will be ruled by YHWH, the God of Jacob, and its center will be in Zion/Jerusalem, the center of Israel. The subjects will listen to YHWH's word as it will be proclaimed in Zion/Jerusalem. Thus, on one level, YHWH will be the sovereign in that universal empire, but on a different level, it is implied that the necessary human intermediaries, the brokers of YHWH's word, are to be Jerusalemites, and likely Jerusalemite literati — one may note also that the book of Micah is referred to as YHWH's word. It is unlikely that it is mere chance that the authorship and readership of a text that advance such claims, and of the book of Micah as a whole, are among the Jerusalemite literati. Of course, within this discourse both the success of the empire and the worthiness of its ruler, as well as the associated value of the faithful brokers of this ruler, are taken for granted. The image of world peace and the eradication of the subject's lacks characterize and dramatize this success. Does such a dream of universal empire say nothing in particular to the readership of the text about themselves?

It seems that the opposite is true: it says a great deal about their dreams for the future and their self-understanding. Since these imperial dreams are developed against the background of a world that at least on the surface denied their potential, they may be seen as an expression of the dreams of grandeur of the actually powerless, or as another instance of "the self-reassuring triumphalism of a weak and unsuccessful tribe" (Greenspahn, 109). In any case these dreams, and the worldview implied by them, function as a significant religious compensator (see above).

Scholars usually mention that v. 5 conveys a particularistic approach. If this verse refers to the circumstances before the establishment of the future empire, which includes the present situation of the readers and the literary setting of the audience of the textually inscribed speaker, then it conveys a message quite consonant with that of vv. 1-4. If the verse characterizes the glorious future in which the nations are allowed to keep their gods, even when they obey YHWH and YHWH's word, then it may be considered particularistic, but it would be a matter of opinion and perspective whether it is more or less Israel/Zion-centered than the dream expressed in vv. 1-4. (Cf. the very positive characterization of the sailors in the book of Jonah.)

All in all, it seems that Mic 4:1-5 is not only Israel/Zion/Jerusalem-centered, but that it also serves to communicate a strong reaffirmation of the community in which and for which the book of Micah was written, and the community's theological tenets, particularly against the background of the actual situation of this postmonarchic, most likely Jerusalemite, and surely Jerusalemite-centered community. Moreover, this strong reaffirmation is consistent with the place of 4:1-5 within the book, because after the extreme high point of the violent dispossession reported in 3:12, one may expect that a reference to a profoundly pure world will follow (→ 2:1-5, Intention). This is the case in 4:1-5.

The discussion here addresses the meaning of the text in that original community. The issue of how this famous text was read, reread, and understood by later communities of Christians and Jews through the centuries is beyond the scope of this work.

Bibliography

P. R. Ackroyd, "A Note on Isaiah 2:1," *ZAW* 75 (1963) 320-21; W. S. Bainbridge, *The Sociology of Religious Movements* (New York: Routledge, 1997); J. Barr, "Hypostatization of Linguistic Phenomena in Modern Theological Interpretations," *JSS* 7 (1962)

85-94; W. Brueggemann, "'Vine and Fig Tree': A Case Study in Imagination and Criticism," *CBQ* 34 (1981) 188-204; G. W. Buchanan, "Eschatology and the 'End of Days,'" *JNES* 20 (1961) 188-93; E. Cannawurf, "The Authenticity of Micah IV.1-4," *VT* 13 (1963) 26-33; H. Cazelles, "Qui aurait visé, à l'origine, Isaïe II 2-5," *VT* 30 (1980) 409-20; R. J. Clifford, *The Cosmic Mountain in Canaan and the Old Testament* (HSM 4; Cambridge: Harvard Univ. Press, 1972); M. Fishbane, *Biblical Interpretation in Ancient Israel* (Oxford: Clarendon, 1985); E. S. Gerstenberger, *Psalms, Part I, with an Introduction to Cultic Poetry* (FOTL XIV; Grand Rapids: Eerdmans, 1988); B. Gosse, "Michée 4,1-5, Isaïe 2,1-5 et les rédacteurs finaux du livre d'Isaïe," *ZAW* 105 (1993) 98-102; F. E. Greenspahn, *When Brothers Dwell Together* (Oxford: Oxford Univ. Press, 1994); J. C. Hoffman, "Structure and Anti-Structure in Social Processes," in Hoffman, *Law, Freedom and Story* (Waterloo, Ont.: Wilfried Laurier Press, 1986) 71-102; T. Jacobsen, *The Harps That Once . . . Sumerian Poetry in Translation* (New Haven: Yale Univ. Press, 1987); E. Lipínski, "באחרית הימים dans les textes préexiliques," *VT* 20 (1970) 445-50; E. Nielsen, *Oral Tradition* (SBT 1/11; London: SCM, 1961); J. J. M. Roberts, "The Davidic Origin of the Zion Tradition," *JBL* 92 (1973) 329-44; E. H. Scheffler, "Micah 4:1-5: An Impasse in Exegesis?" *OTE* 3 (1985) 46-61; B. Stade, "Bemerkungen über das Buch Micah," *ZAW* 1 (1881) 161-72; J. G. Strydom, "Micah 4:1-5 and Isaiah 2:2-5: Who Said It First? A Critical Discussion of A. S. van der Woude's View," *OTE* 2 (1984) 25-28; E. Tov, *Textual Criticism of the Hebrew Bible* (Minneapolis: Fortress, 1992); H. Wildberger, *Isaiah 1–12* (tr. T. H. Trapp; Minneapolis: Fortress, 1990); J. T. Willis, "The Structure of Micah 3–5 and the Function of Micah 5₉₋₁₄ in the Book," *ZAW* 81 (1969) 191-214; idem, "The Expression *acharith hayyamim* in the Old Testament," *ResQ* 22 (1979) 54-71; A. S. van der Woude, "Micah IV.1-5: An Instance of the Pseudo-Prophets Quoting Isaiah," in M. A. Beek et al., eds., *Symbolae Biblicae et Mesopotamicae. FS F. M. T. de Liagre Böhl* (Leiden: Brill, 1973) 396-402.

SECOND READING, 4:6-8

Structure

I. Statement about the gathering of the exiles to Zion and
   of YHWH's reign over them   6-7
   A. Opening formula pointing to the future and marking
      the following text as YHWH's saying and drawing
      attention to it   6aα
   B. Divine announcement of (future) salvation:
      gathering the "lame"   6aβ-7a
   C. Divine announcement of YHWH's reign over Israel
      in Zion   7bα
   D. Concluding formula pointing to the future of the future   7bβ
II. Statement about Jerusalem as the capital of YHWH's reign   8
   A. Introduction by means of vocatives   8aα
   B. Body of the statement   8aβ-b

This second READING in 4:1–5:14 consists of two subunits. The first is clearly set apart from its context by an opening and a closing formula, both of which provide temporal information. This subunit addresses a common topos in announcements of salvation that was not present in the first READING: the gathering of the dispersed (see Westermann, *Prophetic Oracles*, esp. 105-13). This type of announcement presupposes the theological concept of the exile as a most significant deficiency from which Israel suffers, and whose removal is hoped and expected at some indefinite point in the future. Mic 4:7 joins in this regard 2:12-13; 4:9-14 (i.e., the following READING in this SET OF READINGS); 7:11-12; and similar announcements in other prophetic books (e.g., Zeph 3:18-19, 20; on the particularly close relation between Zeph 3:19 and Mic 4:7 see Ben Zvi, *Zephaniah*, 256-58).

Clear links bind this subunit to the preceding READING, including both language (cf. *lĕʿôlām wāʿed*, "forever and ever," and *wĕʿad-ʿôlām*, "forevermore," in vv. 5 and 7, respectively; *gôy ʿāṣûm*, "strong nation," in vv. 3 [pl.] and 7; *har ṣîyôn*, "Mt. Zion," in v. 7 and the multiple references to Mt. Zion and the temple in vv. 1-4) and theme. Regarding the theme, the issue of the rulership of YHWH from Zion is developed in v. 7, and then addressed again in v. 8 (notice also *har ṣîyôn*, "Mt. Zion," and *bat-ṣîyôn*, "Daughter Zion," in vv. 7b and 8, respectively; and *mālak*, "be king," and *mamleket*, "kingdom," in these verses).

The second of these subunits (v. 8) is associated with 4:6-7 (cf., e.g., Westermann, *Prophetic Oracles*, 103, 109, 122); but also with 4:9–5:1 (NRSV 5:2). That is, it is claimed that it serves as a Janus, double-duty unit (just like 5:1 [see below]; cf. the role of 1:5, 8-9) that brings together and creates a strong sense of textual coherence between 4:4-7 and 4:9–5:1. This sense of coherence is communicated not only by thematic relations but also by the fact that 4:8 contains the necessary information to understand the pronominal suffixes in v. 9; that is, the readers of v. 9 are asked to understand it on the basis of the language and the information conveyed in v. 8. It is worth noting that the sonorous link created between *ʾattâ* ("you") and *ʿattâ* ("now") in vv. 7bβ and 8 appears again between vv. 8 and 9 (and then 4:14 and 5:1).

The first subunit (4:6-7) may be divided into four literary parts. The first (4:6aα) consists of a multipurpose introductory formula created by the combination of two formulas: *bayyôm hahûʾ* ("on that day"), usually used to introduce a text and to associate it with an undetermined future; and *nĕʾum-yhwh* ("YHWH's saying"), which marks the text as a direct quotation from YHWH, legitimizes it, and functions in a way analogous to a focus marker in the sense that it draws the attention of the readers to the marked text. (On *nĕʾum-yhwh* see Parunak; Meier, 298-314.) This combined formula (with or without an initial *wĕhāyâ*, "it shall be") occurs elsewhere in prophetic literature (e.g., Jer 4:9; 30:8; Hos 2:18 [NRSV 16]; Zeph 1:10; Zech 12:4; 13:2), and in the book of Micah at the beginning of another READING in this SET OF READINGS (see Mic 5:9 [NRSV 10]).

The second part (4:6-7a) is the statement regarding the gathering of the exiles. It is presented in the text as an utterance by YHWH, both because of the preceding formula ("YHWH's saying"), and because only YHWH can be described as uttering these words. The saying itself is related to its immediate literary context (see, e.g., *gôy 'āṣûm*), interacts with contexts within the book of Micah, and uses lexical items that are usually associated with this type of discourse. Thus the pair *qbṣ–'sp* ("gather"–"gather") occurs elsewhere in the book in 2:12 (cf. Isa 11:2; 62:9; Ezek 29:5; Joel 2:16; Hab 2:5; Zeph 3:8; etc.). The theologically laden term *šĕ'ērît* ("remnant") occurs here as in Mic 2:12; 5:6, 7 (NRSV 7, 8); and 7:18 (cf. also the sound combination of *šĕ'ērît wĕhan-nahălā'â* ("remnant and her that was cast far off," in 4:7 [but see Williamson, 364-65], and *šĕ'ērît nahălātô*, "the remnant of his possession," in 7:18). The references to *rā'/â* ("evil," "disaster," "harm," "affliction") in 1:12 and 3:11 reverberate through the expression *wa'ăšer hărē'ōtî* ("which I have harmed" or "which I have afflicted"), which is attributed to YHWH in v. 6. The reference to Israel as *ṣōlē'â* ("lame") and *niddāhâ* ("one cast off") does not occur in other passages in Micah but appears elsewhere in prophetic literature in Zeph 3:19, on a similar note; regarding the image of Jacob/Israel as "lame" see Gen 32:32.

The third part (Mic 4:7bα) consists of a reference to YHWH's rule as a king over Israel and in Zion (cf. Isa 24:23; Ps 146:10). The underlying issues were implied in the preceding READING (Mic 4:1-5) but are now explicitly brought forward. The speaker is again unclear. It may be the human prophetic speaker or it may be YHWH (the reference to YHWH in the 3rd person in 4:7bα does not preclude YHWH as the speaker, as mentioned in the discussion of 2:5; see also Judg 2:22; 6:26; 1 Sam 10:19; 2 Sam 12:9; 1 Kgs 17:14; 2 Kgs 20:5; Isa 49:7; Jer 14:10; 17:5; 23:16; 26:2; 27:16; Zeph 3:12; Mal 1:4; cf. Revell, §27.3; for similar instances in the book of Micah, see 2:5; 4:10; 6:5).

This subunit opens and closes with formulaic language. The fourth part (i.e., 4:7bβ) consists of the expression *mē'attâ wĕ'ad-'ôlām* (lit., "from now on and forever"), which is usually used to close a literary unit or a subunit within a unit (see Isa 59:21; Pss 113:2; 115:18; 121:8; 125:2; 131:3) with a positive remark about the unlimited extension in time of the circumstances mentioned in the unit. It is worth mentioning that in Mic 4:7bβ, the beginning of the good period is in the undetermined future mentioned at the beginning of 4:6 and, accordingly, the expression may be rendered as "from then on and forever" (e.g., Allen, 328) or "for ever from that time forward" (REB). In other words, the concluding expression points to a future that stands in the future of the time referred to by the expression "that day," but significantly it does so by using the word *'attâ* ("now"), which invites the rereaders of the book to partake in that future, to enter into the literary and utopian world described in this text.

The second subunit (v. 8) in this READING consists of an introduction made by vocatives and in which — because of the literary context in which the text is set — Jerusalem must be addressed as a male rather than as a female character (see *bat yĕrûšālayim*, "Daughter Jerusalem" [e.g., 2 Kgs 19:21; Zeph 3:14; Zech 9:9; see Mic 4:8b] or *bat-ṣîyôn*, "Daughter Zion" [e.g., Isa 16:1; 52:2; 62:11; Jer 6:2; Zeph 3:14; Zech 9:9; Ps 9:15 (NRSV 14)], and which may also be translated as "Fair Jerusalem" and "Fair Zion"; so NJPSV). Although the pervasive characterization of Jerusalem as a female character is present in this verse too (and cf. Mic 1:13; 4:10, 13; note that even the dispersed of Israel, who are identified at some level with Jerusalem [see below], are represented by fem. forms in vv. 6-7), the link created by *'attâ* and *'attâ* (see vv. 8, 9, 11, 14, and 5:1 [NRSV 2]) requires that the textually inscribed speaker address Jerusalem/Zion in the 2nd masc. sg. (i.e., *'attâ*). (For examples of the literary play on *'attâ* and *'attâ* beyond the book of Micah, see Gen 26:29; 1 Kgs 12:4; Ezek 7:2, 3; Jonah 4:2, 3.)

Of course, as in other sections in the book of Micah (e.g., 2:1-5), that the words uttered by the speaker in one speech reported in the book depend on those uttered in another speech in close proximity in the book militates against the idea that we have before us the very words said by an actual speaker on two different occasions. This observation and those advanced before (e.g., → 2:1-5, Genre) indicate that the implied author constructed the voice of the speaker with the readership of the book in mind.

Images and motifs conveyed elsewhere in the book (particularly in 2:12-13, which deals with similar matters) reverberate in 4:8. See, for instance, the reference to *'ēder* ("flock") in reference to Israel in 2:12 and 4:8, and the image of YHWH as king in 2:13 (also cf. 1:9 and 15 with 4:8).

Genre

Some have argued that 4:6-8 is an oracle of salvation (e.g., Westermann, *Prophetic Oracles,* 109). It is more precise to say that the text is written so as to evoke in its readers the genre expectations usually associated with announcements of salvation, which may or may not have been part of the actual life of postmonarchic Israel within which the authorship and readership of the book of Micah — to be distinguished from potential forerunners and sources — are to be found. In any case, the readers of the book faced not a living prophet announcing salvation to them but a written text in which they read and reread about an ideal future described in terms of a saying of YHWH (v. 7) and a statement attributed to a godly voice (be it divine or human or a voice that overlaps both), both of which are included in a literary unit that is phrased so as to interweave with the literary units surrounding it in the book, and with other read sections. The genre of the unit is therefore a READING about the ideal future that is placed within a SET OF PROPHETIC READINGS dealing with the same matter, and that is to be read and reread in the light of its *Sitz im Buch.*

Setting

As in all the other READINGS in this unit (and as in 2:1-5 and other READINGS in the book), the setting of the speaker's words is left as open as possible. Moreover, even the implied past of the speaker (i.e., the dispersion, YHWH's harming of Israel; see vv. 6-7a) is not described in the text in such a way that it must be tied to any particular historical event, be it at 701 BCE, 587 BCE, or any disaster to Israel. Indeed, the text suggests that the readers are to contextualize rather than historicize when they approach the text. This is consonant with the activity of reading and rereading the book of Micah. The potential to understand "the lame condition of Israel" against many possible backgrounds and referents is conducive to multiple rereadings and multiple identifications by the rereaders, all of which contribute to the meaning of the text as reread by the community.

In relation to the community, something may be learned about the intended readership of this READING (as of the other READINGS in this set) from this text. Just like the textually inscribed audience of the speaker in the text, this readership accepts the Jerusalem-centered theology of Israel in the postmonarchic period and shares a world of knowledge that includes, among other things, a self-perception of Israel as a group who suffers from a lack, the idea of "exile," and the hope and image of the "gathering of the exiles." (See Intention below.)

The text here does not claim or ask its rereaders to understand it as part of the celebration of the temple's dedication, nor does any subunit or part of a subunit in 4:6-8. The same holds true for any possible temple or nontemple liturgy. From the use of a few expressions that do occur in the Psalms but not only there (e.g., *mēʿattâ wĕʿad-ʿôlām,* "from now on and forever," appears also in Isa 9:6 [NRSV 7]; 59:21), it does not follow that the text was used in or likely understood as a liturgical text. At best, this observation may suggest that these expressions were part of the world of knowledge of the authorship and the intended readership of Mic 4:6-8. (For a different approach, see Wolff, *Micah,* 124-25; see also Lescow, "Redaktionsgeschichtliche Analyze.")

The implied construction of the present of the community (see Intention) as being lame, cast away, dispersed, in need of gathering, powerless, and the like neither confirms nor precludes any possible setting in the Achaemenid period (as opposed to a so-called exilic, i.e., Neo-Babylonian, setting; cf. Mays, 102), because the temple community in Persian Yehud considered itself still in exile (on this issue see Ezra 10:7 and passim in Ezra-Nehemiah; cf. Knibb; Ben Zvi, "Looking"), still in need of YHWH's restoration, and still powerless.

Intention

The main intention of the piece is to reaffirm the main tenets of the readership by describing — and one may say inventing and reinventing — the future. The first of these addresses the certainty of YHWH's gathering the dispersed of Israel and the king from Zion. Every gathering of the dispersed implies undoing the results of past actions (YHWH's harming Israel) and a return to a kind of predisaster situation. In any case, the future is imagined as more like the distant, glorious past than the present or closer past, when YHWH acted against Jerusalem/Zion. The issue of return to the preexilic situation is advanced explicitly in the second statement (notice the reference to *hammemšālâ hāri-ʾšōnâ,* "the former dominion," in v. 8). That it is brought to the forefront is consistent with the legitimizing function of claims to restoration in the ancient Near East in general and in the postmonarchic discourse of Israel in particular (see Ben Zvi, "Inclusion").

Whether one of the intentions of this unit by itself is to convince its readers that the future described here includes the restoration of the Davidic dynasty to a position of leadership (cf. Wolff, *Micah,* 125) is debatable. Indeed, the text expresses a combination of equivocal and unequivocal claims. The latter concern the leadership of YHWH as king (cf. Exod 15:18; Isa 24:23; Obad 21; Pss 93:1; 96:10; 97:1; 99:1; 146:10; 1 Chr 16:31), the former the human ways in which this leadership will be manifested in Zion/Jerusalem. On the one hand, the reference to the kingdom of the "Daughter of Jerusalem" does necessarily imply a Davidide as a king in Jerusalem, particularly in the context of v. 7. The reference to *hammemšālâ hāri'šōnâ,* "the former dominion," is again inconclusive, since the whole expression itself occurs nowhere else in the HB/OT, and *memšālâ* alone is used in reference to YHWH's rulership (e.g., Ps 103:22), a Davidic ruler (e.g., 2 Kgs 20:13//Isa 39:2), or a foreign king (e.g., Jer 34:1). On the other hand, the clear reference to a new David in Mic 5:1 (NRSV 2) (i.e., in the next READING in this SET OF PROPHETIC READINGS), along with the textually inscribed request to co-textualize readings, and the bond between these two READINGS created by their sharing of v. 8, all seem to suggest a (veiled?) Davidic connotation in v. 8. I must stress, however, that the image of YHWH's kingship does not necessarily stand in tension with that of the reign of a Davidide (see, e.g., 1 Chr 16:7, 31; 17:14; and the suzerain role of YHWH in Psalm 2).

In sum, the text in vv. 6-8 does not advance but does not exclude the possibility of a Davidide's rule over Jerusalem. The reference to Jerusalem as a capital of a past kingdom may have evoked the image of the leadership of the Davidic dynasty. Significantly, the issue will be addressed again, from a different perspective, in the next READING. Not only is the text written so as to suggest that one READING is supposed to inform the other, but rereaders of the book of Micah were most likely aware of 5:1 (NRSV 2) when they read 4:6-8.

Although not an overt intention of the text, the equivalence between Zion and Israel ("the flock") and between the acropolis, Ophel (of Zion), and the "tower" of the flock in v. 8 (cf. Isa 32:14) strongly communicate the Jerusalem-centered worldview of the authorial voice (cf. the reference to Jerusalem as the "gate," i.e., the fortification, the stronghold of YHWH's people, Israel, in Mic 1:9).

Similarly, the text suggests a self-image of Israel prior to its gathering (see vv. 6-7). It is constructed metaphorically as a lame female who has been driven away, as an afflicted woman. Since the group represented by these images is the one that will turn into a "great nation," there is no reason to assume that it stands for a section of Israel rather than all of Israel (cf. Shoemaker, 165, among others). If so, this image of powerlessness points to a self-understanding of the present status of the community within which one finds the authorship and readership of the book of Micah from their own perspective. This image of Israel stands in sharp contrast with the anticipated and hoped-for Israel of the future that is described as *gôy 'āṣûm,* "a mighty nation." Significantly, here (and in Zeph 3:19) the people who will live in that future are referred to by masc. forms (including the masc. pl.; see v. 7b) rather than by fem. forms. (For Wolff this shift points to the secondary character of v. 7b [*Micah,* 115];

but this assumes that authors will not resort to changes in grammatical persons for rhetorical purposes; cf. Micah 1.)

Bibliography

M. A. Knibb, "The Exile in the Literature of the Intertestamental Period," *HeyJ* 17 (1976) 253-72; E. Otto, "Techniken der Rechtssatzredaktion israelitischer Rechtsbücher in der Redaktion des Prophetenbuches Micha," *SJOT* 5 (1991) 119-50; H. Van Dyke Parunak, "Some Discourse Functions of Prophetic Quotation Formulas in Jeremiah," in R. D. Bergen, ed., *Biblical Hebrew and Discourse Linguistics* (Winona Lake, Ind.: Eisenbrauns) 489-519; J. T. Willis, "Micah IV 14–V 5 — A Unit," *VT* 18 (1968) 529-47.

THIRD READING: FROM THE PAST TO THE FUTURE, 4:8–5:1 (NRSV 2)

Structure

I. Opening *wĕ'attâ* ("and you") section: statement about Jerusalem as the capital of YHWH's reign	4:8
A. Introduction by means of vocatives	8aα
B. Statement	8aβ-b
II. First *wĕ'attâ* ("and now") section	9-10
A. Set of rhetorical questions related to Israel's understanding of YHWH's role/status	9
B. Note of disaster (exile)	10a-bα
C. Note of salvation (return from exile)	10bβ
III. Second *wĕ'attâ* ("and now") section	11-13
A. Note of disaster: nations gathering to dishonor Zion	11
B. The (enemy) nations' lack of understanding of YHWH and YHWH's plan/plot	12
C. Note of salvation: defeat of the enemy nations	13
IV. Third *wĕ'attâ* ("and now") section	4:14
A. Note of disaster (including reference to dishonoring YHWH)	14a
B. Note of salvation	14b
V. Closing *wĕ'attâ* ("and you") section	5:1
A. The new David	5:1

This reading is both delimited and structured by explicit, textually inscribed markers. The reading shows an envelope created by the two sections that open with *wĕ'attâ*, "and you." In both cases the term immediately following *wĕ'attâ* contains a reference to a place or location that stands in this text as a symbol. Both sections also address similar kingly issues. The three *wĕ'attâ*, "and now," sections share, in addition to their opening, a similar basic structure. All address first disaster and then announce salvation. The role of the announcement of future salvation in the third *wĕʿattâ* section is taken by the final *wĕʿattâ* section, which functions as both the envelope pair of 4:8 and the salvation remark necessary (see co-texts) to conclude the third *wĕʿattâ* section, as well as an integral part of the next READING (see below). The multiplicity of roles of certain sections and phrases in the book of Micah has been noticed before (e.g., 1:5; 4:8). It is worth stressing, however, that this feature communicates the intertwined character of different textual units or subunits either within the frame of a particular READING or at a higher structural level, among subunits belonging to different READINGS. Thus there can be no doubt that the presence and wording of these phrases or sections depends on their *Sitz im Buch*. This conclusion stands in clear tension with the assumptions that the texts before us represent (at least, in the main) the actual words of a historical prophet as he pronounced them on different occasions and before different audiences.

Among additional markers pointing to the literary unit of this READING, one may mention the pun on the openings (i.e., *wĕʿattâ* and *wĕʿattâ;* cf. 2 Sam 7:25-29 and notice that a few additional features of 2 Sam 7:25-29 are present in one way or another in either this or the next reading, 5:1-5; see the structural role of *wĕʿattâ* and the use of the expressions *ʿad-ʿôlām,* "for eternity," *yigdal šimmĕkā,* "magnify the name of"; this evidence suggests both a shared lexical inventory and common structural devices that may be activated when similar issues or needs are raised), the use of the double fem. imperative forms in 4:10, 13, and the reference to "counselor" and "counsel" (vv. 9, 12). This READING shows also numerous links to other READINGS in this SET OF READINGS. Among them one may mention the reference to *mālak,* "be king," in 4:7 in close textual proximity to *melek* ("king") in 4:9, the reference to YHWH as *šōpēṭ* ("ruler," "judge") in 4:14 and the text in 4:3; the similar or identical references to "numerous peoples" (see 4:2, 3, 11; 5:7); the contrastive references to *qbṣ* ("gather") in 4:6, 12; the similar case of the forms from the root *nṣl* ("save, deliver") in 4:10; 5:7; those to *yôlēdâ* ("a woman in labor") in 4:9, 10; 5:2; and the sound play between *tārîʿî rēaʿ* ("you [fem. sg.] cry out loudly") in v. 9 and *hărēʿōtî,* ("I have afflicted") in v. 6 (cf. Luker).

The structure of the opening *wĕʿattâ* section was already discussed in relation to 4:6-8. As an integral part of 4:9–5:1, 4:8 is written to indicate to the readers a close bond between this verse and 5:1. Significantly, the envelope created by the two verses moves the attention of the readers from Jerusalem to Bethlehem, and associates the restoration of the old rule exercised by or from Jerusalem to the new David who will come from Bethlehem (on *mamleket lĕbat-yĕrûšālāim* see Hillers, *Micah,* 56). This shift is also marked by the contrastive choice of nouns from the root *mšl,* from *memšālâ,* "dominion," in 4:8 to *môšēl,* "ruler," in 5:1.

The first *wĕʿattâ* section (4:9-10; the *waw* there is implied; see *BHS* and cf. the textual situation in the Tg.) opens with a series of rhetorical questions. On one level the questions are addressed by the textually inscribed speaker, the prophetic voice, to the implied audience of this speaker against some undefined circumstances in the world of the book. On a second level the intended readership is supposed to identify with the addressees, to see these questions addressed to them as well. The lack of any narrative anchoring the speech to a particular setting is to allow for this identification. Of course, distance does exist too. The text is attributed to the monarchic period (see 1:1) and the exile is still in the future from the perspective of the audience in the world of the text, but not so from that of the rereaders of the book. The answers to these questions are obvious: yes, the "Daughter of Jerusalem" (i.e., Israel) has — in monarchic as well as postmonarchic times — a king, YHWH (see v. 7; see, e.g., already Ibn Ezra, Radak, Abrabanel; cf. Jer 8:19), and their "counselor" (cf. v. 12) has not been lost. (Regarding YHWH as *yôʿēṣ,* "counselor," cf. Jer 32:19.)

Yet the theological problem reflected in the text is that, in spite of YHWH's being Israel's king and wise advisor, Israel suffers greatly as if it had no king or advisor from the two viewpoints that can be discerned here. From the perspective of the monarchic audience addressed by the speaker, in the world of the text, Israel will be exiled to Babylon. From the perspective of the readership of the text, not only was monarchic Israel (i.e., Judah; → 1:2-16 and bibliography there) led to exile, but also they themselves — that is, the readership — recognize their king to be YHWH, and yet in the world of real-politik, they (postmonarchic Israel) seem to be kingless, powerless, and, from their own perspective, in pain, like the woman in labor mentioned in the note about disaster that follows (on that image cf. Jer 6:24-26, a unit within which a few motifs found in Micah occur). It is only anticipated, but still worth stressing, that the text is construed to encourage the identification of the readership with the addressees in the book (cf. Deuteronomy).

The note of disaster in vv. 10a-bα opens with two imperatives in the 2nd fem. sg., addressed to Daughter Jerusalem, which are similar to those that open the note about salvation in the second *wěʿattâ* section. In this note, however, the reference to the painful labor of the woman leads to the mention of the exile in Babylon. (Once the shift from Daughter Jerusalem to Daughter Bethlehem is advanced in the READING, a connoted sense of birth is advanced.) Pain was not in vain (see 5:1). This section, like all the *wěʿattâ* sections, concludes with a note about the resolution of the lack or deficiency created by the circumstances described in the note of disaster: YHWH will rescue and redeem the exiles (v. 10bβ).

A number of scholars have claimed that the references to *melek,* "king," and *yôʿēṣ,* "counselor," in v. 9 concern a human king, and that the situation described here points most likely to the events during Sennacherib's campaign (e.g., Hillers, *Micah,* 59). It is true that these terms may be used for a human or a divine king. Yet the following points seem to turn the balance of the evidence against this position.

1. The literary context in which the verse is situated in the book suggests a divine figure.
2. The text mentions neither Sennacherib nor the events of 701 BCE; in fact, there is no mention of any precise historical circumstances, except the reference to the exile to Babylon.

3. The text does not provide any clear signal to the readers that they should understand the text against a particular historical narrative, but sets many markers indicating to them that the verse is part and parcel of a larger unit, this READING, which in turn is an integral part of a SET OF READINGS.

The proposals to understand the references to "king" and "counselor" as pointing to a human being are consistent with a tendency to give priority to the possible settings in which a historical prophet in the 8th century BCE could have proclaimed either the text of the section, or a speculative forerunner of it over the actual reading of the text. In other words, it points to a reading of the relevant section or fraction thereof that does not take into account its immediate literary context or the world of the book of Micah, but rather is fully contextualized within a proposed historical narrative or metanarrative, be it related to the events in 701 or 586 (e.g., Mays, 104-5). The same tendency is responsible for the proposal to emend or reconstruct the original text by the replacement of "Babylon" with "Assur." This replacement is not based on any textual source, or on any grammatical, lexical, or syntactic problem. Rather it is based on what likely could have said by a historical 8th-century prophet who faced the Assyrian crisis to a living audience at that time (cf. Hillers, *Micah*, 59; Alonso Schökel and Sicre Díaz, 2:1059).

Moreover, some scholars consider that the tension in the text between the claim that YHWH is Israel's king and that the people will still be exiled requires the hypothesis of two different speakers, namely, the false prophets and the true prophet (van der Woude, "Micah in Dispute"; Alonso Schökel and Sicre Díaz, 2:1054-56). Again, it might be possible that this is the case if one envisages a historical prophet talking to an audience and trying to persuade them that Jerusalem will be defeated and its people deported. But if one works with a text to be read and reread and that above all expresses and shapes the theological thought of an intended postmonarchic readership, then it is obvious that this tension is part and parcel of their theological thought and their understanding of their past. Moreover, from their perspective YHWH was surely Israel's sovereign even when they were exiled to Babylon.

Two final observations regarding this first *wěʿattâ* ("and now") section (vv. 9-10), one concerning style and the other content. First, this section shows some repetitions and puns on words and sounds (e.g., the emphatic repetition of *šām*, "there," in v. 10; of *yôlēdâ*, "a woman in labor," in vv. 9, 10; the assonance between the two imperatives in v. 10). The section is not different in this regard from other sections (notice the repetition of consonants in *bt-yrwšlm-mmlkt — mmšlh*) and elsewhere in the book (e.g., 1:1-16; 3:1-12).

The second observation points to the message conveyed in v. 10 that "Israel" is "exilic Israel," exiled Judah. This theological or ideological construction is ubiquitous in biblical literature from the postmonarchic period (see Ben Zvi, "Inclusion"). The emphatic reference to *šām*, "there" (i.e., Babylon), as the place where the salvation of all of Jerusalem (which symbolically stands for Israel) will take place, is noteworthy. The same is to be said of the use of the roots *nṣl* and *gʾl* ("rescue, save," and "redeem," respectively), which in this context evokes associations with the delivery from Egypt (see Exod 6:6; significantly, the return from Babylon is portrayed in terms reminiscent of — or even more glorious than — the exodus from Egypt in Isaiah 40–55 and Ezra; see, e.g., Isa 52:12 and cf. Exod 12:11 and Deut 16:3; see also Whybray, 50; on the ideological horizon of these themes, Ben Zvi, "Inclusion"). Of course, the reference to Babylon as "there" points also to the perspective of the speaker in the text, who is most likely in Judah (cf. Ps 137:1), or more precisely Achaemenid Judah (i.e., Yehud).

The second *wĕʿattâ* ("and now") section (vv. 11-13) contains three sub-units that provide a clear thread of thought. The first deals with impending disaster associated with the gathering of "many nations" against Jerusalem (v. 11); the second advances their characterization as unaware of YHWH's plan or plot against them and of YHWH as their opponent (v. 12); and the third reveals, under those circumstances, the expected defeat of Zion's enemies and along with it the salvation of Jerusalem (v. 13).

The image of the nations gathering to attack Jerusalem/Zion (or Israel) opens other pericopes associated with salvation (e.g., Ps 46:6-8 [NRSV 5-7]; Isa 17:12-14; 25:6-8; Ezekiel 38–39; Joel 4:9-16 [NRSV 3:9-16]; Zech 12:2-4, 8-9; 14:1-3, 12-15). It presents the problem that is supposed to be resolved by YHWH's activity, whether or not mediated by Israel. The nations gathering against Jerusalem/Zion are characterized as powerful in worldly terms. But they are also characterized as in opposition to YHWH and, accordingly, within the logic of the worldview of the composers and readers, as doomed to destruction. On the theological or ideological issues associated with the judgment of the nations in prophetic literature and on their not knowing YHWH's plan, as opposed to the authorship and readership of this text, see below. For other instances of the use of the image of YHWH's plan or plot against foreign nations see Isa 14:26-27; Jer 49:20-21; 50:45-46.

The literary device of describing characters through the attribution of short direct speeches to them has been found elsewhere in the book of Micah (e.g., 2:6-7; 3:12; 4:2; 7:10; cf. the numerous cases of speech attributed to YHWH). The nations themselves are characterized through this device in this SET OF READINGS in 4:2, though in a form very different from the one in 4:11. Their purpose is now to pollute or to profane Zion/Jerusalem and to dishonor it (cf. Ps 79:1). To be sure, within the world of the authorship and readership of the book, such a statement is an act of defiance against YHWH, and as such leads to doom. Thus the declaration of the nations allows the text to shift its focus easily and smoothly from the confrontation between the nations and Zion/Jerusalem to that between the nations and YHWH (cf. Isa 36:1–37:13//2 Kgs 18:13–19:13; and notice the interweaving of the two motifs in, e.g., Isa 29:1-8; Ezekiel 38–39; Obadiah; Psalm 2).

Within the postmonarchic discourse or discourses of Israel there was already an association between Israel's defeat and a profanation — which in an honor-shame system is to be associated with dishonor — of either what is considered to be holy by YHWH or of YHWH's name (cf. Isa 43:27-28; Ezek 7:21-24; 22:16; 24:21; 39:7; Dan 11:31; see below). These actions, even if committed by YHWH, are not consistent with a display of public honor (see, e.g., Ezek 20:9, 14, 22; 39:7).

The particular image of the nations' defeat is developed according to the agrarian model of the threshing floor (cf. Jer 51:3), and on the use of animals to thresh the sheaves. Thus the characterization of Daughter Jerusalem or Zion as a woman groaning in birth pains shifts to that of an extremely strong cow. Notice the reference to a "horn of iron" and to "bronze hoofs," which emphasizes strength rather than the creation of the mimetic image of a threshing cow (the fem. pronominal references point to a "cow" rather than an "ox") that will beat the sheaves (i.e., the nations) into pieces. This metaphorical image is also likely to connote an association between the imagery of this *wĕʿattâ* section (vv. 11-13) and the following one (4:14–5:1), in which the symbolic Bethlehem (i.e., "house of bread") figures prominently.

The final note in this second *wĕʿattâ* section (vv. 11-13) points to the devotion of the nations' wealth to YHWH, which is another theme present in depictions of the future (e.g., Hag 2:6-7; cf. the explicit future *ḥērem* against the nations themselves, rather than the devotion of their "gain" and "wealth" in Isaiah 34). Also the reference to YHWH as *ʾădôn kol-hāʾāreṣ*, "lord of the whole earth," appears elsewhere in Zech 4:14; 6:5; Ps 97:5 (cf. Ps 97:5 and Mic 1:4; also cf. Ps 114:7), and in relation to the "ark of the covenant" in Josh 3:11, 13. In Mic 4:13 the reference to YHWH in these terms explains the transfer of the riches of the nations to YHWH, who is their legitimate owner as the "the lord of the whole earth" (cf. Hag 2:7).

The presence in the MT of the word *wĕhaḥăramtî*, "I will make a *ḥērem*" (v. 13), introduces a note of ambiguity regarding the speaker in the text. The MT shows a 1st common sg. form that leads to an understanding such as "I will make X a *ḥērem*." Of course, one may have expected a 2nd fem. sg. form (leading to "you [here, Daughter Zion/Jerusalem] will make X a *ḥērem*"), as actually found in some ancient versions (LXX, Vg.). Significantly, the affirmation that the *ḥērem* is for YHWH does not rule out YHWH as the speaker in the text (as mentioned before regarding Mic 2:5; 4:7; see Judg 2:22; 6:26; 1 Sam 10:19; 2 Sam 12:9; 1 Kgs 17:14; 2 Kgs 20:5; Isa 49:7; Jer 14:10; 17:5; 23:16; 26:2; 27:16; Zeph 3:12; Mal 1:4; cf. Revell, §27.3; for another instance in the book of Micah, see 6:5). Thus a sense of ambiguity about the identity of the speaker is communicated. This sense is consistent with the tendency to blur the lines between godly voices (either those of a human speaker — the "prophet" — or those of YHWH) that has been found in many readings in the book of Micah. It also creates a sense of association between YHWH and Daughter Zion/Jerusalem in that both may serve the same roles in the text. This sense is consistent with the characteristic tendency in this section to associate conflict with Daughter Zion/Jerusalem with the confrontation with YHWH (see vv. 11-12), and, indirectly, to create a theological and ideological world in which the two (YHWH and Zion/Jerusalem/Israel) are tied together. The latter is, significantly, a major claim reflected and communicated by the book of Micah (see, e.g., 4:1-5). The ancient translations remove the ambiguity in favor of an unequivocal 2nd person fem. form.

Proposed emendations of *tehĕnāp*, "let her be profaned, polluted," in v. 11 (e.g., Wellhausen, 142; Ehrlich, 436; cf. *BHS*) are worth mentioning given the importance of this term for the present analysis. But the text does not have to represent a plausible point of view of the nations, from their own perspective as it were, in accurate, historical terms. It must instead evoke in the readership a particular characterization of the nations: they hold the viewpoint that the implied author wishes to attribute to them for rhetorical reasons in this pericope. This being the case, there is no convincing support for these proposals (see Hillers, *Micah,* 60-61).

The manner in which this second *wĕʿattâ* section (vv. 11-13), and particularly its contents, relates to those present in the first and third one is discussed under Genre.

The third *wĕʿattâ* section (4:14–5:1) shows the same basic structure found in the others. It contains a note of disaster (v. 14) followed by a note of salvation (v. 15). This section is characterized by a considerable number of puns that are based on assonance. Thus one may observe the presence of (1) *titgōdĕdî bat-gĕdûd* ("Daughter of a troop [i.e., of an attacking troop; cf. Job 19:12] lacerate yourself [in mourning]"; for this and other readings of this text, see, among others, J. M. P. Smith, 100-101; Renaud, 197-98; Allen, 341; Mays, 114; Hillers, *Micah,* 62; Petrotta, 114-18; Schwantes); (2) *šēbet* ("rod") and *šōpēt* ("judge") (see Willis, "Micah IV," 533 n. 1); (3) *lĕḥî* ("cheek") and *lehem* ("bread") (as part of "house of bread = Bethlehem"); and (4) *yāṣāʾ* ("shall come forth") and *môṣāʾōt* ("origin"). The pun on words in *titgōdĕdî bat-gĕdûd* (which is based on a contrast between the meanings of the Hitpolel forms of the Hebrew roots *gdd* I, "make incisions upon oneself," "lacerate oneself in mourning," and *gdd* II, "roam about," "come as a troop," "gather in troops"; cf. Luker, 293) is clearly reminiscent of similar puns in 1:10-16. From this observation it does not follow that 4:14 "belongs" to 1:10-16, or that the same human author is responsible for both texts (cf. Lescow, "Komposition," 213-15). It follows, however, that the text is written to communicate to the intended readers a sense of textual closeness that goes beyond the level of the particular READING and its immediate contexts, so as to evoke or activate in the readership their memory of previous sections in the book.

The note of disaster in v. 14 describes the nations as dishonoring not Jerusalem/Zion but the "judge of Israel." The question of who is referred to as "the judge of Israel" has received much attention. The most promising approach to the question is to focus on the text itself. Given that this is a note about disaster for Israel, it is clear that the term "the judge of Israel" stands for the "ruler of Israel" rather than "the one who judges and punishes Israel (notice that the 3rd masc. pl. *yakkû,* "they strike," points to the nations mentioned in the previous section). Yet "the judge and ruler of Israel" is clearly an ambiguous designation. Moreover, it is set within a literary section in which there is no reference to a particular time, place, location, or anything that may anchor the events in a particular event either in history — as reconstructed within the community in which the text was written and first reread — or even in the world of the text. Aside from the obvious, that is, that the "daughter of troops" (i.e., Jerusalem/Zion) is under siege (whether literally or figuratively), the text is not written to allow for a single identification but rather to be as general as possible. Thus the text does not ask the intended readers to identify this ruler of Israel with a single historical figure (e.g., Hezekiah), or necessarily to evoke the image of the charismatic rulers of Israel in the book of Judges. Moreover, in addition to a human ruler, "the judge of Israel" may also point to the divine one (see Gen 18:25; Isa 33:22; cf. Pss 96:13; 98:9; 1 Chr 16:33; cf. also the epithet in Gen 18:25 with that in Mic 4:13). Within the context of this SET OF READINGS and esp. Mic 4:3, there is some support for the idea that the "judge of Israel" here may also refer to YHWH.

Such a position assumes that the reference to "striking the cheek" is not meant literally but indicates an affront to YHWH. This understanding of the term "the judge of Israel" is supported by the text, the imagery, and the implicit logic of the previous section (vv. 11-13). There, the confrontation between the nations and Zion moves swiftly to that between the nations and YHWH. Dishonoring Zion/Jerusalem is considered to be an affront to YHWH that calls for YHWH's response. In this unit Jerusalem's siege or an attack that caused Zion to display mourning rituals is constructed as an affront to YHWH, as striking YHWH's cheek, at it were. As mentioned above, within this world of discourse the misfortune of Israel connotes the image of displaying YHWH's dishonor; see Ezek 20:9, 14, 22; Ps 79:9-10; cf. Jer 14:21.

Within this discourse the display of dishonor leads directly to the doom of the perpetrator, which in the world of the text is represented by the note of salvation in Mic 5:1. Still, the note itself brings back to the forefront the image of a human ruler, although one supported by YHWH. Thus the text does not communicate ambiguity but creates a textual space in which there is blurring and even possible overlap between images of divine and human rulers. As such it conveys that the two are associated and stand as opponents of the nations who stand against YHWH, YHWH's selected king, or Israel (cf. Psalm 2).

Two notes regarding v. 14: first, regarding "striking the cheek" in v. 14, see 1 Kgs 22:24 (//2 Chr 18:23); Job 16:10; Ps 3:8 (NRSV 7); Lam 3:30; cf. Isa 50:6. The action points clearly to a display of dishonor; see esp. Lam 3:30. Second, as for YHWH suffering, as it were (a display of dishonor is to be considered as some level as "suffering"), because of Israel's misfortune, → Mic 1:8. For a different approach, see Kapelrud (399-400), who understands "the judge of Israel" as pointing to the human king of Israel, and interprets his humiliation in terms of a New Year Festival similar to the Akkadian Akitu ritual. This understanding is important for Kapelrud's position that "chs. iv and v look like a collection of or an imitation of ritual texts intended for use at a great festival . . . this festival was the great Autumn and New Year festival" (Kapelrud, 403).

The explicit association of Bethlehem with Ephrathah in 5:1 is worth mentioning. Bethlehem is identified as Ephrathah in Gen 35:19 and 48:17, and there (as in Gen 35:16) it is bound with the story of the death and burial of Rachel. Significantly, the geographical term Ephrathah does not occur in the Deuteronomistic History, nor is it associated with David elsewhere in the HB/OT, except in Ruth 4:11 and Ps 132:6. The reference to Bethlehem as one of the smaller clans of Judah is consistent with the common stress on the unlikely character of those chosen by YHWH (cf. Judg 6:15; 1 Sam 9:21), and which serves to maximize their successes and YHWH's role in achieving them (see Greenspahn, 106-7, et passim).

Genre

The three *wĕʿattâ,* "now," sections (4:9-10, 11-13; 4:14–5:1) evoke the genre and the expectations of prophetic announcements of salvation. In each of them, a character identified with Jerusalem/Zion/Israel is addressed against a background of misfortune and it is announced to that character that those circumstances will drastically turn around. If the addressees will be exiled, then they will return; if a great army of many peoples attacks them, then they will rise and vanquish the attackers, and maintain the honor of Jerusalem; if they will be under siege, they will be saved by a new David. In all these announcements the speaker is a godly voice, be it the prophetic or the divine speaker, or a combination or blend of both. Moreover, the speaker may identify with the addressees (see 4:14), and the rereaders are certainly asked to identify themselves with the addressees, and to some extent with the godly speaker or speakers too (cf. 4:14).

Yet one should note that an analysis of these three announcements points to their existence in the world of the text rather than outside that world. They do not correspond with an orally delivered prophetic announcement in a real-life situation.

To begin with, the first of these three sections not only presupposes the presence of the first *wĕʿattâ* section (v. 8) but also determines its position in the text as being just prior to the first *wĕʿattâ* section (vv. 9-10) (see the reference to the 2nd person fem.). The second *wĕʿattâ* section (vv. 11-13) presupposes the first one (see the reference to the 2nd person fem.), and the third (4:14–5:1) assumes the presence of the second. Neither the referent of "daughter of troops" nor the identity of the attackers is understandable unless they are read in a way that is informed by vv. 11-13. Moreover, the third section is written to advance the second and last *wĕʿattâ* section, whose presence presumes the existence of the first one. For the proposal that 4:14 is only a fragment of an original and now lost text that did not include 5:1 but some other text that supplied the same trend of thought found in 4:9-10, 11-12, see Hillers, *Micah,* 62. This proposal is not only fully speculative but also stands against Ockham's razor, which states that things not known to exist should not be postulated as existing unless it is absolutely necessary. Moreover, this proposal does not explain the text of the book of Micah.

The three *wĕʿattâ,* "and now," sections (4:9-10, 11-13; 4:14–5:1) are clearly written to convey to the reader a sense of textual coherence and a request to read and reread them one in the light of the other; that is, these sections inform each other. I must stress that the literary unit composed of these three sections neither resembles nor attempts to resemble closely a possible, real-life, oral announcement made by a prophet to a group of people (who from a rhetorical and theological or ideological stance were identified — or asked to identify themselves — with Jerusalem/Zion) at the time of a most threatening attack against monarchic Jerusalem by foreign foes, be they Assyrians, Babylonians, or any other historical enemy. For rhetorical reasons it is unlikely that the people under such circumstances would be told at the same time and place that they are going to be (1) defeated and carried to exile, and then and only then saved; and be (2) victorious to the degree that they will trample many peoples and surely not go into exile. A contradictory message lasting seconds and delivered to a live audience is not the most likely address to the people under such dire circumstances, nor is it likely to be remembered verbatim.

On the other hand, the three *wĕʿattâ*, "and now," sections are consistent with, and inform one another within, the frame of a textually inscribed literary unit, namely, a written text to be read and reread as a collage of images that evokes an expected future. The readership of such a text does not consist of people who are personally involved in a severe military crisis that spells imminent doom to them. Rather, this is a group of highly literate readers and rereaders who reflect on past misfortunes that happened in the monarchic period, as constructed in the text and within the frame of their world of knowledge. From this perspective, the three *wĕʿattâ* sections point to the hopes of the authorship and readership of the text. The announcements of salvation there are presented from *their* viewpoint, perhaps partially fulfilled (4:10) but mainly unfulfilled (e.g., 4:13; 5:1). Thus one may conclude that the words of the speaker to the addressees in the world of the text are constructed and presented for the sake of the intended rereadership of the book, rather than the textually inscribed addressees. As such, the appropriate genre for this text is a READING, or, to be more precise, a PROPHETIC READING.

Setting

As in previous units in the book of Micah, within the world of the text there is no particular historical setting in which the words of the speaker to the addressees are set. There is no reference to Hezekiah (cf. Hillers, *Micah,* 59), Jehoiachin (cf. Mays, 105), Zedekiah (cf., Mays, 105), Sennacherib, or any individual king, friend or foe. There is no reference to specific circumstances that may anchor the utterance of the speaker's words to a particular event (cf. Bordreil, esp. 28), beyond the rhetorical requirement that the starting characterization of Jerusalem/Zion is one of a strong misfortune, and the reference to the Babylonian exile in 4:10. To be sure, this characterization then leads, in the world of the book, to that of its future salvation. The repetition of the precise temporal marker, *wĕʿattâ* ("and now"), does not point to a request to read the text in a way that is strongly informed by the particular historical conditions that obtained at some precise point in the past. Here *wĕʿattâ* is more of a literary device that fulfills structural and affective functions. The latter targets the intended audience of the text, who are invited repeatedly to identify themselves with the monarchic-period addressees in the text (and occasionally with the speaker; see the 1st common pl. pronominal reference in v. 14), and always with the concepts of Israel/Jerusalem/Zion. This request of identification expresses and shapes a basic principle in the worldview of the authorship and readership of the book, and of the postmonarchic communities.

The conspicuous binding of the different subunits together into a single text suggests a tendency away from historicized or mimetically oriented readings (after all, the three *wĕʿattâ* sections are unlikely to be pronounced one after the other and in oral form) and toward a composition and reading that are mark-edly co-textual, that is, a composition and reading and rereading that are gov-erned by the *Sitz im Buch* of each subunit. This points to the genre of the text as a PROPHETIC READING. Yet genre is deeply related to setting. The setting of this READING is that of the other READINGS that comprise this SET OF PROPHETIC READINGS, namely, 4:1–5:14, which as a literary product is aimed primarily to those bearers of high literacy who were able to read and reread prophetic books.

Intention

The main intention of this unit is to convey an association between the past and the future. The envelope of the *wĕ'attâ* sections expands on the issue of the manifestation of YHWH's kingship in the future that was advanced in 4:7. The envelope links the former dominion (i.e., in the past) with the future one, and shifts from the (past and future) seat of the kingdom to the identity of the past and future king, a "David," or metaphorically from Jerusalem to Bethlehem. The final focus is clearly on the future David. His role is associated with an image of the future in which the true and full will of YHWH will be mani-fested on earth, and in which the divine economy will truthfully correspond to what is held as divine instruction by Israel. It is worth mentioning that the presence of a Davidide in Jerusalem does not negate the sovereignty of YHWH or the manifestation of YHWH's kingdom (cf. 4:7; and see, e.g., Psalm 2 and 1 Chr 17:14). The envelope conveys an expression of hope and an image of this ideal future in terms of a powerful Davidide.

All three *wĕ'attâ* ("and now") sections deal with the link between the past and the future. The past is here characterized as a period of hardship, mis-fortune, and displays of dishonor. Yet these images of the past lead to mes-sages of hope. Indeed, these images represent the necessary negative circum-stances that are to be turned around in the future. Descriptions of salvific acts require the presence of a situation from which someone has to be saved. Yet from the perspective of the intended readership, the distress is in the past and perhaps is considered to persist in their present — as understood by this public — and at least metaphorically. But the announcements of salvation are either only partially fulfilled (4:10) or most often not fulfilled at all. Given the au-thority that the text claims for itself, the message of the text is that these an-nouncements will surely be fulfilled in the future; accordingly, the entire sec-tion is a message of hope.

While this message of hope is unequivocal, there is considerable equivocality regarding the particular image of the future. In fact, not only this READING but the entire SET OF READINGS (chs. 4–5) asks the intended reader-ship to imagine a set of future scenarios that are not logically congruent but point to a situation in which different approaches and emphases regarding the expected future should inform one another. Indeed, it is most likely that the tapestry created by their multivocality represents the multiple voices, images, and approaches that were evoked in postmonarchic Israel when they attempted to describe what an ideal future might be.

In contrast with 4:1-5, these units and particularly the middle *wĕ'attâ* section associate the salvation of Israel with the defeat and shame of many nations (also cf. 5:6-8). This section explicitly advanced a horizon of thought similar to that in the tripartite prophetic books in which Israel's suffering is followed by the nations' suffering and then by salvation for Israel (and at times the nations too; cf. 4:1-5). The main difference with some of these books regards the characterization of a saved Israel, which is described here as taking an active role in the divinely driven thrashing of the nations. These images of the future may be interpreted in terms of dreams of power by the powerless, a relatively common phenomenon. In addition, they are consistent with a world of thought in which the actual power of foreign nations is not seen as an indication of their status as blessed by YHWH, but of their situation as not yet punished by YHWH (cf. 4:10, 11, 12). On the horizon of thought expressed by the mentioned tripartite structure and in particular about the world as a truthful or misleading manifestation of status before YHWH, see Ben Zvi, "Understanding"; idem, *Zephaniah*, 325-46.

Two of the *wĕ'attâ* sections address other significant issues in addition to those mentioned above. The first section (4:9-10) deals with the question of the presence of YHWH alongside that of defeat and exile. The rhetorical question, "Is there no king in you?" in 4:9 has to be answered affirmatively: there is a king in Jerusalem — YHWH. But YHWH's kingship was not a guarantee against exile. It certainly did not prevent the exile to Babylon, and accordingly Daughter Zion had every reason to "writhe and groan." Rather, YHWH's kingship in the world of the book provides hope that the terrible situation (i.e., exile) will be reversed in the future.

From the viewpoint of the postmonarchic community within which and for which this text was written (notice the explicit reference to the exile to Babylon), YHWH was surely the king of Israel. But YHWH's kingship could not have been considered a guarantee that their status in worldly terms would be higher than that of other groups. Rather, the earthly status of the Israelite postmonarchic communities could be described only as close to powerlessness in relation to that of the superpowers of the time. Still, YHWH was their king. YHWH's kingship provided hope for their future rather than power and worldly status in the present.

The second *wĕ'attâ* section (4:11-13) constructs a world in which the nations are unaware of YHWH's plan against them. But who is aware of YHWH's plan? Certainly the intended readers of the unit who may read about them in a book that is considered YHWH's word, that is, the book of Micah. Of course, this book and the divine knowledge that it purports to communicate is not available to "the nations" as opposed to the readership of this book and those taught or told by the literati who are able to read and reread it (cf. Ben Zvi, *Obadiah*, 97-97).

In sum, the intention of the text is to address theological and ideological issues that are central to the thought of the intended community of readers, and to instill in them hope for a better, ideal future, which is not disassociated from, but reverses, the tragic images of the past.

Bibliography

P. Bordreuil, "Michée 4:10-13 et ses parallèles ougaritiques," *Sem* 21 (1971) 21-28; A. B. Ehrlich, *Miqra kePeshuto*, vol. 3 (1901; repr. New York: Ktav, 1969); F. E. Greenspahn, *When Brothers Dwell Together* (Oxford: Oxford Univ. Press, 1994); S. J. Schwantes, "A Note on Micah 5:1 (Hebrew 4:14)," *AUSS* 1 (1963) 105-7; R. N. Whybray, *Isaiah 40–66* (NCB; Grand Rapids: Eerdmans, 1981); J. T. Willis, "Micah IV 14–V 5 — A Unit," *VT* 18 (1968) 529-47.

FOURTH READING: FROM A DAVIDIDE TO THE COLLECTIVE "WE," NAMELY, "ISRAEL": A DREAM OF "PEACE," 5:1-5 (NRSV 2-6)

Structure

I. The new Davidide and the circumstances of his rule	1-3
A. The announcement of a new David	1
B. Motive clause characterizing the period prior to the reign of the new David	2
C. The shepherding (i.e., reign) of the Davidide and its character	3 (+ 4aα)
II. A dream of peace	4-5
B. Focus marker	4a
C. The image of overcoming "Assyria"	4b-5

The strong link between v. 1 and v. 2 is communicated conspicuously by the presence of a clearly dependent clause at the beginning of v. 2 (notice *lākēn*, "therefore"). Thus v. 2 could not have opened a new READING. (On the relation between 5:1 and 4:8–5:1, → 4:8–5:1, Structure.)

The use of words from the root *r'h* ("shepherd") in vv. 3, 4, and 5 and of *'ereṣ* ("land") in vv. 3 and 5, along with the thematic relation between the references to the ideal future and king and to peace, suggest that section II here is not only closer to section I than to the next READING (vv. 6-8), but also that sections I and II were probably intended to be reread as two — albeit diverse — parts of a single READING rather than two fully independent literary units. (On these issues cf. Luker, 296; Westermann, *Prophetic Oracles*, 122-24; Mays, 118-20; but also Willis, "Micah IV 14–V 5"; Hillers, *Micah*, 69; Hagstrom, 65-67; etc.)

One may notice also that *wĕhāyâ zeh šālôm* in 5:4 is a multivalent, multiduty, Janus expression. In relation to the preceding text, it suggests to the readers the following meanings: (1) "and he [the Davidide] will be the one of peace" (see *IBHS*, §19.5.d; cf. NRSV), and (2) "and that [i.e., the situation described above] shall be peace" (cf. Job 21:2; see "and that shall afford safety," NJPSV). Yet it also opens and characterizes the following text (cf. Lev 7:1, 11; Deut 15:2; 19:4; Siloam inscription 1, *ANET*, 321; etc.), in which case it conveys a meaning akin to "this or that shall be peace [namely, if or when As-syria . . .]" (cf. RSV). (The presence of *wĕhāyâ* ["it shall be"] is consistent with the future orientation of the text and with the system of markers of textual coherence of units and subunits that open with *wĕhāyâ* in close textual proxim-ity; see Mic 5:4, 6, 7, 9; cf. 4:1.) Of course, whereas double-duty expressions surely bind literary units and emphasize contextuality, they do not define the hierarchical status of the linked units. Whether sections I and II are indeed sec-tions within one READING or are better understood as separate though related READINGS within a SET OF PROPHETIC READINGS cannot be decided on the grounds of a double-duty expression or microunit (see 5:1). (For a summary of research regarding *wĕhāyâ zeh šālôm* see Willis, "Structure," 201-2 n. 53; see also Cathcart, "Notes.")

On the surface the most significant difference between sections I and II is probably the shift of the focus of the text to the characterization of the future "peace" through a hypothetical example ("If Assyria . . . ," or, in paraphrase, "imagine a world in which if Assyria . . .") or through a description of the cir-cumstances that will reign in that ideal future ("when Assyria . . ."); cf. Isa 11:1-9. A closer analysis points rather to the shift of focus from the new Davidide to the inclusive "we" (notice the change in pronominal suffixes from vv. 2b-3 ["his brothers," i.e., "the exiles"; "his God," i.e., YHWH] to vv. 4-5 [e.g., "our land," and the five 1st common pl. markers in vv. 4-5]). Since the latter is identified with "Israel," the shift brings to the forefront: (1) the speaker in the text, (2) the addressee of that speaker, and at a different level (3) the authorship and the readership of the text. The result is a text in which the figures of the Davidide and the people flow into each other and thus be-come associated (notice also that the people [pl.] are those described as suffer-ing until the coming of the Davidide). Thus an important theological point is conveyed: the future, ideal Davidide is not to be understood as separate from that transgenerational "we" with which the authorship and rereadership of the text identified themselves, and which they called Israel. Significantly, the fo-cus on "we" leads to the next READING in the set (5:6-8) in which Israel stands at the forefront.

Like all the other READINGS, 5:1-5 contains key expressions that appear elsewhere in the SET OF READINGS of which it is an integral part, for instance, the reference to the woman in labor (see 4:9, 10; 5:2), though here, as opposed to the situation in 4:9-10, the image points to the end of suffering and the be-ginning of a new "golden" era. (For other markers of textual coherence, see Luker.) The unit contains also the important marker *'attâ*, which, given its roles in the previous READING (see 4:8–5:1), must be noticed. Significantly, the *'attâ* of this READING is syntactically and thematically different from that in the preceding one. The latter opens the mentioned "now" sentences, whereas the *'attâ* in this READING follows *kî* ("for"), which leads to a translation of *kî 'attâ* as "for now," and opens only a subordinate clause.

Among the literary devices present in the unit, the likely purposeful use of ambiguity — even if it does not lead to lasting indeterminacy — to connote association between particular items merits mention. The first verset of v. 3 may be understood as "he [the Davidide] will stand and rule [lit. 'shepherd'] by the might of YHWH" (see Hillers, *Micah*, 64-65), or as "he [YHWH] will stand and rule [lit. 'shepherd'] with might." The text in the second verset, "by the majestic name of YHWH, his God," strongly suggests that the former understanding is the main intent in the text, yet it also conveys a sense of closeness between the two possible ideal rulers (YHWH and the Davidide) to which the first verset might have referred. This sense of relationship between these two theological or ideological figures is consistent with the explicit claims of the text in v. 3a. Moreover, it is intensified by a second instance of ambiguity that relates the two figures in v. 3b. The subject of *yigdal* ("grow greater" or "magnify") in v. 3b may be understood to be (1) the Davidide; cf. 2 Sam 5:10, though the reference to "ends of the earth" is somewhat awkward if this is the case in this context (see Intention below); but see Zech 9:10; Pss 2:8; 72:8; or (2) "the name of YHWH, his God," or "YHWH, his God" (v. 3a); see 2 Sam 7:22, 26; Pss 35:27; 40:17 (NRSV 16); 70:5 (NRSV 4) (also cf. Ps 104:1; Num 14:17). Even if one accepts that the main rereading was likely the former (1), it is difficult to deny, within this context, that it is more than probable that a connoted meaning like the latter (2) was also conveyed.

Other stylistic devices found in this text include the pun on *yĕšûbûn* ("they shall return") and *yāšābû* ("they shall dwell [securely]") (cf. Num 35:32; Judg 21:23; 2 Sam 1:1; 15:19; 2 Kgs 2:18; 19:36; Isa 37:37; Jer 42:10; Hos 14:8 [NRSV 7]; Neh 8:17); the pair *'md* ("stand") and *yšb* ("sit" or "dwell") (cf. Ps 1:1); and perhaps a connoted pun on the aurally similar *'elep* ("thousand") and *'alĕpê* ("clans of") in Mic 5:1 (cf. Petrotta, 89-92; and cf. Matt 2:6).

One may notice that the change to the 1st person plural in Mic 5:4-5 is understood as an invitation for the readers to strengthen their identification with the speaker or speakers and the addressees in the world of the book, an identification that is consistent with the concept of Israel held by the authorship and the readership of this text. One may compare this approach with that of those who have concluded that the change to the 1st person plural "would seem to indicate that 5:4-5 functions as a communal response to 5:1-3" (Hagstrom, 66-67; see 60 n. 59). Among others, Wolff (*Micah*, 135) understands this change as an indication of different authorship and considers 5:4b-5a a late interpolation. Gordon (161) refers to these verses as "widely regarded as secondary." Wolff, among other redaction critics, considers a number of sections in 5:1-3 secondary as well; he reconstructs an older text in which v. 3 follows v. 1 (*Micah*, 135-36, 145-46).

Genre

The text communicates a message of salvation that may be compared with, for instance, Isa 11:1-9. Because of its contents one may consider it an announcement of a royal savior (cf. Isa 11:9), and as such one may associate it with the motif of the return of the exiles (cf. Zech 9:9-12) and with victory over enemies (cf. Am 9:11-12; see also Psalm 2). I must stress, however, that the intended readership of the text accesses that message when it reads the text. Moreover, the readership is invited to read the text in a particular manner. They are asked to identify themselves with the implicit addressees to whom the words of the speaker are intended within the world of the text, to overhear the words of the speaker, and even to identify with the speaker by the end of the unit (vv. 4-5). They are also asked by coherence markers to read and reread the text in the context of other READINGS within this literary set (i.e., chs. 4–5). Mic 5:1-5 contains not only the usual links to other READINGS but even a double-duty verse (5:1). In sum, 5:1-5 is a written text to be read and one that evokes the possibly oral genre of the independent announcement of salvation in general, and of the announcement of a royal savior in particular.

Setting

The words of the speakers in 5:1-5 point to an undatable, open future. In addition, the readers of 5:1-5 are not asked to imagine the speaker or speakers as uttering their words at a certain date, against the background of particular historical events or the like. Also there is no specific characterization of the addressees beyond that they are "Israel," and that they are living under circumstances far inferior to what they thought they should be (see v. 2a). This openness is somewhat contrasted with the clear requests to the intended readership to understand the unit as textually coherent with the units in its textual vicinity (see the mentioned links). All this is consistent with the situation that obtains in other READINGS, and it suggests a request to the readers to contextualize (i.e., to approach the unit from a perspective that is informed by the other literary units in its textual vicinity) rather than to historicize their reading. It suggests also an attempt to maximize the identification of the readers with the characters in the text, along with all the affective elements with which this identification is associated. Of course, the intended link between the readers and the characters set in the past of the readership serves to shape an image of the latter that is at least partially based on the image that they construct of their past. In this regard, and only in this regard, may one say that the text "historicizes" the community of rereaders, that is, it shapes among them an identity and characterization that is based on their own construction of their history.

The world of knowledge implied in the text includes: (1) the concept of an exile that is associated with YHWH's temporal will (see v. 2aα); (2) the expectation of new Davidide, a royal savior who will exist in some association with YHWH; (3) the association of salvation with the return of the "brothers" (of the Davidide; and of the [re]readership) to the children of Israel (i.e., Judah/Yehud, i.e., the [re]readership of the text; see v. 2); (4) a theological construct in which Israel is identified with Judah and with the postmonarchic communities in which the book of Micah was written and reread (see Ben Zvi, "Inclusion"); (5) a symbolic world in which both Assyria and "the land of Nimrod" (i.e., Babylon; see Gen 10:6-10) may function as representatives of the foes of Israel, a symbolism that in itself is not unexpected given the history of the kingdoms of Judah and Israel and the recollection of their history in biblical literature; and (6) a tradition that associates Babylon with Nimrod.

The use of the pair Assyria–Babylon as the archetypal mighty nations that may invade Israel suggests a symbol that comes out of a recollection of the past. It is worth mentioning in this regard that Assyria is not to be understood literally in some places in the HB/OT (see Lam 5:6; Ezra 6:22; Zech 10:10-11). To be sure, from the reference to Assyria and Babylon in a parallel structure in which the first position is taken by Assyria, it does not follow that the text had to be written during the period of Assyrian hegemony over Babylon.

Thus this text contributes to understanding the world of the literati for whom, at least primarily, this READING was written and within whom one is to locate the authorship of this text as an integral part of this SET OF READINGS about the future. This worldview and world of knowledge is consistent with that of the (implied) authorship and (intended) readership of the book of Micah as a whole. Both point to a postmonarchic community.

For studies and different approaches to 5:4-5 in particular, see, for instance, Renaud, 234-39, 250-54, and the extensive bibliography there; Willi-Plein, 90-95; Mays, 117-20; Willis, "Micah IV 14–V 5"; for the position that vv. 4-5 belong to the false prophets who confront the words of Micah, see van der Woude, "Micah in Dispute," esp. 255; de Waard; Saracino; and Alonso Schökel and Sicre Díaz, 2:1056, 1061. Some scholars associate at least a reconstructed core of 5:1-5 with the historical events of 701 BCE, despite the lack of reference to them in the text (e.g., Willis, "Micah IV 14–V 5"). Shaw (156-60) associates the text with the events of 734 BCE. Other scholars (e.g., Wolff, *Micah,* 134-49) advance a redactional history of the text that includes different historical settings; for an extensive discussion of the date of 5:1-3 from a redaction-critical perspective see Renaud, 239-50; regarding 5:4-5 see ibid., 250-54. One may mention also that Saracino (268-69) attributes the text of 5:4-5 to pseudoprophets whose champion was Zedekiah; Crook associates with it the events that surround the revolt against Athaliah, and understands the reference to Assyria in terms of the circumstances in 841 BCE.

Intention

The main intention of this READING is to provide or strengthen the hope of a better, indeed, ideal future for the readership of the text. This hope is presented in terms of a future reversal of the present situation, an explanation of the present situation and above all of its ephemerality (see v. 2) in terms of living characterized by the lack of an ideal Davidide. The ideal Davidide is presented in the text in a manner that associates him with YHWH. This is the reason that traditional Christians and Jews who interpret this text in a manner informed by their religious traditions have often considered this unit to point to the Messiah. From a historical-critical perspective, and without entering into the question of which concept or concepts of the Messiah were upheld by the most likely primary readership of the book of Micah, the text is clear that the mentioned Davidide is not a regular king (i.e., someone like Zedekiah or Hezekiah) but an ideal king whose time has not yet come, and whose actions, power, and dominion actually originate with YHWH.

This ideal king is also deeply associated with Israel. Within the world of the text, the might of the future king leads to the might of the people (vv. 4-5), and perhaps significantly, even in vv. 1-3, it is not the ideal king per se who will vanquish the exile (i.e., return the people), but rather the people who will return. Thus the main emphasis in the text seems to move from the figure and power of the ideal king to that of Israel.

Verses 4-5 also express and shape an image of the ideal future. Indeed, they provide a characterization of what is meant, from the perspective of the authorial voice, by šālôm ("peace"). The description points to a situation of security from foreign invasion, defeat, and the destruction that goes along with it. If the mightiest worldly armies attack, they will not only be defeated, but their territory will be ruled by rulers appointed by a now hegemonic Israel. The motif of reversal is clear, because during the periods of Assyrian and Neo-Babylonian hegemony, those empires imposed rulers on the countries of the area, and those who fought against them were most often the target of successful military campaigns carried out by the hegemonic center. Motifs of reversal, explicit and implicit, abound in biblical literature (e.g., Obad 17); the defensive position regarding war adopted in this text is found elsewhere in the ancient Near East (see, e.g., Saracino) and in the HB/OT; notice that even the conquest of most of the land in Joshua is described in terms of defensive warfare (Joshua 9–11). For the position that "peace" in "this shall be peace" (Mic 5:4aα) is not to be understood from a political perspective but from that of "the common people who wanted to lead their lives in peace and quiet," see Westermann (*Prophetic Oracles,* 134).

It is worth noticing the balance, or, perhaps better, interrelatedness, created by the combination of vv. 1-3 and 4-5. Whereas the Davidide is the ruler of Israel, the Israelites are those who will assume the central role and appoint rulers over the nations that attack them. Moreover, whereas Assyria and Babylon will be governed by a substantial number of rulers appointed by humans, Israel will be ruled by one Davidide who is chosen by YHWH. (On rulers appointed by humans, see *něsîkê 'ādām,* "princes [or chieftains] of [appointed by and representing] humans"; on the genitive of agency see *IBHS,* §9.5.1; cf. *maś'at mōšeh,* "the tax imposed by Moses" [2 Chr 24:6]; also cf. the multiple meanings conveyed by the expression *měšîah yhwh,* "YHWH's anointed"; see 1 Sam 24:7; 26:9; 2 Sam 1:14, 16; Lam 4:20; cf. Mays, 120.)

Thus the text conveys a sense of coherence between the unique character of the Davidide vis-à-vis other rulers and that of Israel vis-à-vis the nations as symbolized by Assyria and Babylon. The numbers seven and eight in v. 4b may point to either a recourse to typological numbers or a reference to undefined numbers (cf. Haran, esp. 256; Clines, esp. 89); in any case they convey the sense of a substantial number. (For another instance of a seven-eight construction in the HB/OT, see Qoh 11:2; regarding other ancient Near Eastern texts see Cathcart, "Notes.") The word *'ādām* (here "human") is sometimes emended to *'ǎrām* ("Aram"), partially on the basis of the understanding of the text in relation to historical circumstances in the 8th and 7th centuries BCE (see, e.g., Hillers, "Imperial Dream"); for an understanding of the last two versets in v. 4 as meaning "we shall raise against him the seven evil ones and the eight biters of man [or of the earth]," see Saracino.

Bibliography

K. J. Cathcart, "Notes on Micah 5,4-5," *Bib* 49 (1968) 511-14; idem, "Micah 5,4-5 and Semitic Incantations," *Bib* 59 (1978) 38-48; D. J. A. Clines, "The Parallelism of Greater Precision: Notes from Isaiah 40 for a Theory of Biblical Poetry," in E. R. Follis, ed., *Directions in Biblical Hebrew Poetry* (JSOTSup 40; Sheffield: JSOT Press, 1987) 77-100; M. B. Crook, "The Promise in Micah 5," *JBL* 70 (1951) 313-20; R. P. Gordon, "*K/kī/ky* in Incantational Incipits," *UF* 23 (1992) 161-63; M. Haran, "The Graded Numerical Sequence and the Phenomenon of 'Automatism' in Biblical Poetry," in G. W. Anderson et al., eds., *Congress Volume: Uppsala 1971* (VTSup 22; Leiden: Brill, 1972) 238-67; W. Harrelson, "Nonroyal Motifs in the Royal Eschatology," in B. W. Anderson and W. Harrelson, eds., *Israel's Prophetic Heritage: Essays in Honor of James Muilenburg* (New York: Harper, 1962) 147-65; D. R. Hillers, "Imperial Dream: Text and Sense of Micah 5:4b-5," in H. B. Huffmon, F. A. Spina, and A. R. W. Green, eds., *The Quest for the Kingdom of God: Studies in Honor of George E. Mendenhall* (Winona Lake, Ind.: Eisenbrauns, 1983) 137-39; S. Mowinckel, *He That Cometh* (tr. G. W. Anderson; New York/Nashville: Abingdon, 1956); F. Saracino, "A State of Siege: Mi 5 4-5 and an Ugaritic Prayer," *ZAW* 95 (1983) 263-69; J. T. Willis, "Micah IV 14–V 5 — A Unit," *VT* 18 (1968) 529-47; idem, "The Structure of Micah 3–5 and the Function of Micah 5₉₋₁₄ in the Book," *ZAW* 81 (1969) 191-214.

FIFTH READING: TWO IMAGES OF THE FUTURE RELATION BETWEEN THE REMNANT OF JACOB/ISRAEL AND THE NATIONS, 5:6-8 (NRSV 7-9)

Structure

I. The first image	6
A. Opening	6aα
B. First and second similes	6aβ
C. The *'ăšer* clause	6b
II. The second image	7-8
A. Opening	7aα
B. First and second similes	7aβ
C. The *'ăšer* clause	7b
D. Volitional conclusion	8

The close structural similitude and the almost word-by-word repetition of the opening of sections I and II create a sense of cohesiveness within the READING and set this unit apart from the preceding and following units. These verses also show clear, textually inscribed markers that set this unit apart from its textual surroundings. In other words, the text ʾ ʿe clearly invites the rereaders to understand one section of this unit in a way that is strongly informed by the other, as two sides of a close-knit unit.

Of course, as is the case with other READINGS within this set, the text of the unit does not suggest total independence from its textual environs. Thus one may notice the occurrence of the following: (1) an opening *wĕhāyâ* ("and it shall be") in 5:6, 7 and in 4:1; 5:4, 9; (2) *šĕ'ērît* ("remnant") in 5:6, 7 and in 4:7; cf. the similarity in sound between the opening clauses in 4:1, 5:7, and 5:8; (3) *'ammîm rabbîm* ("many nations") in 5:6, 7 and in 4:3; (4) *gôyîm* pointing to "the nations" in 5:7 and in a substantial number of instances in this set (e.g., 4:2, 3, 11; 5:14); (5) *'ādām* ("human") in 5:6 and 5:4; (6) *wĕ'ên maṣṣîl* ("and there is no deliverer," i.e., "and there is none who can save") in 5:7 and *wĕhiṣṣîl* ("he shall save/deliver") in 5:5; notice also *wĕ'ên maḥărîd* ("and no one shall/can make [them] afraid") in 4:4; (7) *'ēder* ("flock") in 5:7 and 4:8 (also cf. 2:12-13); (8) the use of the root *krt* at the conclusion of 5:8 and in 5:9-12; (9) the triple repetition of the 2nd person masc. sg. suffix in 5:8 that prefigures its fourteen repetitions in the following six verses; (10) the presence of *bĕqereb* ("in the midst") in 5:6, 7 and of *miqqirbekā* ("from your midst") in 5:9, 12, 13; and (11) the pun on sounds between *'aššûr* ("Assyria"), which appears three times in 4:4-5, and *'ăšer* ("that") in 4:6, 7 (cf. *'ăšêreykā* ["your *asherim*"] also in 5:13).

While each particular instance may be explained as coincidental, the cumulative weight of all these instances within a short text points not only to a text that conveys to the rereaders a sense that it should be read and reread as part and parcel of a larger text, but also a text that was carefully written to convey that sense. Mic 5:6-8 is therefore strongly dependent on its literary contexts within this SET OF READINGS. There are some connections also between this text and units elsewhere in the book of Micah; on *bahămôt ya'ar* in 5:7 and *bāmôt yā'ar* in 3:12 → 3:1-12, Structure.

At least on the surface, the close structural similitude between sections I and II stands in sharp tension with the diametrically different images that the two sections evoke in the readership. Whereas in one of them the remnant of Jacob will be a blessing (on "dew" as blessing see, e.g., Gen 27:28; Deut 33:28; Hos 14:6 [NRSV 5]; Zech 8:12; Ps 133:3; Prov 19:12; note that the only other occurrence of the pair *ṭal-rĕbîbîm* — i.e., dew showers — is in Deut 32:2), in the other it will be like a lion that tramples and tears "the prey" (i.e., the nations; note the sharp contrast between the simile of the dew and the lion in Prov 19:12). Again, this clear combination of similar structure and contrastive message is hardly accidental. Moreover, it is unlikely that the authorial voice instructed the readers to easily solve the tension between the two opposite images by either associating the "good nations" with one image of the ideal future (5:6) and the "bad nations" with the other (5:7-8; this proposal has already been advanced by Abrabanel); or by interpreting the two images as pointing to a progression in time that is presented in reverse chronological order in the book, namely, first the nations will suffer a stern defeat at the hands of the remnant of Jacob, and then the same remnant will be like YHWH's dew (i.e., a most beneficial element) for them (cf. Allen, 355, among others), or even by attributing one of the sayings to the godly speaker and the other to the ungodly pseudoprophets (e.g., Alfaro, 59; Vargon, 155; among others). The simple fact is that the authorial voice did not include any textually inscribed marker that indicates or even hints at any of these options. This lack of markers cannot be easily explained away in this case, given that the same voice chose to present a text in which so much is quite conspicuous and unequivocal (e.g., its close relation to the units in its textual vicinity, the structural similitude between sections I and II, and the tension between the images of the future developed in each section). In other words, the text does not seem to have been written so as to indicate to its readers that they should understand it in any of these ways. In any case, one must take into account that the structural similarity and the particular choice of words strongly associate rather than dissociate the two sections. The solution to the mixed message of the unit is more likely to be found within the context of the multiple different but yet related voices about the future that characterize not only this READING but the entire SET OF READINGS, to which it is so unequivocally associated by textual markers (cf. 4:1-5 and 4:8–5:1 and the different sections in the latter).

This unit, like others before, also exhibits its share of ambiguity and even polyvalence at the service of its rhetorical goals. The two relative *'ăšer* clauses refer back — at least at the connoted level — to both the remnant of Jacob and what this remnant is compared to (e.g., dew, a lion), thus strengthening the simile. Moreover, the choice of verbs in the first clause creates an additional level of double meaning because the text connotes two different images depending on which referent one associates primarily with the *'ăšer* clause. The verbal pair *qwh* and *yḥl* in the Piel occurs also in Isa 51:5, where it is usually rendered as "wait for . . . hope," and in Job 30:26, where it is often translated as "looked for . . . waited for." The pair may convey the meanings "wait," "tarry," "delay," but also "look for," "hope," and "trust." If one associates the *'ăšer* clause primarily with the "dew" or "showers" (rather than with the remnant of Jacob), then the text suggests that they (i.e., dew or showers) "do not depend upon people or wait for any mortal" (NRSV), and therefore advances the point that the blessing ("dew" or "showers") that the remnant of Israel shall bring is inevitable, because it depends not on humans but on YHWH (notice also the expression *kĕṭal mē'ēt yhwh,* "like dew from YHWH," in v. 6). If the *'ăšer* clause is associated primarily with the remnant of Jacob, then the text suggests that the remnant of Jacob in that ideal future shall not look for a person or hope or put its trust in humans but rather in YHWH (cf. Weiser, 277; Vargon, 154; NJPSV). This pious, future Israel will then be a blessing for the nations. To be sure, these two readings are not alternatives, but they together advance the claim of the text that it is certain that at some point in the future the remnant of Jacob will both put their trust in YHWH and be a blessing to the nations.

Finally, an additional connoted meaning is shaped by the rhetorical strength of the simile and by the influence of the actual agrarian realities of the area in the discourse of the people. Since dew or showers cannot be withheld from the land without risking the very existence of human society (see Hag 1:10), the presence of a remnant of Jacob (i.e., the divine dew) is required for the existence of the nations. As in Mic 4:1-4, the "universalistic" tone of the text (cf. Westermann, *Prophetic Oracles,* 126, among others) actually reflects and communicates great claims about Israel's status, within its own discourse.

For the position that the two similes here are understandable in the light of a preexisting book of Hosea (see Hos 5:14 and 14:6 [NRSV 5]) and for a short summary of research, see Jeremias; for the position that "dew" may carry a hostile sense rather than blessing, cf. Hillers, *Micah,* 71. For an explanation of the tension between sections I and II in diachronic terms (i.e., vv. 7-8 are a later gloss) see, for example, Westermann, *Prophetic Oracles,* 207; cf. Anbar.

Verse 8 may be understood as a wish, an exhortation to Israel, a promise or statement about the future, a prayer addressed to YHWH, or as conveying all these meanings. As in other cases, that the text is written so as to allow both YHWH and the remnant to take the role of the addressee connotes some degree of closeness between the two. If the 2nd person sg. is understood as pointing to Israel, then the reference fulfills an affective function in relation to the readership of the text who identifies itself with Israel. If the 2nd person sg. is understood as pointing to YHWH, then the reference prepared (or "misprepared"; → 5:9-14) the reader for the next unit (note the use of the root *krt,* "cut off," in v. 8 and in vv. 9, 10, 11, 12).

Genre

Both sections in the READING evoke in the readership the type of discourse of an announcement of salvation. Yet the pericope is written to be read as one unit; that is, the text strongly suggests to the intended readers that they should approach the sections one in the light of the other. Moreover, the text of the pericope also indicates that it should be read within its *Sitz im Buch,* that is, as an integral part of a written text, chs. 4–5. The latter was designed to be read as a SET OF PROPHETIC READINGS about the ideal future by those literati able to read such a text, and the book of Micah of which it is part. All the other READINGS in the mentioned set, vv. 6-8, ask the readership to address the question of the ideal future, and in fact provide two snapshots or images that characterize two different perspectives from which this future may be conceived. As such, the genre of this unit, like the others in the set, is best described as a PROPHETIC READING that deals with and imagines the ideal future. The rhetorical purposes served by evoking the genre of possibly oral announcements of salvation include the connotation of certainty, legitimization, and the general suitability and elasticity of this type of discourse.

Setting

The pericope is written from a perspective that assumes exile and dispersion, and it refers to Israel in terms of the "remnant of Jacob." One may also conclude that the text reflects the perspective of a community that considers itself to be an underdog, that sees itself as less powerful than "the nations." Taking into consideration this perspective and the written and literary character of the READING, along with its emphasis on the strong relationship between the text of this READING and its *Sitz im Buch,* then the likely setting of the writing and reading of the text is similar to that of the other READINGS in this set and the book of Micah as a whole: a postmonarchic community of literati. (For a different position based on a particular reconstruction of the textual history of this and related texts, see Wolff, *Micah,* 153-54.)

Yet I must stress that this is not the setting of the speaker's words within the world of the text. In that world the setting of the speaker's words (and in v. 8 even the identity of the addressees) is left wide open. Vv. 6-8 are not anchored in particular events (whether in the world of the text or beyond it), nor are they associated with any ruler, time, place, or even type of social interaction. This openness enhances the ability of the readers to identify with the text and increases its affective impact.

Intention

The READING conveys hope for the community by evoking images of an ideal future that shall be. These images reduce the dissonance between the actual status of the community and its claims about what is to be its proper role in the divine economy and its own image of the status that it will have in the world that shall be. Both images may be considered within the category of a dream of power by the powerless. Yet they characterize the future in different ways and point to different manners in which power may be constructed and imagined.

The first image reassures the readership that at one point in the future the remnant of Jacob will rely on YHWH, and then it will be a blessing over the nations, and that in the ideal future that reflects the will of YHWH, Israel (i.e., that remnant) will be as necessary to the existence of the nations and the world as dew and showers.

The first image constructs a world in which Israel enjoys a role superior to that of the nations but is yet supportive of and vital to them. The second image develops a hostile image of the relationship between the nations and the remnant. This image is similar to those advanced in the "oracles against the nations" sections in the prophetic books and in the announcements of reversal (i.e., this time Israel is the powerful lion and the nations the powerless "flock"). Like the first image, this second one is presented as being consistent with YHWH's point of view. The roles that these "belligerent" kinds of images fulfilled in prophetic literature seem to go beyond the level of the dream of power by the powerless. They serve to explain the present world of the authorship and primary readership within a theological or ideological framework that preserves their understanding of themselves within the divine economy. The superior status of the nations that is taken as self-evident in these sections (notice also the stressed use of the term "remnant") is thus constructed not as reflecting a particular blessing from YHWH — which is denied from Israel — but rather as still being in the status of the not-yet-judged, punished, or trampled, as opposed to Israel, which has already passed this stage and, although actually a remnant, will exert an irrepressible force. (On the issues raised here see Ben Zvi, *Zephaniah,* 325-46; idem, "Understanding.") In this regard it is worth mentioning that also in section I Israel is characterized as one that will exert an irrepressible force over the nations and an unparalleled status, though in this case for their own benefit (cf. Shoemaker, 181).

Finally, the invitation to the readership (i.e., postmonarchic communities who upheld a Jerusalem-centered theology) to identify with the remnant of Jacob reflects and shapes their understanding of themselves as Israel, a theological construct that is ubiquitous in the HB/OT. (Cf. Ben Zvi, "Inclusion.")

Bibliography

M. Anbar, "Rosée et ondées ou lion et lionceau (Michée 5,6-7)," *BN* 73 (1994) 5-8; J. Jeremias, "Tau und Löwe (Mi 5,6f)," in F. Crüsemann, C. Hardmeier, and R. Kessler, eds., *Was ist der Mensch . . .? Beiträge zur Anthropologie des Alten Testaments. FS H. W. Wolff* (Munich: Chr. Kaiser, 1992) 221-27.

SIXTH READING:
DIVINE PURGE AND OBEDIENCE, 5:9-14 (NRSV 10-15)

Structure

I. Opening formula pointing to the future and marking the
   following text as YHWH's saying ... 9a
II. Description of the future purge ... 9b-14
   A. First *wĕhikrattî* ("I [YHWH] will cut off") microunit ... 9b
   B. Second *wĕhikrattî* ("I [YHWH] will cut off") microunit ... 10
   C. Third *wĕhikrattî* ("I [YHWH] will cut off") microunit ... 11
   D. Fourth *wĕhikrattî* ("I [YHWH] will cut off") microunit ... 12
   E. *Wĕnātaštî* ("I [YHWH] will uproot") microunit ... 13
   F. *Wĕ'āśîtî* ("I [YHWH] will execute [in anger and wrath]")
      microunit ... 14

The unit is interrelated to the other units in its close textual environment as mentioned above, but as in the preceding unit it shows a salient degree of textual coherence, which in this case is communicated by, among others, a six-fold repeated opening with a *w-qṭl* verb in the 1st common sg. that is identified with YHWH (see v. 9aβ): "I [YHWH] will. . . ." Moreover, the first four instances in this sixfold pattern exhibit the very same opening, the verbal form *wĕhikrattî* ("I [YHWH] will cut off"; cf. v. 8, *yikkārētû*, "they will be cut off"). Furthermore, three of these microunits show an additional *w-qṭl* verb in the 1st common sg. at the opening of their second colon: *wĕha'ăbadtî*, *wĕhārastî*, and *wĕhišmadtî*, all of which can be rendered as "I will destroy." In addition, the 2nd masc. sg. pronominal suffix occurs fourteen times in the unit, and the expression *miqqirbekā* ("from your midst") three times within the same verses. All these features, along with some syntagmatic relations among the objects described in the future divine destruction, communicate to the rereaders that 5:9-14 is to be understood as a literary unit.

In addition, the precise combinations of verbal forms and direct objects are unique. The Hiphil of *krt* is not attested elsewhere with the following direct objects: *sûsîm*, "horses" (it occurs only once in the entire HB/OT with *sûs*, "horse," as its direct object; see Zech 9:10); *'ārê 'arṣekā*, "the cities of your land" (or "cities," for the sake of argument); *kĕšāpîm*, "sorceries"; the noun form *pāsîl* meaning "statue"; and the noun *maṣṣēbâ*, "pillar." Moreover, the Hiphil form of *'bd* is not found elsewhere with *merkābâ*, "chariot," as its direct object; nor *ntš*, "root out," with *"asherim"*; nor *šmd* in the Hiphil with *'ārîm*, "cities," or even with *'îr*, "city." Furthermore, the expression *'śh bĕ'ap* is not found elsewhere except in Ezek 5:15 (but cf. Jer 18:23), and *hrs* in the Qal with *mibṣār*, "fortress," as its direct object appears also once elsewhere (Lam 2:2).

To be sure, the occurrence of each of the mentioned expressions may be explained individually as a simple case of activating the language of the authorship and audience. It is unlikely, however, that the pattern of occurrence of the entire set of expressions mentioned above is accidental. It seems more likely that it points to an effort to keep the unit distinct from other texts that are related to the matter of ritual purges that are present in other books (cf. Ben Zvi, "Deuteronomistic"). In other words, the precise language conveys a sense of dealing with a known issue (notice the syntagmatic pairs of objects and see below; see also Isa 2:6-8) but in a distinctive manner and, given the textually inscribed markers of interrelatedness mentioned above, in a manner that is consistent with the *Sitz im Buch* of this unit.

The first part of the introduction shapes the other half of the main envelope that encompasses chs. 4 and 5 (see 4:1). In addition, it anchors 5:9-14 to the preceding text formally (notice the *w-qtl* form) and by the reverberation of the opening (cf. 4:1; 5:4, 6, 7). Moreover, it also serves to set one of the basic characteristics of the world evoked here: it is a future world. It is about the substantial change — enacted by YHWH — that will happen in a future time ("on that day") from the perspective of the speaker, and at least to some extent, the (re)readership too, and implicitly about the future world that will be created by these actions (cf. 4:1, 6). The combination of the two formulas — *bayyôm hahû'* ("on that day") and *nĕ'um yhwh* ("YHWH's saying") — occurs also in 4:6. (For a discussion of that combination see the commentary there.)

As in the previous unit, the conspicuous structural unity and the unequivocal choice of words that it conveys are all present in the text, showing a substantial openness to a multiplicity of rereadings. Who is to be purged by YHWH? Who is the one referred to by the rhetorical device of mentioning "you" fourteen times within a few verses? At first, it seems that it is Israel (cf. Exod 20:4; Lev 19:26; 26:1; Deut 4:28; 5:8; 16:21-22; 27:15; Isa 2:6-8; Jer 1:16). If so, the text here is to be understood as an announcement of judgment against Israel. Although such a text would stand in tension with vv. 6-8, similar textual circumstances occur elsewhere (see Isaiah 2). Yet it is also true that within the general discourse in which this unit was written and read and reread, the choice of objects to be destroyed points to the encompassing motif of reliance on something other than YHWH (cf. Hillers, *Micah*, 72-73; Vargon, 158; Mays, 126-27). If so, the unit may be understood in association with v. 6b. Within the frame of this understanding, the drastic purge initiated and carried out by YHWH is necessary to achieve the remnant of Israel that shall rely only on YHWH. The purge is thus the main preparation for the role given to Israel in v. 6, and therefore may even be considered a "blessing," despite the fact that it involves, among other things, the destruction of Israel's fortified cities. If so, the readers are asked to evoke the image of an announcement of judgment eventually to turn it around and interpret it as an announcement of salvation. Judgment and destruction are then seen as a purge that leads to salvation, as in other types of utopian discourse. This approach is consistent with the perspective that understands the welfare of "the nations" and their worldly superior status not in terms of a particular blessing but of a not-yet-punished status ($\rightarrow$ 5:6-8, Intention). But if so, what will be the status of "the nations" after their judgment? (On these issues, see Ben Zvi, *Zephaniah,* 325-46; idem, "Understanding.")

All these considerations are very close to the text and the worldview or worldviews shaped and represented by that text. V. 14, which is formally quite similar to the other verses in the unit and may be understood as the conclusion to which they lead, clearly refers to *haggôyîm* ("the nations") as the object of YHWH's actions. These nations are further characterized as those who have not listened to YHWH. V. 14 strongly undermines the exclusiveness of an understanding of vv. 9-14 as referring to Israel alone. To be sure, it may be claimed that *haggôyîm* ("the nations") actually refers to Israel (cf. Vargon, 157), but this seems an ad hoc forced interpretation (notice also the pl.: "the nations"), and, in any case, it does not remove from the text the connotation of *haggôyîm* as pointing to "the nations."

Diachronic explanations, namely, that some editor added a note of judgment against the nations to an announcement of judgment against Israel (e.g., J. M. P. Smith, 116-17; Alvarez Barredo, 109), may at best propose a possible — though still hypothetical — reconstruction of the history of the text but cannot explain it. This is so because it is abundantly clear that the text asks its readers to understand it in a way that is informed by the proposed redactional history of the text. Not only is there no textually inscribed marker indicating to the readers that they should follow such a mode of reading, but the clear textual coherence within the unit strongly suggests the contrary: the readers are asked to approach this unit as such, as a unit.

If so, the reference to "the nations" in v. 14 impinges on the understanding of the entire unit. Two approaches are then possible. According to the first, the reference to Israel in vv. 9-13 and to the nations in v. 14 is to be explained in diachronic terms within the future created by the speaker within the world of the text. In other words, YHWH will first purge "Israel" and then "the nations that have not listened to YHWH." From the perspective of a postmonarchic community, the divide between v. 13 and v. 14 may represent a situation with which they may identify. If so, Israel has already suffered its portion, and, most importantly, they themselves live in the after-purge period; as for the nations, they still "wait" to be punished (cf. Ben Zvi, *Zephaniah,* 325-46; idem, "Understanding"). Significantly, in this case, the textual cohesiveness of the text suggests that both purges are part of a single, divine act.

The second approach is to maintain that, as in 1:5, the text is written so as to be read in two different ways depending on whether the reading is informed mainly by the beginning of the unit or by its end. If the intended reader approached the text in the light of its beginning, then Israel is the referent because of the reasons mentioned above. But if the reader approached the text in the light of its conclusion, then "the nations" are the referent in vv. 9-13. If the latter is the case, then YHWH will associate some of Israel's characteristics with the nations, because YHWH will purge them of whatever YHWH does not accept in Israel (cf. 4:1-4; cf. also Kapelrud, 402-3; and notice that the expression "not listen to" or "not obey" [lōʾ-šmʿ] YHWH is at times explicitly associated with Israel's cultic misbehavior; see, e.g., Jer 25:6-9).

In fact, these two readings and the one suggested by the first approach are complementary. Given the general context of the book of Micah, where textual ambiguities and polyvalence abound, and the careful choice of words to produce rhetorical effects that characterize this unit in particular, it is hardly accidental that the text of this READING allows multiple readings. If so, textual polyvalence — at the very least at the connoted level — would have served several functions, as in many other occasions in the prophetic literature: (1) to provide a textually compact way of expressing a relatively complex set of ideas, (2) to draw the attention of the reader to the ambiguity itself and to the issues of identity and YHWH's will regarding Israel and the nations around which the ambiguity is centered, and (3) to contribute to the rereadability of the text. (On these issues → 1:2-16; see Ben Zvi, *Obadiah,* 4, et passim.)

As in many other instances, ambiguity and polyvalence are here contrasted with unequivocality. Whereas the "you" may be discussed, the "I" is not open to debate: it is YHWH who will act, it is YHWH who spoke these words, and it is YHWH's announcement and message that the readers learn when they read this READING within the book of Micah.

Genre

The unit seems to evoke the genre of an announcement of judgment against Israel, but it certainly defamiliarizes the genre (→, e.g., 1:2-16; 2:1-5), and in manifold ways. For instance, it allows ambiguity regarding the identity or identities of those to be punished — is it Israel, the nations, or both? Moreover, the announcement may communicate salvation, though in the future (cf. Alonso Schökel and Sicre Díaz, 2:1063, among others). In addition, the unit is also well bonded to the other units in its close textual environment within the book. None of these features is consistent with an oral and independent, prophetic announcement of judgment against Israel that is addressed to an actual audience.

At the level of the book, I consider this unit, like all others in this set (and in the book of Micah), as a PROPHETIC READING.

Setting

Some scholars have read this account in the light of the conditions during the time of Jotham (e.g., Vargon, 163-64) or, most often, Hezekiah (e.g., Willis,

"Authenticity"). The case for the former is based on a characterization of Jotham's days as a time of military building, materialism, and pride. The latter proposal is based on a claimed association between the text here and the reform (or, better, purge; cf. Linville, 23) of Hezekiah. The debate goes on about the historicity of Hezekiah's reform (see, e.g., Handy). But even if, for the sake of the argument, one would grant that Hezekiah carried out the reform described in Kings (or in Chronicles), there is no unequivocal relation between what YHWH is described as saying that YHWH will do in Mic 5:9-14 and Hezekiah's reform according to the historical narratives in the HB/OT. No source claims that as part of his purge (or reform) Hezekiah systematically and willingly destroyed all of his own fortified cities and strongholds (for the rendering "all" here see Ringgren) and disarmed his own army. Moreover, it is almost unthinkable that any ancient Near Eastern king would have actually promoted and carried out such a reform, though see 5:9, 10, 13b (cf. Hillers, *Micah,* 74).

I must stress that there is no differentiation in the world of 5:9-13 between the future purge of (a) cities and army and (b) against cultic objects and practices. Such a differentiation is foreign to the claim of the text, which not only brings (a) and (b) together but also contains no textually inscribed cue that suggests to its readers that they should take one literally and the other hyperbolically. Such readings represent an effort to domesticate the text so as to rationalize and historicize it (e.g., to claim that 5:9-13 served to support the reforming efforts of Hezekiah and accordingly must be dated between the beginning of that reform and 701 BCE; see Olyan, 16-17). In sum, there is no reason to assume that the main purpose of the text is to communicate to the intended readership something that the text is not saying at all.

Moreover, to imagine a future world in which YHWH will purge Judah, or "Israel," of the cultic objects and practices mentioned in 5:11, 12, 13a also does not require a Hezekian setting, because this imagery is consistent with a post-586 setting (see, e.g., Deuteronomy 4). In addition, the position that the text is written to show and communicate a clear Deuteronomistic style fails to explain the persistent authorial tendency to combine common verbal forms and their grammatical objects in uncommon ways (see above). This combination suggests an effort to individualize the text and to set it apart from similar texts in other books. On these issues see Ben Zvi, "Deuteronomistic."

When one considers all this, the fact remains that 5:9-14 is written to be an open text. It is neither historicized nor asks its intended readership to historicize it. It is not anchored to any particular set of historical circumstances. The only textually inscribed markers pointing to the manner in which the text is intended to be read point to a request to read it in terms of its *Sitz im Buch,* that is, to understand 5:9-14 within its literary setting in the book.

The actual social setting in which the reading of the text was likely to take place, and for which 5:9-14 as part of the book of Micah was intended, is the group of postmonarchic literati within which one is likely to find the authorship and readership of the book.

Much of the past scholarship on 5:9-14 has focused on the question of whether the text is "authentic" (i.e., goes back to the words of a historical prophet named Micah) or inauthentic, or alternatively which verses within the unit are authentic and which are not (see, e.g., Willis, "Authenticity," and the extensive bibliography mentioned there; cf. Willi-Plein, 95-97; Mays, 124). Leaving aside the issue of the value judgment expressed by the word *authentic,* in this commentary I focus on the book of Micah and its primary readership; → 1:2-16, Structure.

Intention

As in all the other READINGS in this set, the text attempts to describe or to imagine an ideal future. In this READING this future is the result of YHWH's purging action. All that may encourage reliance on anything but YHWH is taken away. Indeed, the ideal world suggested by the text evokes a completely different society and geography from that known to the readership. There will be no fortified cities, no strong armies to maintain and to fear (cf. 4:3-4). There will be an end also to cultic practices and objects that are not consistent with the will of YHWH. But is this new world confined to Israel alone? V. 14 seems to deal with this question. To be sure, the verse within this context allows more than one reading, and it is reasonable to assume that it reflects the presence of multiple theological or ideological voices in this regard and in this type of discourse. Significantly, one of those allowed readings is that the new world may also include "the nations."

Bibliography

L. K. Handy, "Hezekiah's Unlikely Reform," *ZAW* 100 (1988) 111-15; J. L. Linville, *Israel in the Book of Kings* (JSOTSup 272; Sheffield: Sheffield Academic Press, 1998); S. M. Olyan, *Ashera and the Cult of Yahweh in Israel* (SBLMS 34; Atlanta: Scholars Press, 1988); H. Ringgren, "The Omitting of *KOL* in Hebrew Parallelism," *VT* 32 (1982) 99-103; J. T. Willis, "The Authenticity and Meaning of Micah 5:9-14," *ZAW* 81 (1969) 353-68.

PROPHETIC, DIDACTIC READING ABOUT DIVINELY ORDAINED BEHAVIOR, 6:1-8

Structure

I. Introduction	1-2
A. First summons	1a
B. Second summons	1b
C. Third summons	2
1. The summons itself	2a
2. Reason for the summons; conclusion	2b

The thematic and structural unity of 6:1-8 is easy to recognize. Indeed, most scholars treat the pericope as a unit (e.g., Hillers, *Micah,* 75-79; Wolff, *Micah,* 163-84; Vargon, 166-84; Alvarez Barredo, 112-22). The only question has been whether sections III and IV (vv. 6-8) should be treated as standing on the same hierarchical level (structurally) as vv. 1-5 and vv. 9-16. The dialogical character of the text and the lack of any introduction to the speeches and speakers in vv. 6-8 (contrast with v. 9) suggest that vv. 1-8 should be taken as one unit. Such an understanding is reflected also in the system of open and closed paragraphs found in the MT. (The text of 6:8-10 is not preserved in Mur 88, but notice there the *vacat* between 5:14 and 6:1.)

Although 6:1-8 is constructed in the text as a unit, it is also presented in such a manner as to communicate to the intended rereaders that it is an integral part of the book of Micah, particularly of chs. 6–7. The unit is linked to the preceding one by the verbal form from the root *šm'*, "listen" or "hear" (see 5:14 [NRSV 15]; on this link see also Luker, 298). The strongest links, however, are between this unit and the following texts in chs. 6–7, as almost universally recognized. The most significant of these links is the one created by the dialogical structure of 6:1-8, given the dialogical character of all the units in chs. 6–7, and of chs. 6–7 as a whole (see, e.g., Mays, 9-10; Hagstrom, 102-3, 106-13; Shoemaker, 184-85). As expected, the choice of words in the text shapes a set of cross-references and a sense of textual coherence through the repetition of terms. Thus, for instance, *rîb,* "complaint," occurs in 6:1, 2; 7:9; *'ammî/ô,* "my/his people," in 6:2, 3, 5; 7:14. One may also notice the multiple occurrences of words from roots such as *špṭ* (basic meaning akin to "judge") in 6:8; 7:3, 9 and *ḥṭ'* (basic meaning akin to "sin") in 6:7, 13; 7:9, 19; or the noun *ṣĕdāqâ* (basic meaning akin to "justness and loyalty"; see *HAL,* 3:1006) in 6:5; 7:9.

As with all other units in chs. 6–7, links to other sections in the book of Micah are also suggested to the readership of 6:1-8. Among the most conspicuous is that between 6:1-2 and 1:2 (see also 3:1, 9), but see also 4:3aβ and 6:2b, and the references to "my/his people" in 1:9; 2:4, 8, 9; 3:3, 5; 6:2, 3, 5.

The introduction consists of three summonses and a motive clause that also serves as an interpretive key for the ensuing text. Perhaps the most salient feature of the summons is the constant, fluid play on the identity of speakers and addressees. The speaker in the first summons (6:1a) is most likely a human one, the prophetic voice. The addressees, however, are not identified.

The first summons creates the expectation that the following text will be directly associated with YHWH. Given that there are no clear markers to the contrary in 6:1b, it seems that the following text was constructed to suggest to the readers that they should understand it as YHWH's direct speech (cf. Meier, 117, 213), rather than as the words of the human voice to whom the first summons is attributed. If this is the case, then the addressee, who is referred to here as a 2nd person masc. sg. (see *qôlekā,* "your voice," in 6:1), may be Israel, particularly since the same pronominal reference points clearly to Israel in 6:3 (see also 6:2). But the addressee may also be the speaker in the first summons (e.g., Renaud, 302). If one follows the first approach, then the text, because of the closeness and dependence of the two speeches, would evoke an association between YHWH's voice and the prophetic voice. This feature has been seen in many other instances in the book of Micah (e.g., 2:1-5, 6-11). If one follows the second approach, the text would evoke some association between the prophetic character and Israel. Of course the two approaches may exist side by side, informing each other in a text written so as to be read and re-read.

Furthermore, if one maintains that the speaker in the second summons is to be identified with that of the first summons rather than with YHWH, which is also a possible alternative, then YHWH is the likely addressee. If such is the case, then the speaker serves as a master of ceremonies or officer of the court in a trial-like scene, addressing Israel and YHWH with different messages to each (see Hagstrom, 89-91).

In addition, even the actual contents of this second summons may be understood in more than one way. One may take *qûm rîb 'et-hehārîm* as (1) "up, make a complaint with the mountains," "up, accuse the mountains," "up, remonstrate with the mountains," or the like (cf. Isa 50:8; Jer 2:9; Prov 23:11; Neh 13:17; see Wolff, *Micah,* 164); or (2) "up, plead to [or 'unto'] the mountains" (cf. the use of the preposition *'et* in Lev 13:49; see Radak; Wellhausen [143] and others [cf. Hillers, *Micah,* 75] emend the text, from *'et* to *'el,* "to"); or even (3) "plead (your case) before [or 'in the presence of'] the mountains" (cf. Isa 30:8; see Watson; NRSV). If reading (1) is followed, then the mountains are accused. Of course, the value that the implied author wished to associate with the accusation depends on whether (a) the speaker is YHWH and the addressee is Israel, in which case it may be ironic; (b) the speaker is YHWH and the addressee is the prophetic personage of v. 1, in which case not only will it be ironic, but it will also be a legitimate accusation; or (c) the speaker is the prophetic voice and YHWH is the addressee, in which case the accusation will also be valid but roles will be inverted in relation to (b). Of course, if readings (2) and (3) are followed, then the mountains are not accused of anything; their function would be that of witnesses. The situation here is reminiscent of that in (→) 1:2, except that 6:1b allows even more readings.

The third summons may continue YHWH's speech, despite the reference to YHWH in the 3rd person, as mentioned before regarding 2:5; 4:7, 10 (see Judg 2:22; 6:26; 1 Sam 10:19; 2 Sam 12:9; 1 Kgs 17:14; 2 Kgs 20:5; Isa 49:7; Jer 14:10; 17:5; 23:16; 26:2; 27:16; Zeph 3:12; Mal 1:4; cf. Revell, §27.3; also Mays, 128). It may also be and usually is understood as the speech of the human speaker of the first summons, who returns to the forefront (e.g., Hillers,

Micah, 75; Renaud, 32). The addressees of the speech in the world of the text are not Israel (or YHWH) anymore but the mountains and *hā'ētānîm mōsĕdê 'āreṣ,* "the streams from the foundations of the earth" (cf. Hillers, *Micah,* 75-76). (Some scholars, e.g., Allen, 362, have rendered *'tnym msdy 'rṣ* as "enduring ones, earth's foundations"; while others [e.g., Wellhausen, 143; Mays, 128; cf. Renaud, 291-92] emend the text to read *ha'ă'zînû mōsĕdê 'āreṣ,* "listen, O foundations of earth"; cf. Judg 5:3; Isa 1:2, 10; 32:9; Jer 13:15; Joel 1:2; Pss 49:2 [NRSV 1]; 54:4 [NRSV 2]; 84:8 [NRSV 7]; 143:1; Job 33:1; 34:2, 16; but see Barthélemy et al., 3:755-56.)

In sum, the three summonses are written in a manner that allows for a substantial degree of polysemy. The text is open-ended and seems to suggest a multiplicity of voices that build a tapestry. In this tapestry the voice of the prophetic speaker is on the one hand associated with that of YHWH, a feature that occurs many times in the book of Micah and that is supported by the dependence of the language that the implied author places in the human and the divine mouths. On the other hand, the prophetic voice is also associated with Israel, a feature that is also found several times in the book.

In addition, the question of whether others are to face trials because of the misdeeds of Israel reverberates in these verses, as in 1:2. The consistency between these connoted meanings and similar claims advanced elsewhere in the book, along with the ubiquitous tendency in the this book (and in other prophetic books) toward polysemy (or at least ambiguity), and the contribution of polysemy and ambiguity to the rereadability of the text suggest strongly that the depth of meanings conveyed by the multivocality of 6:1-2 is not accidental. The polysemic character of the unit — or, at the very least, the numerous ambiguities created by the text as it stands — cannot be explained away by a reconstructed editorial process. The readers still had to deal with the text, and there is no reason to believe that they did so in a way that was constantly informed by their knowledge of its redactional history. For an example of redactional approaches to 6:1b, see Renaud, 303-4.

Against the background of this "sea of open ends" that characterizes the text, it is worth stressing that a few of its features and claims are sharply unequivocal. As the explanation for the summons (6:2b) states explicitly, YHWH has a complaint and accuses "his people" of something. Given the emphasis on "his" (i.e., YHWH's), one is to expect that the complaint has to do with a lack in the required behavior of Israel as the particular client of this divine patron (cf. 2:6-11; notice the emphatic repetition of "my/his people" in relation to Israel; cf. 2:4, 8, 9; 3:3, 5 and 6:2, 3, 5). To be sure, within the patron-client discourse, such a lack is a way of dishonoring the patron. People accused of such behavior will likely try to prove that they had in fact honored or attempted to honor the patron. These considerations act as a prelude and interpretive key for the rest of the READING. (Regarding the centrality of the patron-client system in ancient Israel and the ancient Near East, see Hobbs; Lemche.)

In addition, it is clear that the sequence of 2nd-person addresses that point, in part, to Israel serves an affective function in regard to the readership of the text. As in the previous cases, the call to hear is addressed to the readership. They are supposed to pay attention to the text, to overhear the voices of the textually inscribed speakers, and to identify with the addressees (→ 1:2; 3:1, 9).

The first divine speech in the ensuing dialogue between Israel and YHWH concerns YHWH's salvific deeds toward Israel. Within this context YHWH's mention of them stands as a strong reproach or accusation. YHWH advances a self-characterization as a good patron (notice the connotation of "loyalty" that is carried by the word *ṣĕdāqâ;* cf. *HAL,* 3:1006). This character-ization is supported both by the divine authority that the divine voice carries and by the accepted traditions of Israel. The rhetorical implication of YHWH's presentation is that Israel has no reason to fail in fulfilling its obligations as YHWH's client.

The aforementioned actions of YHWH are all associated with events be-longing to the foundational era within the shared discourse of the authorship and the intended readership (namely, the exodus from Egypt; the Balak-Balaam story, Numbers 22–24; and the crossing of the Jordan, Joshua 3–4). No event may be even vaguely associated with the monarchic period, the time in which Mic 1:1 sets the world described in the book, or the postmonarchic pe-riod, which is the most likely time of the composition of the book of Micah as such. The reason for that particular choice is partially the categorization of the historical narratives that appear or are reflected in the Pentateuch as founda-tional, as opposed to all other historical narratives. A second reason may be the implicit tension between the description of YHWH's mighty deeds in favor of Israel and the circumstances of Israel in the world of the book, in the common postmonarchic recollection of the monarchic period and in the present circum-stances of the postmonarchic community (cf. Ben Zvi, "Looking"). Moreover, it is worth noting that contrary to some other retellings of Israel's past (e.g., Joshua 24; Psalm 106; Nehemiah 9; see also Ezekiel 20), the short references in Mic 6:4-5 stop before the conquest of the land itself; that is, they conclude with the equivalent of Joshua 4.

The two addresses are linked to one another not only by their *Sitz im Buch* but also by their opening with the same vocative, *'ammî,* "my people," and by the rhetorical questions that begin with *mâ,* "what" (vv. 3, 5). Both ad-dresses advance similar concerns in a similar manner. In addition, one may easily notice the (contrastive) repetition of verbs from *'ānâ,* "answer," in vv. 3 and 5. Yet the first address shows a series of 2nd-person pronominal suffixes that provide additional cohesiveness to that microunit and set it apart, along with the new *'ammî* opening, from the following microunit (i.e., v. 5; notice also the contrastive pun between *hel'ētîkā,* "I have wearied you," and *he'ĕlitîkā,* "I have brought you up [from Egypt]"; see Renaud, 302; Hagstrom, 91; Anderson, 192).

The opening with the vocative *'ammî* (vv. 3, 5) on the one hand points to and characterizes the addressees of YHWH in the world of the book and indi-rectly stresses their unworthy behavior, but on the other hand it asks the read-ers of the book to identify with the addressees. After all, they too are "YHWH's people." The repeated marker of question *mâ,* "what," serves to in-troduce the reference to YHWH's past deeds in favor of Israel, and implicitly to condemn Israel. Both the intended readership and the authorship assume that the answer to YHWH's questions is known and was known to those addressed by YHWH in the book. These addressees are never described as questioning YHWH's recollection in any regard or as being surprised by any unknown information.

Although YHWH's presentation of past deeds draws on traditional images (namely, the exodus from Egypt, the Balak-Balaam story, and the crossing of the Jordan; the reference to Miriam might have evoked the memory of the crossing of the Red Sea; cf. Alonso Schökel and Sicre Díaz, 2:1065) and carries some of the lexicon associated with them (e.g., *bêt 'ăbādîm,* "house of slaves"), it shows and communicates a distinctive flavor that is not found elsewhere (cf. the situation in 5:8-14 [NRSV 9-15]; 6:16). For instance, the triad Moses, Aaron, and Miriam appears nowhere else in biblical literature except in Num 12:1, and there in a very different context. The dyad Moses and Aaron, however, appears many times, including the reference in Josh 24:5, which is an integral part of a summary presentation of the salvific acts of YHWH (and of the past of Israel) that also recounts the Balak-Balaam episode (Josh 24:9-10). The idiom *yd' ṣidqôt* ("know righteous, saving acts") in Mic 6:5 is also found only here. Significantly, expressions that do not occur elsewhere in the HB/OT appear also in the response of the people; see *kpp* (Niphal) *lē'lōhîm* ("bow oneself to God") and *'ĕlōhê mārôm* ("high God"). On the grounds of these observations, one is to conclude that the precise choice of words creates a sense that the unit is distinct from other similar texts that may deal with similar matters. Although the text includes the expression *pdh mibbêt 'ăbādîm* ("redeem from the house of slaves," i.e., "from the house of bondage"), which occurs elsewhere only in Deut 7:8; 13:6, it seems that the unit is not written so as to be understood as another piece of Deuteronomistic literature, nor is it textually marked as such (*ṣidqôt yhwh,* usually translated "the salvific acts of YHWH," occurs in Judg 5:11; 1 Sam 12:7; Mic 6:5; Ps 103:6). On these issues see Ben Zvi, "Deuteronomistic"; for a different perspective, see Alvarez Barredo, 112-19; see also Renaud, 318-201; Wolff, *Micah,* 170-71, 183.

Israel's response to YHWH's address is in vv. 6-7. This response is presented to the reader as the speech of an Israelite representing Israel, YHWH's people. The addressee of the Israelite is YHWH. Just as YHWH's speech was constructed around four rhetorical questions, so is that of the Israelite. Just as the implied author constructed a divine speech in the 1st person in which YHWH is referred to in the 3rd person, so is YHWH, the obvious addressee, referred to in the 3rd person in the Israelite's address. The difference here is also significant. In the first instance (6:5), the speech of the superior speaker, YHWH, is constructed as resorting to a self-referential 3rd person so as to convey a sense of power, superiority over, and distance from the subordinate (cf. Shoemaker, 262-64; Revell, §27.3); whereas in the second (6:6-7), the speech of the subordinate refers to the superior addressee in the 3rd person, so as to convey deference and recognition of the inferior status (cf. Shoemaker, 255-59; Revell, §22.3).

Although it is clear that YHWH's address develops an accusation, neither the readers of the text nor the addressees of YHWH in the world of the text are told unequivocally at this stage of which particular transgressions Israel is accused. Since the literary context and the dialogical form of the unit require the speaker in 6:6-7 to respond to the charges, the speaker may be constructed as either accepting YHWH's claim and asking forgiveness or the like, or as pleading not guilty, refuting and rejecting the claims made by YHWH. The second alternative is preferable from the perspective of authorship because of the combined weight of the following considerations: (1) the highlight of the READING is the teaching in 6:8 rather than any announcement of salvation, description of a massive repentance, or the like; (2) a poignant disagreement between the two main characters in a text serves to draw the readers' attention to their precise words, and posits them in a sharp light; (3) the unit is shaped around a basic contrastive dialogical structure; and (4) the contents of the teaching (i.e., "morality") are often mentioned in contrastive patterns, one of which is "morality vs. cult" (see below).

Thus the implied author sets the voice of the Israelite to rebut YHWH's claim as presented in the preceding verses and to defend YHWH's people (see the "my/his people" references in those verses) before YHWH's accusation. The basic line of defense adopted by the Israelite in the text characterizes this speaker as one who assumes the following: (1) YHWH is the deity (patron) of the Israelites; in other words, YHWH is correct in saying that Israel is his people; (2) the client (Israel) has an obligation to honor its patron (YHWH); (3) the salvific traditions mentioned by YHWH in the previous speech are truthful and are accepted without any reservation; (4) sacrifices are a way of honoring YHWH; and (5) YHWH's complaint is likely to refer to a lack in the sacrificial system (cf. Isa 43:22-24; Mal 1:6; and the world of the audience addressed by YHWH in texts such as Isa 1:11-15; Ps 50:7-13). Point (4) is based on the fact that the entire defense advanced by the Israelite addresses only one issue that was not mentioned by YHWH in the previous verses: the cult. Thus the speaker is construed as uncooperative in the conversation (i.e., as someone who answers a question with a matter that has nothing to do with the words of the other interlocutor), or this line of defense assumes that the speaker thought that YHWH had cultic issues in mind. The latter is the preferred option, since it is most unlikely that the speaker is construed as uncooperative in this case (and the more so, given the mentioned examples of Isa 1:11-15; 43:22-24; Mal 1:6; Ps 50:7-13). Of course, points (1), (2), (3), and (4) are shared by the authorship and readership of the text, by the Israelite speaker and YHWH, as well as by any "good Israelite" within this type of religious discourse. The required negative characterization of that speaker therefore has to be conveyed through point (5); on this issue see below. (Within the world of the text the Israelite is required to reject YHWH's explicit accusation of misconduct, which rejection is considered to be just; such a personage cannot be characterized in a neutral or positive way.)

YHWH's previous speech included four sharp rhetorical questions. The speech of YHWH's contender is likewise shaped around four rhetorical questions. The difference between the two cases, however, is most significant. When the superior asks the inferior rhetorical questions there is no deference but rather a strong statement (cf. 1 Kgs 2:22); when the inferior asks the superior rhetorical questions, this is likely to represent a polite and effective way of communication that allows the superior to retake the initiative and reaffirm the message conveyed by the inferior (cf. Abraham's dialogue with YHWH in Genesis 18; also 1 Kgs 22:7).

The four rhetorical questions advanced by the Israelite speaker represent an attempt to bring YHWH to recognize that there is no cultic fault in Israel, a recognition that within the world of this personage would have been tantamount to asserting that the previous accusation has no basis. The first question deals with the common issue of the manner in which a person should come before YHWH (cf. Ps 95:2; see also Vargon, 176, and bibliography there). The first question leads directly to the second (notice also the repetition of verbal forms from *qdm*, "come before"), which the speaker assumes that YHWH will have to answer affirmatively. There is nothing unexpected in the claim that Israel is to offer *'ōlâ* sacrifices (usually referred to as "burnt offerings") to YHWH (cf. Lev 28:3). Although the speaker in Mic 6:6bβ may sound somewhat hyperbolic in the choice of calves instead of lambs, such a hyperbole is understandable given the circumstances surrounding this speech in the world of the book (cf. Ps 66:15; Lev 9:3; etc.); in any case the text does not go as far as mentioning heifers, which are much more valuable than calves.

Yet the speaker anticipates that YHWH will have to answer the third and fourth rhetorical questions negatively. First the hyperbolic quantities mentioned in the third question and then the quality (i.e., the identity) of the offering in the fourth and heightening line are advanced so as to preclude a divine affirmation that this is what YHWH requires. One should note that this characterization of the speaker suggests that in the world described by the implied author and communicated to the readers of the book, neither the quantities mentioned in v. 7a nor the type of offering mentioned in v. 7b is part of YHWH's cult as practiced by the speaker, and by implication Israel. One may notice that the implied author does not construct any godly voice in the text — neither YHWH nor the prophetic voice — as accusing or reproving Israel because of child sacrifice. This is so because this is not an issue in the text; the text instead assumes the opposite, that such was not the case. The question of whether there was some form of child sacrifice in historical Israel during the monarchic period is another matter, and it stands beyond the scope of a commentary on Micah (on these issues see, e.g., Heider, and bibliography there).

On the stylistic level, the shift between the first and the second set of two questions is suggested by a change in the subject of the verb, from "I" to "YHWH." The question moves from "what should I do before YHWH?" to "does YHWH (really) wish this?" (in 6:7a, and implicitly also in 6:7b). Should YHWH respond in such a way, the speaker would have thought that the case for the defense was made.

Such a defense fails because here (and in similar cases; cf. Isa 43:22-24) the complaint that YHWH raises does not concern the sacrificial system. In fact, the characterization of the speaker as bringing up sacrificial matters rather than issues of morality is consistent with the topos of "the primacy of morality over sacrifices," which is well known both in the HB/OT (e.g., Isa 1:11-17; Am 5:21-24; Pss 40:7-9 [NRSV 6-8]; 51:18-19 [NRSV 16-17]; Prov 15:8; 21:3, 27) and in other ancient Near Eastern texts (e.g., "The Instruction

Addressed to King Merikare" and "The Tale of the Shipwrecked Sailor"; see M. Lichtheim, *Ancient Egyptian Literature* [3 vols.; Berkeley: Univ. of California Press, 1973-80] 1:106, 214, respectively). On this issue see Weinfeld, 189-93. Moreover, as Weinfeld (189-90) has shown, such a topos is not unexpected in a text that evokes the *rîb* pattern. In other words, following the combinations of themes and patterns known to both the authorship and primary readership of Mic 6:1-8, the implied author constructed a speaker who represented the Israel of the world of 6:1-8. By extension, this Israel is presented as a flawed character who wrongly thought that YHWH's accusation had to do with sacrifices and who was not aware of the well-known theological position, and literary pattern, that proclaims the primacy of morality over sacrifices.

The construction of this image of Israel calls, in the world of the book, for a strong restatement of that position. This is the issue that YHWH in the world of the text and the author of the book wished to bring forward from the outset, and toward which the text moves in stages to its climax in 6:8, namely, that YHWH (the patron) requires from Israel (the client) a certain moral behavior, which is expressed in 6:8 as: "Do justice, love kindness [or 'faithful love,' which may refer to the interpersonal obligation of the client to the patron; cf. Lemche, 125-26; Malina] and walk wisely with your God" (cf. Hillers, *Micah,* 75-76; also Hyatt, and see Hillers's qualification of Hyatt's position; cf. Ginsberg, 84). Whereas the Israel of the world of the book is about to hear this divine teaching from YHWH's mouth, the intended readers are about to read and reread about it, as they access this unit within the book of Micah.

Genre

The unit, particularly its opening, is constructed so as to evoke the images and associations of a lawsuit, the so-called *rîb* pattern. The cumulative effect of the references to *rîb* (3 times in 6:1-2), the presence of the expression *'ănēh bî* ("answer me!" or "testify against me," 6:3), and particularly the appeal to natural elements (6:1-2) are likely to activate in the readers the image of the (usually considered to be) imitations of legal procedures that appear in several prophetic books (e.g., Isa 1:2-3, 18-20; 3:13-15; Jer 2:4-13; Hos 4:1-3; cf. Westermann, *Basic Forms,* 199). To be sure, none of these features alone necessarily requires the readers to read and reread the text in a manner informed by their image of a lawsuit, or an imitation thereof (cf. Daniels, 350-54), but all these features together suggest that the text hints for rhetorical purposes (perhaps even misleadingly; see below) at more than a simple verbal dispute between a superior (YHWH, the patron) and a subordinate (Israel, the client). (On "prophetic lawsuits" see Nielsen, and the bibliography discussed there; cf. Daniels.)

In sum, it seems that the unit is presented to the intended readers in a manner that suggests to them that they should read it in way that is informed by their knowledge of legal procedures and lawsuits. Some of the features associated with the simile of a lawsuit fulfill important affective and structural roles in this text. For instance: (1) the opening serves to draw the attention of the readers to the text (see 6:1-2; cf. 3:1, 9; → 1:2); (2) the opening, the series of imperatives, the vocatives, and the emphasis on the use of the 2nd-person address serve to develop affective responses in a readership that identifies itself with Israel; (3) the images serve to bring forward and express the tension between YHWH and Israel that is so significant in this text; (4) a lawsuit simile develops the text in a way that is consistent with the dialogical character of chs. 6–7 and accordingly provides a sense of textual coherence within chs. 6–7 (but see below); and (5) the simile and the literary features that it brings along create a sense of textual coherence within the book of Micah by bridging 6:1-8 and chs. 1–3, which contain other units that evoke the image of a lawsuit (cf. the similar openings in 1:2; 3:1, 9). This bridge provides a kind of envelope around the SET OF READINGS about the future found in chs. 4–5. Moreover, if the prophetic lawsuit evoked (and borrowed) some features of international suzerainty law (cf. Harvey, among others), then the activation of this literary model could have further contributed to the communication of the typical scheme of the accusation of the suzerain or patron (YHWH) against the vassal or client (Israel).

Yet it is also clear that the text suggests to the intended readers that the image of legal procedures should not be taken too literally, and certainly not in a mimetic form. Indeed, the text clearly contradicts the expectations raised by a lawsuit simile. For instance, the identities of the accusers, accused, judge, and perhaps even the presider of the session if the last is not identified with the judge are not clear. It is often unclear who is speaking and to whom. In addition, there is no clear, explicit accusation in 6:3-5. This feature is necessary in the world of the text because it allows the author to construct the speaker as one who misunderstands YHWH's complaint, but it is less than consistent with actual legal procedures. Moreover, there is no verdict, no sentence at the conclusion of the "legal procedures." Instead, the text has a short instructional saying and attributes it to the accuser. In fact, the addressees in the world of the text (and certainly the intended readership of the book) are brought forward not for the purpose of being judged and condemned but to be persuaded (or at least the speaker aims at persuading them) of the value of the short instructional saying (see Intention). That the image of a lawsuit is raised but then its expectations are contradicted by the text is not surprising in the book of Micah, in which defamiliarization is a common rhetorical device. In this and other instances, defamiliarization serves to shape the salience of and to call attention to the unexpected features and, particularly in this case, to the heightened conclusion in 6:8. Significantly, the text in 6:1-8 contradicts the clear tendency in the "prophetic lawsuits" that appear in the prophetic books not to allow a defense speech (cf. Nielsen, 5, et passim). Vv. 6-7 provide precisely this type of speech.

Some have proposed that 6:6-8 reflects the genre of or belongs to a temple entrance liturgy and that these verses should be associated with priestly torah (cf. Pss 15:1-5; 24:3-6; Isa 33:14b-16; also Hag 2:11b-12; see Koch, 54-56; Begrich, 249-51; cf. Wolff, *Micah,* 167-68; Daniels; Renaud, 320-23; also Gerstenberger, 86-88, 117-18; as well as the relevant objections advanced in

García de la Fuente, "Liturgias"; significantly, some of the scholars who understand 6:6-8 as a "Torahlike question and answer" dissociate it from 6:1-5; see Westermann, *Basic Forms,* 204). Even if one leaves aside for the sake of the argument the doubts that linger regarding the existence of this genre or its expression in texts such as Pss 15:1-5 and 24:3-6 (García de la Fuente, "Liturgias"), the interpretation as an entrance liturgy or a priestly torah is strongly undermined by the cumulative weight of the following considerations: (1) YHWH is the likely speaker in Mic 6:8; (2) priests are not mentioned at all in 6:6-8, and the rhetorical contrast between sacrifices and morality is present in various literary formats, many of which do not involve priests at all; (3) the language in these verses cannot be characterized as priestly (see *qdm,* "come before"; *kpp* in the Niphal, "bow oneself down"; see Hillers, *Micah,* 78); (4) there is no reference to entering a temple, nor to anyone wishing to enter a temple; moreover, neither is it necessary to understand the rhetorical questions of the Israelite as pointing to an actual situation beyond the world of the book, nor does the text attempt to be mimetic (see, e.g., the defamiliarization of the lawsuit; → 1:2-16; 2:1-5, 6-11; 3:1-12; and 5:9-14; the text is not written so as to maximize its resemblance to an actual dialogue between people at the gates of the temple, or anywhere); (5) the dialogical character of 6:1-8 is related to that of chs. 6–7, and does not necessitate the assumption of particular genres, nor an explanation grounded on a well-defined *Sitz im Leben* rather than a *Sitz im Buch;* (6) the basic structure of the entrance liturgies consists of question, response, and promise (cf. Pss 15:1-5; 24:3-4; Isa 33:14b-16; see Gerstenberger, 117-18); there is no such promise in Mic 6:6-8; and (7) for reasons expressed above, it is difficult to separate 6:6-8 from 6:1-8, which as a whole cannot be considered an entrance liturgy. Yet it would not be unreasonable to assume that if postmonarchic, probably synagogal texts such as Psalms 15 and 24 (see Gerstenberger, 88-89, 118-19) were part of the discourse shared by the implied author and the intended readership of the book of Micah, then the dialogical structure in this section of Mic 6:1-8 might have evoked an association with other dialogical texts such as Psalms 15 and 24 that deal with ethics and morality.

In sum, it is preferable to consider Mic 6:1-8 in its entirety as a PROPHETIC READING of didactic character (cf. Wolff, *Micah,* 170-72), which is integral to the book of Micah (see also Setting and Intention). It is a text written to be read and reread and with a clear didactic slant. The text, particularly in its opening, does evoke the mental image of legal procedures rather than of simple verbal disagreement for rhetorical purposes and thwarts them for the same reasons. This READING might have evoked associations with texts such as Psalms 15 and 24.

Setting

The didactic dialogue advanced in 6:1-8 is not anchored in the world of the text to any particular circumstances, place, location, time, or the like. In this regard 6:1-8 is like other READINGS discussed above. The text does not ask the readers to historicize and particularize it; to the contrary, it attempts to keep it as open as possible, within the basic frame of the book of Micah.

Although one cannot rule out a priestly or perhaps better a liturgical setting for an hypothetical textual forerunner of 6:1-8, this unit, as an integral part of the book of Micah and a text that asks its readers to avoid approaching it in a manner that associates it with any particular event or liturgy, cannot be associated with those settings. It is a text to be read carefully (as required, among others, by its polysemy), repeatedly, and in a manner informed by its *Sitz im Buch.* All of this suggests that the primary readership for which this READING was composed, in its present form at least, consisted of those literati, bearers of high literacy, who were able to read and reread this type of literature. In this regard, this unit is not different from the other READINGS in the book of Micah. (Watson [67] suggests that the *Sitz im Leben* of 6:1-8 is "where priests sit in judgment of cases that deal with the questions of the covenant and the cult . . . and where, as judges in a trial, they [i.e., the priests] might be expected to give their verdict in a form indigenous to the priestly office.")

This unit sheds some light into the world of knowledge of that readership. The audience of the book is supposed to be aware of some foundational traditions of Israel (the exodus from Egypt, the Balak-Balaam story, and the crossing of the Jordan), and of the literary as well as theological and didactic commonplace of the primacy of morality over sacrificial worship. To be sure, this primacy was not understood as meaning that sacrifices had no important role; rather, it meant that the sacrifices of the sinners have no efficacy.

Several scholars have advanced the idea that 6:1-8 (and chs. 6–7) is to be associated with the northern kingdom of Israel (e.g., Burkitt; van der Woude, "Three Classical Prophets," esp. 48-53; → 1:1). Nothing in these verses requires such a setting. The only piece of relevant information that may elucidate the public for whom the text was composed (at least in its present form) is that the intended readership of the text is imagined as being aware of the traditions of the exodus from Egypt, the Balak-Balaam story, and the crossing of the Jordan. These traditions were certainly known by the literati of postmonarchic Israel, within which one is to find the primary readership of the book of Micah. (For responses to the northern setting proposal from different perspectives, see Wolff, *Micah,* 170; Renaud, 325-26; Vargon, 165-66.)

Intention

On the surface, the text is a well-crafted didactic READING whose aim is to inculcate the teaching expressed in 6:8. The purpose of this teaching is to develop a life that is coherent with YHWH's will. The contents of the teaching are not surprising (cf. Prov 21:3; 15; Jer 9:23 [NRSV 24]; 22:3) and somewhat vague on details. It is possible that Mic 6:8 serves as a short, easily memorized saying, somewhat similar to those in Proverbs, whose purpose is to encapsulate a much larger stance (cf. the Golden Rule).

Thus it is not surprising that "no other saying in the book of the prophet Micah is cited so often or has become so influential" (Wolff, *Micah,* 182). For centuries 6:8 was understood as encapsulating a comprehensive stance regarding YHWH's requirements. To be sure, these requirements were grasped from the perspective and in a way consistent with the theological discourse of the interpreters of the verse (see, e.g., *b. Mak.* 24a; *b. Sukk.* 49b; cf. Radak on 6:8).

The focus of this commentary is on the primary readership of literati for which the book of Micah, as a book, was intended, and on their possible rereadings of the text. For that purpose, it is worthwhile to address concepts and associations in the discourse of postmonarchic communities that were likely evoked by textually inscribed markers, such as the choice of words and expressions. Mic 6:8 connotes that what YHWH requires is not the life of some thing, but the living of the person who stands before YHWH in a way that is consonant with YHWH's will (cf. Mays, 142; on these matters see also Isa 1:11, 17; Collins, 193-95, and bibliography there). This divine will includes a requirement from the audience to behave in accordance with some of YHWH's attributes (cf. Lev 19:2), while at the same time maintaining a constant awareness of the unbridgeable gap between humanity and YHWH. To do justice is a well-known divine attribute. In fact, the expression *'śh* (Qal) *mišpāṭ* ("do justice") occurs with YHWH as the subject in a substantial number of texts in the HB/OT (e.g., Gen 18:25; Deut 10:18; Pss 9:5, 17 [NRSV 4, 16]; 146:7). Similarly, *hesed* (usually translated as "kindness" or "steadfast love"; the term often conveys the meaning of "loyalty" and "interpersonal duty" as well) is another well-known divine attribute mentioned explicitly in numerous texts (e.g., Exod 34:6-7; Num 14:18; Pss 33:5; 101:1; 119:124). Whereas these two attributes are clearly associated with YHWH in the theological discourse of the period (cf. Vargon, 181-82), the third element in Mic 6:8, the demand to *haṣnēaʿ leket ʿim-ʾĕlōheykā* (usually translated as "to walk humbly with your God"; cf. Vargon, 182), points to the unbridgeable difference between human beings and YHWH. Moreover, the term *ʾādām* ("human being") often occurs in the semantic field shaped by the opposition God–human (e.g., 1 Sam 15:29; 16:7; Isa 31:3; Ezek 28:2, 9; Mal 3:8; Ps 144:3; 1 Chr 21:13; 29:1). The use of the supposedly superfluous vocative *ʾādām* in Mic 6:8 seems a rhetorical device to foreground and emphasize this difference between YHWH and the audience, both in the discourse of the characters in the world of the text and in the discourse of the reading community (cf. the widespread use of *ben-ʾādām,* "a person who belongs to the category of human," i.e., "human being," in the book of Ezekiel).

To be sure, the attributes of doing justice and *hesed* are not associated only with YHWH in the HB/OT. They occur in reference to kings (e.g., 2 Sam 8:15; 1 Kgs 10:9; 20:31; Prov 20:28; 2 Chr 32:32; 35:26; cf. Jer 33:15; Neh 13:14), and individuals other than a king or ruler (e.g., Isa 57:1; Ezek 18:27; 33:14, 19; Prov 11:17; Ps 119:121). The context of Mic 6:8 and the choice of the word *ʾādām* clearly align this verse with those pointing to individuals as such. Mic 6:8 communicates a message of personal duty and responsibility for fulfilling that duty. This is consonant with the emphasis on the role and responsibility of individuals in society in other places in Micah (e.g., ch. 2).

On a different level other issues arise. For instance, the READING reaffirms the salvific traditions of Israel and of YHWH. It also provides hope that the tensions between Israel and YHWH can be resolved if Israel follows the right path, stresses the essential status of Israel as YHWH's people, even at a time when YHWH is in conflict against Israel. The combination of these motifs connotes hope for future salvific acts. The READING emphasizes the importance of historical memory. The emphatic call to remember in v. 5 is noteworthy in this regard (cf. Exod 12:25-29; Deut 26:1-9; et passim).

Finally, the READING also points to the importance of being able to read and study this sophisticated type of literature.

Bibliography

G. W. Anderson, "A Study of Micah 6:1-8," *SJT* 4 (1951) 191-97; J. Begrich, "Die priesterliche Torah," in W. Zimmerli, ed., *Gesammelte Studien zum Alten Testament* (TBü 21; Munich: Kaiser, 1964) 232-60 (= BZAW 66 [Berlin: Töpelmann, 1936] 63-88); F. G. Burkitt, "Micah 6 and 7, a Northern Prophecy," *JBL* 45 (1926) 159-61; A. Yarbro Collins, "Finding Meaning in the Death of Jesus," *JR* 78 (1998) 175-96; D. R. Daniels, "Is There a 'Prophetic Lawsuit' Genre?" *ZAW* 99 (1987) 339-60; O. García de la Fuente, "¿Liturgias de entrada, normas de asilo o exhortaciones proféticas?" *Aug* 9 (1969) 266-98; E. S. Gerstenberger, *Psalms, Part I* (FOTL XIV; Grand Rapids: Eerdmans, 1988); H. L. Ginsberg, "Notes on the Minor Prophets," *ErIsr* 3 (1954) 83-84 (Heb.; Eng. summary, p. IV); J. Harvey, "Le 'rîb-Pattern,' réquisitoire prophétique sur la rupture de l'alliance," *Bib* 43 (1962) 179-96; G. C. Heider, *The Cult of Molek: A Reassessment* (JSOTSup 43; Sheffield: JSOT Press, 1985); T. R. Hobbs, "Reflections on Honor, Shame, and Covenant Relations," *JBL* 116 (1997) 501-3; A. V. Hunter, *Seek the Lord! A Study of the Meaning and Function of the Exhortations in Amos, Isaiah, Micah, and Zephaniah* (Baltimore: St. Mary's Seminary and University, 1982); P. Hyatt, "On the Meaning of Micah 6,8," *ATR* 34 (1953) 232-39; K. Koch, "Tempeleinlassliturgien und Dekaloge," in R. Rendtorff and K. Koch, eds., *Studien zur Theologie der alttestamentlichen Überlieferungen. FS G. von Rad* (Neukirchen: Neukirchener Verlag, 1961) 45-60; N. P. Lemche, "Kings and Clients: On Loyalty between the Ruler and the Ruled in Ancient 'Israel,'" *Semeia* 66 (1995) 119-32; T. Lescow, *Micha 6,1-8: Studien zur Sprache, Form und Auslegung* (Stuttgart: Calwer, 1966); B. A. Levine, "An Essay on Prophetic Attitudes toward Temple and Cult in Biblical Israel," in M. Z. Brettler and M. Fishbane, eds., *Minḥah le-Naḥum: Biblical and Other Studies Presented to Nahum M. Sarna* (JSOTSup 154; Sheffield: Sheffield Academic Press, 1993) 202-25; B. J. Malina, "Patron and Client: The Analogy behind Synoptic Theology," *Forum* 4 (1988) 2-32; K. Nielsen, *Yahweh as Prosecutor and Judge: An Investigation of the Prophetic Lawsuit (Rîb-Pattern)* (tr. F. Cryer; JSOTSup 9; Sheffield: University of Sheffield Press, 1978); Th. Pola, "Micha 6,7a," *BN* 86 (1997) 57-59; P. Watson, "Form Criticism and an Exegesis of Micah 6:1-8," *ResQ* 7 (1963) 61-72; J. T. Willis, "Review of *Micha 6 6-8* by T. Lescow," *VT* 18 (1968) 273-78.

PROPHETIC READING EXPLAINING
THE REASONS FOR DIVINE JUDGMENT
AGAINST THE MONARCHIC "CITY," 6:9-16

Text

The text in 6:9-13 has presented a number of difficulties to readers through the ages. The ancient versions, the work of medieval commentators as well as critical scholars of the Hebrew Bible in our time, and the translations of the text in modern languages all point to a variety of perspectives and possibilities (see Barthélemy et al., 3:758-68). In addition, there is no general agreement regarding the literary image advanced in v. 14, and there are some textual issues in v. 16. The following rendering is based on a plain understanding of the text (i.e., excluding, e.g., connotations suggested by puns on words, to be discussed in the body of the commentary below):

(v. 9aα)   The voice of YHWH calls to the city:

(v. 9aβ)   — Wisdom is to fear your name[a] —
(v. 9b)   "Hear the staff[b] and the one who appoints it.
(v. 10a)   Are there still in the wicked house wicked treasures
(v. 10b)   and the cursed [or abhorrent][c] scant ephah measure?
(v. 11a)   May I be a just [or beyond reproach] person with untrue scales
(v. 11b)   and a bag with crooked stones?

(v. 12aα) whose [the city's][d] wealthy are full of violence
(v. 12aβ) and whose dwellers speak falsehood,
(v. 12b)   and their tongue is deception in their mouth.

(v. 13a)   As for me, I have made [or make] painful [or grievous, sore] your smiting,[e]
(v. 13b)   making you desolate because of your sins:
(v. 14aα) you shall eat, but not be satisfied
(v. 14aβ) your excrement will remain in your inside;[f]
(v. 14bα) you shall conceive, but not give birth;[g]
(v. 14bβ) and whoever shall be born, I will give to the sword.
(v. 15a)   You shall sow, but not reap;
(v. 15bα) you shall tread olives, but not anoint yourself with oil;
(v. 15bβ) (you shall tread) grapes, but not drink wine.

(v. 16aα) The statutes of Omri were kept[h] and all the deeds of the house of Ahab,
(v. 16aβ) and so you followed [or walked in] their counsels;[i]
(v. 16bα) therefore I must make you a desolation, and her [the city's] dwellers an object of hissing;
(v. 16bβ) and you shall bear the scorn [and dishonor] of my people."

a. The reading implies a repointing of the final *tsere* in *yr'h* to *qametz;* cf. Ps 86:11.
b. Cf. Isa 10:5; 14:5; and esp. 18:27; cf. also Mic 4:13.
c. Cf. Num 23:7-8; Prov 24:14, 24.
d. See v. 9a.
e. That is, "smiting of you"; cf. Isa 53:10, and see Hillers, *Micah,* 80-81.
f. Cf. Vargon, 192; and *DBHE,* s.v. *yšḥ;* but see also Ehrman, and the different proposals in Cathcart and Jeppesen; cf. García de la Fuente.
g. Cf. Vargon, 192-93; Driver, 268.
h. Passive meaning of Hitpael; a less likely alternative, "he [or anyone, everyone] behaved as one who keeps. . . ."
i. See *IBHS,* §33.3.c.

Structure

Despite the numerous discussions regarding the exact meaning of the text of this pericope, scholars widely agree that it is a literary unit within the book. In fact, most scholars have treated it as a unit (e.g., Hillers, *Micah,* 80-82; Mays, 143-49; Alvarez Barredo, 119-22). Its scope is clearly delimited by the conclusion of the previous READING in 6:8 and the clear new beginning in 7:1 (see, e.g., Hagstrom, 96; for a different position see Shoemaker, 202-5). As in all other cases, the READING is also linked to other READINGS in its textual vicinity in the book. Not only is the description of the wrongs of the city the opposite of *mišpāṭ* ("justice"; see 6:8; cf. Prov 16:11-12) but also the strong tendency toward sibilant alliteration in Mic 6:9-12 (see, e.g., Luker) is adumbrated already in *ăśôt mišpāṭ* (v. 8). The reference to "walk [or follow]" at the conclusion of the unit in 6:16aβ points toward a contrastive image to the "walk [or follow]" referred to in 6:8 (cf. Hagstrom, 119). In addition, the summons in v. 9 is reminiscent of those in 6:1, 2 (and other texts in Micah; see below) but also of 5:14 (NRSV 15). The next READING in the book, 7:1-7, relates to 6:9-16 because of its contents (see there; on 6:9-16 as an integral part of chs. 6–7, see Hagstrom, 102-13). In addition, as elsewhere in the book of Micah, some elements in this unit are suggestive of other READINGS in the book. Among them, the most salient is the call to hear (see 1:2; 3:1, 9; 6:1-2). One may also notice that the transition from the description of wrongs to the description of the corresponding divine action — or from "accusation" to "punishment" — in v. 13 (i.e., "as for me") seems reminiscent of the contrastive shift in (→) 7:7 and in 3:8, although in the latter different Hebrew words occur, and the context is different.

Markers of textual coherence within the unit include lexical repetitions and associations, such as the three occurrences of *rešaʿ* ("wicked") in vv. 10-11; the five *wĕlōʾ* clauses ("but not" in the translation above) in vv. 14-15; the opposition between "I" and "you" in vv. 13-15; *mirmâ* ("deceit") in v. 11 and *rĕmîyâ* ("falsehood") in v. 12. Moreover, v. 12 (twice) and v. 16 show pronominal suffixes that point to the city mentioned in v. 9, and presuppose a reading of 6:9-16 as a unit. (For redaction-critical reconstructions of the textual development of this unit see Lescow, "Redaktionsgeschichtliche Analyze," 103-5; Renaud, 335-36; Wolff, *Micah,* 188-90).

A main feature in this unit is the fluidity and ambiguity of speakers and addressees. This is the result of the implied author's play on, and purposeful intermingling of, two different scenarios: (1) YHWH's direct speech to the city and its dwellers, and (2) the prophetic voice telling someone else — identified also as Israel — about YHWH's talk to the city. To be sure, both direct speeches (that of YHWH and that of the prophetic voice in which YHWH's speech is embedded) are constructed by the implied author so as to achieve a certain impact not on either of these two audiences in the world of the book but on the intended rereaders of the book.

The first microunit (v. 9aα) introduces, although in a somewhat unusual form (see Wolff, *Micah,* 191), the direct speech of YHWH. The choice of *qrʾ* ("cry") rather than any other verb usually used to mark direct speech (e.g., *ʾmr,* "say") is perhaps due to either a desire to communicate some sense of distance to be overcome between speaker and addressee (in other words, to convey a sense akin to that of a summons), which may be represented by Eng. "call," or to include some affective element from the speaker's perspective, which may be represented by Eng. "cry out" (cf. 2 Kgs 11:14), or both. (On these issues, though mainly from the perspective of narratives, see Meier, 213, 338-41; C. Miller, 331-32.)

In this READING *qôl yhwh,* "YHWH's voice," is presented as an articulated voice, and mainly as a metonymical reference for YHWH. Such a choice of reference implies that speech is a main and salient attribute of YHWH. Notice the emphasis on language communication in the conclusion of the description of the wrongs of the city in vv. 12aβ and 12b. It is also clear that the meanings associated with *qôl yhwh* in Psalm 29 (or Isa 66:6) are not present here at the plain level. Whether the intended rereaders of the text are totally unaffected or uninformed by those meanings when they approach this text is debatable.

I should stress that the text in v. 9aα leaves the ensuing words of YHWH without a clear temporal anchor. When is YHWH saying (or "crying out") these words? Or when will YHWH be saying these words? How long will YHWH be "crying out" these words? These and similar questions receive no unequivocal answer. The openness of the text here and elsewhere allows multiple readings.

Similarly, although the context of the book of Micah clearly suggests that "the city" is monarchic Jerusalem (so, e.g., Mays, 146; Allen, 377; Wolff, *Micah,* 190; cf. Lam 1:1, et passim), the text still keeps open the possibility of other readings, in which "the city" may stand for any city besides monarchic Jerusalem. (The hypothesis that "the city" here refers to Samaria has been supported by Alonso Schökel and Sicre Díaz, 2:1038; van der Woude, "Three Classical Prophets," 50; Willis, "Reapplied," 70-71; among others. This hypothesis is integral to that of the northern origin of this text and of chs. 6–7; for a critique see Setting below.)

The text suggests to the readers that they are supposed to understand the voice of the presenter of YHWH's speech as different from YHWH and as a human prophetic voice. In the context it is obvious that this voice addresses an Israelite audience, whereas YHWH addresses "the city" with which "Israel" is supposed to identify, but with which it is not coterminous. In v. 9aβ the human voice suddenly shifts to a comment formally addressed to YHWH (see "your name") but meant to be overheard by the audience of this voice within the world of the text and by the readers.

Significantly, the theme of this parenthetical saying is reminiscent of, but not exclusively associated with, wisdom literature (cf. Prov 1:7; 9:10; 15:33; but see also Ps 111:19; cf. Neh 1:11; a similar worldview is expressed in ancient Near Eastern literature other than the HB/OT; see van der Toorn, 38). Moreover, the use of the word *tûšîyâ,* "sound wisdom," which appears here (v. 9) and mainly in wisdom literature (e.g., Prov 2:7; 3:21; 8:14; 18:1; Job 26:3), along with the emphasis on true and false speech, which is also common in wisdom literature, contributes a flavor of wisdom to the text that is not exclusive to v. 9aβ but is present in vv. 9-12 (cf. Kaufmann, 3:277; and see the list of wisdom-like expressions there).

The speaker in v. 9b is YHWH; "the city" is the expected addressee. The city or, better, the people of the city (notice the pl. form in *šim'û,* "hear") are asked to listen to the staff (i.e., the [sound of] the rod of punishment; cf. Isa 30:32; Job 3:18; see also Isa 10:5, 24; Lam 3:1) and above all to YHWH, the one who appointed the staff and who is about to present a speech to this audience (cf. Jer 47:7; see Margolis, 65-66). The word *maṭṭeh* ("staff") rather than the more common *šēbeṭ* is used here perhaps to convey a connotative or associative meaning. The slot of the word following the verb "hear" may be filled by either an object as here (e.g., *šim'û dĕbar-yhwh,* "listen to the word of

YHWH," Isa 1:10; see also Mic 6:1) or by a vocative (e.g., Mic 6:2). The word *maṭṭeh* also suggests the meaning "tribe." Moreover, the expression following *maṭṭeh* is *ûmî yĕ'ādāh*, "and who [or the one who] appoints it," which is phonetically similar to and reminiscent of *mô'ēdāh*, "her [the city's] assembly"; cf. Isa 14:13; Ps 74:4. If so, the text conveys a secondary and connoted meaning akin to: "The voice of YHWH calls to the city . . . : 'Hear, O tribe, and her [the city's] assembly'" (cf. Isa 1:1; Jer 11:2; Joel 4:6 [NRSV 3:6]; Mal 3:4; etc.). Significantly, the existence of this connoted meaning depends on two lexical choices that are clearly possible in biblical Hebrew but usually not favored in biblical literature. The first is the choice of *maṭṭeh* for "rod" rather than *šēbeṭ*, and the second is the reference to *maṭṭeh* as a fem. noun, which allows for the connoted reference back to "city," which is consistent with the salient character of that city in this section of the unit (see v. 9 and the numerous references to it in v. 12). (On the use of a fem. pronominal suffix for *maṭṭeh* see Vargon, 187; on textual emendations of this part of the unit see, e.g., Wolff, *Micah*, 186; but see also Barthélemy et al., 3:761-62; and Hillers, *Micah*, 80 n. c.)

The first section of the characterization of the city is built around two rhetorical questions. Notice the strong presence of rhetorical questions in the previous READING and around the common topos of untrue balance and false weights. This topos occurs many times in the HB/OT (see Lev 19:36; Deut 25:13-16; Ezek 45:10; Hos 12:8; Am 8:5; Prov 11:1; 16:11; 20:10) and in ancient Near Eastern literature other than the HB/OT (e.g., Šurpu, II, 45-46 [see *CANE*, 1689]; "The Instruction of Amenemope," chs. 16-17 [XVII,17–XVIII,19], on which see M. Lichtheim, *Ancient Egyptian Literature* [3 vols.; Berkeley: Univ. of California Press, 1973-80] 2:156-57; see also, e.g., van der Toorn, 19, 162 n. 105; Buccellati, 1689; Vargon, 188-89 n. 17). One may surmise that the widespread attestation of the topos, both in relation to time and in geographical area, is related to a corresponding widespread occurrence of untrue balances and weights, as well as to the rhetorical value and theological message of this literary topos. Given the flavor of wisdom mentioned in relation to v. 9αβ, it is worth noting that *bêt rāšā'*, "wicked house," occurs elsewhere only in Hab 3:13; Prov 3:33; 14:11; 21:12; and *'ōṣĕrôt reša'*, "wicked treasures," in Mic 6:10 occurs elsewhere only in Prov 10:2. Moreover, all the words in Mic 6:11 except one appear in the book of Proverbs and, more significantly, all the words but two appear in a very small subset of the book, that of three verses that deal with these matters in Proverbs (11:1; 16:11; 20:10). One of the two other words is *reša'* ("wicked"), which is common in Proverbs, wisdom literature, and elsewhere in the HB/OT. The expression *ha'ezkeh* ("May I be just?") does not appear in Proverbs, but see Job 15:14; 25:4 (and Ps 51:6 [NRSV 4]). In any case, whereas any particular instance mentioned here if taken in isolation would not provide convincing evidence for a flavor of wisdom in Mic 6:9-12, their combined weight strongly suggests that the text shares lexical items and concepts with wisdom literature and conveys a flavor of wisdom to the readers.

Given the general literary context of 6:11, it is likely that the somewhat unusual *h'zkh* in the Qal stem here ("May I be just?") connotes, in addition to its basic meaning, the meanings carried by the identically written and phonetically similar forms in the Piel or Hiphil stems. These latter verbal forms would render a secondary meaning akin to "Shall I acquit concerning . . . ?" or "Can I pronounce justice when . . . ?" The present text allows a main reading that is enriched and informed by a secondary, connoted reading. Similar cases have been observed in the book of Micah (e.g., and within this unit, 6:9) and in other prophetic books (e.g., Zeph 3:8).

Several scholars have proposed that the original verbal form in v. 11a was in the Piel or the Hiphil rather than the Qal stem, and therefore they emend the text (see, e.g., Wolff, *Micah,* 185; cf. *DCH,* 3:104a, for the Piel proposal; see Shoemaker, 198, for the Hiphil proposal). Renaud (330) considers both readings more probable than the present one.

Although at the primary level YHWH is the speaker in v. 11 (see v. 9aα), the text is written at least to allow and probably to suggest a secondary, affective approach to the text, one in which the intended reader identifies with the speaker: "May *I* be a just person with untrue scales and a bag with crooked stones?" The answer is, of course, no. The didactic character of this reading would be very similar to that of Prov 11:1 and related texts (see above). Moreover, the possibility of a human speaker, as suggested by an identification between the intended rereaders and the speaker constructed in v. 11, raises also the possibility of a tertiary, vaguely connoted meaning: could it be that the addressees of either the human voice that speaks in v. 9a or YHWH (i.e., "the city") are the speakers in v. 11? As mentioned before, one is to expect at least the potential for a multiplicity of meaning in a text that is read and reread many times, and is meant to be so.

The second characterization of the city (v. 12) is syntactically bound to the noun "city" in v. 9aα by the opening 'ăšer, "that." This syntactic link encircles the first description and the (parenthetical) remark in v. 9aβ (cf. 1:1; Jer 1:2). It sets the attention of the reader back to the beginning of v. 9, to the city to which YHWH is (or will be) crying out, and to some extent it may be seen as turning vv. 10-11 into an aside comment (a comment that in English is marked by parentheses or dashes). The focus in v. 12, however, is not on a personified city (as in much of chs. 4–5), but on the inhabitants of the city and their character. There are clear links between the first (vv. 10-11) and the second characterization (v. 12). Among them one may mention the relation between the concluding *mirmâ* ("deceit") and *rěmîyâ* ("falsehood"; see vv. 11, 12); the association between "wealth" and *mirmâ* (see Isa 53:9; cf. Jer 5:27); the word pair *ḥāmās–mirmâ* ("wealth gained by violence" and "wealth gained by fraud," respectively; see Isa 53:9; Zeph 1:9; and Ben Zvi, *Zephaniah,* 102, for the translation); the association between *ḥāmās* and *rešaʿ* ("violence" and "wicked," respectively; see Isa 53:9; Ezek 7:11; Ps 11:5; 140:5; Prov 4:17; 10:6, 11; also see *rešaʿ* and 'āśâ in Isa 53:9); between *šāqer* ("falsehood") and *mirmâ* ("deceit"; see Ps 109:2; Prov 12:17); between *mirmâ* and references to "mouth" and "tongue" (e.g., Pss 10:7; 52:6 [NRSV 4]; 109:2); and the thematic relation between stealing and the description in vv. 10-11. Some lexical choices in Prov 10:2-4 are reminiscent of Mic 6:10-12 as a unit. In addition, one may notice the similarities between the lexical repertoires of Isa 53:9 and Mic 6:10-12.

Whereas the repetition of sibilants that was so significant in vv. 10-11 continues, a combination of the related *r* and *l* sounds, particularly toward the end of the verse, and also that of the sounds *m* and *n,* is also easily noticeable. The sonorous atmosphere of the text is now consistent with the shift of emphasis from false weights and the like to false language, from what is in the "bag" (v. 11) to what is on the "mouth" (v. 12). Significantly, YHWH's condemnatory speech is constructed to climax on references to untrue speech. This emphasis on the importance of speech, true or untrue, is present not only in wisdom literature, where it abounds, but also in prophetic literature (e.g., Zeph 1:9; 3:13; see Ben Zvi, *Zephaniah,* 235-37).

The second characterization of the city in v. 12 states its guilt in common generic terms (for *ḥāmās* see, e.g., Gen 6:11, 13; Jer 51:46; Ezek 7:23; 8:17; 28:16; Am 3:10; Joel 4:9 [NRSV 3:9]; Zeph 1:9; for references to false language, see, e.g., Isa 49:3; Jer 9:4 [NRSV 5]; Ps 109:2). Yet it is precisely the attribution of well-known categories to the city that contributes to the readers' understanding that the expected reaction of YHWH to the wrongdoing of the city is judgment. Thus vv. 10-12 lead directly to vv. 13-15.

Features of curses may appear in announcements of judgment as constructed in the prophetic books (cf. Westermann, *Basic Forms,* 198). YHWH's punishment of the city in vv. 13-15 is described in terms of futility curses (see Hillers, *Treaty-Curses,* 28-29; idem, *Micah,* 82; also see, e.g., Lev 26:26; Deut 28:30-31, 38-40; Hos 4:10; Am 5:11; Zeph 1:13; Hag 1:6; outside the HB/OT, Sefire I A, 21-24, *ANET,* 659).

Significantly, as the text moves into the futility curses, the references to those worthy of punishment shift from the 3rd person (see vv. 9-12) to the 2nd person. Moreover, this 2nd person is emphatically marked by a triple reference to *'attâ,* "you [sg.]," in v. 14 and by about fifteen markers of the 2nd person in vv. 13-14 (i.e., pronominal suffixes and verbal forms that are marked for the 2nd person). Moreover, the text develops a strong contrast between *'ănî,* "I" (v. 13), and *'attâ,* "you [sg.]" (3 times). The reason for the shift is most likely rhetorical, and has to do with the affective power of the 2nd person (Lev 26:26; Deut 28:30-31, 38-40).

Whereas one may have expected the READING to end in v. 5, instead a loop not uncommon in prophetic literature occurs (e.g., Zeph 3:1-8; Obad 7, 12; Mic 2:11; see Ben Zvi, *Zephaniah,* 335-36; idem, *Obadiah,* 73, 144-45; → 2:6-11, Structure). As in other instances, the loop reflects on similar matters from a different perspective or illuminates the issue in a slightly different light. Here the text presents again the issue of the wrongdoing of the people (this time referred to, for the most part, in the 2nd person pl., but also in the 3rd), in terms of the historical reconstructions of Israel's past upheld by the readership of the text. The inhabitants of the city addressed by YHWH are now described as those who follow the rules and deeds of the worst kings imaginable within this discourse in general and the constraints of the *Sitz im Buch* in particular. A reference to people following the "ways of Manasseh" or the like, ways that have led to an anticipation of an announcement of the destruction of the city (i.e., of Jerusalem; see 2 Kgs 21:13; 24:3-4; Jer 15:4), is precluded by the temporal references in Mic 1:1, but Ahab is explicitly compared with Manasseh and his name carries a similar connotation in the reconstruction of the past accepted in postmonarchic times (see 2 Kgs 21:3, 13; cf. 2 Kings 17). In Mic 6:16, as in 1:6-7 and in numerous cases in prophetic literature (e.g., Ezekiel 23) and in 2 Kings 17, for example, the fate of the northern kingdom is evoked — explicitly or implicitly — to advance a reference to the similar fate of Jerusalem.

Although YHWH is constructed in Mic 6:16 as announcing to the city that its fate is destruction (cf. 3:12; Jer 29:18; 2 Kgs 22:19-20), the verse and the unit do not conclude with the announcement of destruction per se, but with YHWH's characterization of those whom YHWH addresses as those who will bear the shame of YHWH's people. In other words, whereas the actions of the addressees deserve severe punishment and such will be executed upon them, Israel remains YHWH's people, despite the deeds of this particular group within Israel. Although the relation between YHWH and Israel will contribute to their shame, this relation is a source of hope for the readers of the book (cf. Mic 2:8; and at the theological or ideological level, 4:9-10).

Genre

The unit evokes the basic features of an announcement of judgment, or better of a prophetic report of YHWH's announcement of judgment (cf. Alvarez Barredo, 119-22; Mays, 144). One section deals with the reasons for the divine punishment, and another announces (and describes) it, and then the same pattern is repeated on a smaller scale (cf. Mays, 144). The unit also evokes curses. But as such the unit is a didactic READING that is an integral part of the book meant to be read and reread. This unit addresses the issue of why YHWH destroyed the "city" (most likely, Jerusalem) of the monarchic period. The answer is, of course: because of the sins of their people. This READING may be classified as a PROPHETIC READING, as are all other READINGS in the book, because it belongs to a prophetic book that is supposed to be read and reread as a particular instance of YHWH's word. (See Snyman for a summary of alternative positions regarding the genre of 6:9-16.)

Setting

Some scholars have claimed that the setting of 6:9-16 is in the northern kingdom, mainly because of the references to Omri and Ahab in v. 16. These scholars usually advance similar northern settings for other units in chs. 6–7 (e.g., Burkitt; van der Woude, "Three Classical Prophets," 50-51; Ginsberg, *Israelian Heritage,* 25-27). The claims regarding other units are discussed as appropriate under Setting in each case. As for 6:9-16, a reference to Omri and Ahab does not require a northern Israelite authorship or readership. Such a reference implies only a group whose cultural memory included a notice about these kings and an evaluation similar to that found in the book of Kings. These conditions certainly obtain in a postmonarchic group of literati who attempt to explain the fall of monarchic Jerusalem, a theme that comes repeatedly to the forefront in the book of Micah. For a different approach, see, e.g., Willis, "Reapplied," 70-71.

Others have claimed that this unit reflects a strong Deuteronomistic redaction (e.g., Renaud, 342-43; Alvarez Barredo, 120-21; cf. Wolff, *Micah,* 190). But it is difficult to maintain that this text was redacted by a socially distinct Deuteronomistic group. It is more consonant with the data that the text as it stands suggests an authorship and readership who share the evaluation of Ahab and Omri present in the book of Kings and for whom some of the language and expressions found in the Deuteronomistic History (and in wisdom literature) were available. Any postmonarchic group of Jerusalemite literati would have satisfied these requirements. Moreover, it is probably not by accident that despite the similarities with Deuteronomistic literature, none of the expressions here is identical with one found in Deuteronomistic literature. For example, *ntn lĕšammâ wĕlišrēqâ ûlĕḥerpâ* ("to make [someone] an object of terror, hissing, and derision") appears in Jer 29:18. The closest expression to this idiom occurs in Mic 6:16, but the differences are clear. Moreover, the topos of "passers-by will shudder" by itself is relatively common in ancient Near Eastern literature (see Hillers, *Treaty-Curses,* 76-78). Finally, the choice of words in Mic 6:16 seems to point to a strong tendency to use unusual combinations within familiar territory. Thus one may note the rare occurrence of *šmr ḥq/h* with *šmr* in the Hitpael (rather than Qal), and the choice of terms such as *ḥuqqôt 'omrî* ("the statutes of Omri") and *ma'ăśēh bêt-'aḥ'āb* ("the deeds of the house of Ahab") that do not occur elsewhere in the HB/OT. Indeed, neither 6:9-16 and 6:16, nor the book of Micah seems to have been written to be understood by the intended readers as Deuteronomistic literature (see Ben Zvi, "Deuteronomistic").

Snyman (337) and others think of "some influence from wisdom circles," because of *wĕtûšîyâ yir'eh šĕmekā* ("it is sound wisdom to fear your name") in v. 9aβ. These words communicate a flavor of wisdom that is not exclusive to v. 9aβ but is present in vv. 9-12. This flavor indicates only that wisdom motifs or features were known to the authorship and intended readership of this unit. This is to be expected, given that both the authorship and the readership of this text are to be found among the bearers of high literacy, the literati (cf. Ben Zvi, "Urban").

A dating of the text ca. 600 BCE advanced by Wolff (*Micah,* 190) and others is based on (1) a textual emendation in v. 13aα that is supported by ancient versions (e.g., LXX, Vg., but see the discussion in Barthélemey et al., 3:767-68); and (2) an assumption that the text must be so explicitly mimetic of current historical events that if YHWH is described as saying "I have surely *begun* to destroy you," then the text must be dated to ca. 600 BCE and not ca. 586 or any time after that. There is no support for this assumption. Moreover, the text here, as elsewhere in the book of Micah, does not ask its readers to imagine a particular setting for the words of any of the speakers in the world of the text. The setting within the world of the book is left as open as possible, within the restrictions associated with 1:1. This openness not only contributes to multiple rereadings but stands in tension with the tight historical mimetism on which the mentioned assumption depends.

As it stands, the text of 6:9-16 reflects on the fall of monarchic Jerusalem. The worldview and world of knowledge of the authorship and intended readership of the READING are reflected in part in the Deuteronomistic historical narrative, in part in wisdom literature, and in part in other biblical texts (e.g., references to futility curses). The openness of the text to multiple readings, connoted meanings, and various degrees of ambiguity not only contributes to the general message of the text but suggests a text meant to be read and reread primarily by a community of literati, as were other READINGS in the book of Micah.

Against this background, a particular feature of the second characterization of the city (v. 12) is noteworthy. The first two parallel versets there are shaped around the pair "its [the city's] wealthy" and "its inhabitants," with "wealthy" and "inhabitants" taking similar roles in the parallel structure. Given that the authorship and primary readership of the book of Micah consisted of urban Jerusalemite literati, the connoted association of the monarchic city with wealth and of its inhabitants with fraud and violence is probably not an accident. These connections reflect a common outline of the reconstruction of Israel's history in the postmonarchic period: monarchic Jerusalem was a great and wealthy city (as opposed to Achaemenid Jerusalem), but its greatness was based on wrongdoing, so YHWH razed it. This basic outline had a great influence on the general discourse of postmonarchic communities, and is consistent with a worldview in which power and wealth in worldly terms are not necessarily an expression of YHWH's blessing but may well characterize one about to suffer divine judgment. Significantly, this worldview is often expressed in prophetic literature (→ 4:9–5:1 [NRSV 2], Intention; Ben Zvi, "Understanding"; idem, *Zephaniah,* 325-46) and is coherent with a self-understanding of postmonarchic Israel as an underdog in earthly terms, a notion also ubiquitous in biblical literature (cf. Greenspahn, 109-10, et passim) and reflecting the actual position of Achaemenid Israel and Jerusalem vis-à-vis the world powers of the time, and even vis-à-vis that of Judah and Jerusalem in the monarchic period. (The population of Jerusalem in the Achaemenid period was about 6 percent of that of late monarchic Jerusalem; on the issues raised by the size of Achaemenid Jerusalem and the production of biblical books, see Ben Zvi, "Urban," and bibliography there.)

Intention

The primary intention of this READING in the book of Micah is to explain the fall of Jerusalem (cf. Renaud, 342) in terms of an authority grounded in YHWH's word: these events were caused by the iniquity of monarchic Jerusalem and its dwellers. The text is didactic in the sense that it alerts its readers to types of actions that lead to YHWH's judgment. These types of actions are described in generic terms to allow the readers to associate them with multiple circumstances in the past, present, or even the imagined future.

The text implies but also reaffirms as YHWH's word the evaluations of Omri and Ahab in the Deuteronomistic historical narratives, and connotes a worldview in which there is a strong emphasis on reliable language. This emphasis on trustworthy speech is more plausible in certain social locations than in others. Leadership that relies strongly on social acceptance is dependent on the acceptance of the assumption that the leaders are trustworthy. The legitimacy of a prophetic book, and of those who claim that it is YHWH's word, depends on a certain assumption about the reliability of the text and those who have primary access to it and who claim that it is YHWH's word. Indeed, all oral education depends on the acceptance of the speech of the educational broker as reliable (cf. Ben Zvi, *Zephaniah,* 236; on the broker roles of the authorship and readership of these texts → 1:2-16, Setting; see Ben Zvi, "Observations").

Bibliography

G. Buccellati, "Ethics and Piety in the Ancient Near East," *CANE,* 1685-96; K. J. Cathcart and K. Jeppesen, "More Suggestions on Mic 6,14," *SJOT* 1 (1987) 110-15; G. R. Driver, "Linguistic and Textual Problems: Minor Prophets II," *JTS* 39 (1938) 260-73; A. Ehrman, "A Note on Micah VI 14," *VT* 23 (1973) 103-5; H. L. Ginsberg, *The Israelian Heritage of Judaism* (New York: Jewish Theological Seminary of America, 1982); idem, "Notes on the Minor Prophets," *ErIsr* 3 (1954) 83-84 (Heb.; Eng. summary, p. IV); F. E. Greenspahn, *When Brothers Dwell Together* (Oxford: Oxford Univ. Press, 1994); Y. Kaufmann, *Toledot Ha'emunah Hayisra'elit* (4 vols.; Tel Aviv: Bialik, 1937-56) (Heb.); C. L. Miller, *The Representation of Speech in Biblical Hebrew Narrative: A Linguistic Analysis* (HSM 55; Atlanta: Scholars Press, 1996); S. D. Snyman, "A Text Intern and Text Extern Investigation of Micah 6:9-16," *NTT* 35 (1994) 332-38; R. Tournay, "Quelques relectures bibliques antisamaritaines," *RB* 71 (1962) 504-36; K. van der Toorn, *Sin and Sanction in Israel and Mesopotamia* (SSN 22; Assen: Van Gorcum; 1985); J. T. Willis, "A Reapplied Prophetic Hope Oracle," in G. W. Anderson et al., *Studies in Prophecy* (VTSup 26; Leiden: Brill, 1974).

READING EXPRESSING TRUST IN YHWH DESPITE AND IN RESPONSE TO SOCIAL DISINTEGRATION, 7:1-7

Structure

I. Speaker's interjection	1aα
II. First description of the wrongful state of society	1aβ-4a
A. Harvesting/gleaning metaphor	1aβ-b
B. Statements of conditions in society	2-3
C. Plant metaphor	4a
III. Expression of confidence in YHWH's redemptive action	4b
IV. Description of the collapse of social cohesiveness (eschatological undertones)	5-6
V. Expression of trust in YHWH	7

Although many scholars consider 7:1-7 a literary unit (e.g., Rudolph, 120-22; Allen, 383-90; Wolff, *Micah,* 200-210; Hillers, *Micah,* 83-86; Vargon, 198-210), there is disagreement regarding its borders or independence. The issue of whether v. 7 is to be associated with, or belongs — originally or redactionally — to 7:1-6 or to 7:8-20 (e.g., Wellhausen, 146-47; Renaud, 357-79; Willis, "Reapplied") has led to considerable debate (see Allen, 384; Wolff, *Micah,* 203; Hillers, *Micah,* 85; Vargon, 199-200). Proposals to divide 7:1-7 into two literary units, 7:1-4 and 7:5-7, or to include the entirety of 7:1-7 into a larger unit (7:1-20), have been advanced (e.g., Reicke; Luker, "Doom and Hope," 188-209).

The text here strongly suggests to its intended readers that they should understand v. 7 in relation to the preceding verses, for several reasons:

1. The unit evokes the literary patterns of complaints, which tend to conclude with an expression of faith (e.g., Pss 6:10-11 [NRSV 9-10]; 13:6 [NRSV 5]; 17:5; 40:12, 18 [NRSV 11, 17]; cf. Hab 3:17-19a). Notice also the common usage of *wa'ănî,* "but I," as a turning point that opens the expression of faith (e.g., Pss 13:6 [NRSV 5]; 31:15 [NRSV 14]; 69:13 [NRSV 12]; Hab 3:18), and see Mic 7:7.
2. The unit shows a thematic a-b-c-b'-c' structure (a = 1aα; b = 1aβ-4a; c = 4b; a' = 5-6; c' = 7) that requires the presence of v. 7.
3. The link between c and c' is enhanced by the repetition of crucial words from the root *ṣph* ("watch" or "wait").
4. The final words in v. 7, *yišmā'ēnî 'ĕlōhāy* ("my God will hear me" or "my God hears me"), seem to present a theological and instructional response to the rhetorical and strongly affective call that opens the unit, *'allay lî* ("How I sorrow!").
5. The type of adversative that appears in v. 7, and that may be rendered in English as "but I," has occurred before in the book of Micah at significant turning points within a single READING (3:8; 6:13), and in any case it presupposes a preceding text. (For support of this position on the basis of sonorous repetitions, see Alonso Schökel and Sicre Díaz, 2:1068.)

To be sure, none of these considerations precludes that the text may have suggested to the intended readership that they should also approach 7:8-20 in association with 7:7 (double-duty verses have been observed before in the book; see, e.g., 5:1 [NRSV 2]; → 7:8-20, Structure). Moreover, whereas the unit shows markers that set it apart from 7:7-20, there is no reason why the primary readers of the book would have repeatedly reread and meditated on one in a way that is not informed by the other (cf. Mays, 152-56).

The main ground for the proposal to divide 7:1-7 into two units, 7:1-4a and 7:4b-7, concerns the formal shift of addressees and the thematic change of imagery that is first taken from the sociopublic and then from the sociofamiliar arena. But such shifts neither necessitate the division of the text nor are they unexpected in the book of Micah.

Among the stylistic features that characterize 7:1-7, the most common is the tendency toward repetition. One may notice (1) the repetition of consonants in *'allay lî,* "How I sorrow!" in v. 1aα (cf. Job 10:15); (2) the presence of the same consonantal pattern, guttural + *lamed* + *lamed,* in *'ōlĕlōt,* "grapes," in v. 1aβ (cf. Pss 40:18 [NRSV 17]; 69:30 [NRSV 29]; 70:6 [NRSV 5]; Lam 3:1); (3) the presence of *'ên,* "not," at the beginning of v. 1b and at the conclusion of v. 2; (4) the occurrence of *'ādām,* "person," in v. 2a and *dāmîm,* "blood," in v. 2b; (5) the presence of *yāšār,* "straight," in vv. 2 and 4 (elsewhere in Micah only in 2:7; cf. 3:9); (6) the close sonorous relation between *'ĕlōhê yiš'î,* "the God of my salvation," *yišmā'ēnî 'ĕlōhāy,* "my God will hear me" (or "my God hears me"), in v. 7 (cf. Isa 43:12; Pss 145:19; 20:9); (7) the sonorous and probably ironic relation between *rā',* "evil," and *rēa',* "fellow" or "friend," in vv. 3 and 5 (cf. Zech 8:17); (8) the pun on *mĕsûkâ,* "thorn hedge," and *mĕbûkâ,* "confusion," in v. 4a-b (cf. the sonorous environment of *mĕbûkâ* in Isa 22:5, which is the only other instance of this term in the HB/OT); and (9) the case of the two words from the root *ṣph,* "watch," in vv. 4b and 7a. Ironical puns on words and rhetorically significant unexpected turns of language are also present to support the message that the world described there frustrates the usual expectations shared by authorship and rereadership. For instance, there is the expression in v. 3 that conveys the sense of "good at wrongdoing." In addition, the usual combination of the words *śar,* "officer," and *šōpēṭ,* "judge," along with the evoked word *šālôm,* "peace," suggests the world that should be, instead of the one described in the text in which *šālôm,* "peace," ends up being *šillûm,* "bribe." The world described in the text is thus presented as far from what the world ought to be. (For additional examples see vv. 5-6. See also the discussion of sonorous effects in Alonso Schökel and Sicre Díaz, 2:1068.)

One of the interesting stylistic features in this unit is the way the implied author plays on the identity of the speaker. Since 7:1-7 follows 6:9-16, and since there is no clearly inscribed marker reporting a change of speaker, the readers may at the very least ponder whether the speaker in 7:1 is YHWH. (The expression "How I sorrow!" does not preclude this interpretation; → 1:8-9 and Structure there.) Significantly, the Tg. seems to be well aware of the possibility of this reading, because here, just as in 1:8, the openness of the text on the matter of the identity of the speaker is explicitly closed (the Tg. adds *'mr nby,* "the prophet said," at the beginning of the verse) so as not to allow or even to suggest a reading that from the perspective of the Tg. was theologically unacceptable, hence mistaken.

If the intended readers of the text considered YHWH to be the speaker in vv. 1-4a, then they would likely recognize a shift of speakers in v. 4b, where YHWH is addressed in the 2nd person. The following shift of addressees from YHWH to the people is not problematic in itself, in the light of instances such as Pss 9:12 (NRSV 11); 31:24 (NRSV 23); cf. Ps 6:9 (NRSV 8). The likely speaker in Mic 7:4b is a default human prophetic speaker, whom the intended readers likely identified with the character Micah referred to in 1:1. Similar shifts between divine and human voices are common in the book (→ 1:2-16, Structure). As in many other instances, the two voices are interwoven within the text, and here it is obvious that the human voice presupposes the divine words reported in the book in the preceding verses. Yet the text remains ambiguous, because there is no clear indication that YHWH is the speaker in vv. 1-4a.

But the text is even more ambiguous. The question of whether YHWH is the speaker in these verses rests on a reading that is mainly informed by its preceding unit in the book, where YHWH is the speaker. If the intended readership approaches 7:1-7 in the light of the following, rather than the preceding, unit, then it is most likely that a feminine voice rather than YHWH would be considered the speaker in 7:1-7 (see 7:10). If one adopts this reading of the text, then since the text evokes some elements of a lament — particularly in the description of the woeful and wrongful conditions, and notice the opening interjection — it is likely that this feminine voice is understood as Daughter Zion/Jerusalem/the city. To be sure, reading the text with a human speaker still remains a valid option.

Thus here, as in 1:5 (→ Structure), the text is conducive to different interpretations of the identity of the speaker depending on whether the readers approach it from a position cued by the following or by the preceding unit in its textual environment. This feature points to the basic character of 7:1-7, namely, its being a READING to be read in a way that is strongly informed by other READINGS in the book of Micah (i.e., a READING that depends on its *Sitz im Buch*).

In sum, the potential voices of three possible speakers — YHWH, Daughter Zion (or Jerusalem), and the human prophetic speaker most likely identified with Micah — populate this unit. Similar instances of a lack of unequivocality regarding the identity of the speaker in the unit along with the multiplicity of voices have been found elsewhere in the book of Micah (→ 1:2-16, Structure; 2:6-11, Structure) and elsewhere in prophetic literature (see Ben Zvi, *Obadiah,* 73-74, 172-74). They are not the result of textual accident but are significant elements in the shaping and conveying of the message (and worldview) of the READING. Here they reflect and communicate a theological relationship among the possible speakers. The three are presented as sharing the possibility of uttering these words and as carriers of "godly" voices. These voices stand in opposition to the implied voices of all those who belonged to the monarchic society described in 7:1-6, that is, to a society in which there is no one who is upright (see 7:2). For another approach to the question of the speaker in these verses and for a summary of several positions, see Hagstrom, 96, 108-9. Regarding the proposal that the speaker in 7:1-7 is a king or his representative and that the setting is that of a proposed Autumn Festival (see Reicke, esp. 351-52), this is neither the plain meaning of the text (note the lack of any explicit reference to the king or to a festival) nor is it a necessary hypothesis to understand the piece.

The identity of the addressees is also of interest. The addressees in the world of the speaker's text in vv. 1-3 are not characterized and seem secondary to the message of the text. What is important here is that the readers overhear the words of the speaker, identify with the speaker, and accept the speaker as one bearing a truthful and godly message. The evildoers who populate the society described by the speaker are addressed in the 3rd person, probably in order to create a sense of distance between the speaker and them; of course, the readers are to separate themselves from evildoers (cf. Ps 1:1; Prov 1:8-33; etc.).

When the speaker expresses confidence in YHWH's action against the evildoers, it is YHWH who clearly takes the role of the addressee. The change is only contextually marked, though emphatically communicated (notice the immediate repetition of the pronominal suffix referring to YHWH). The address to YHWH in the 2nd person in this regard may convey some sense of closeness, particularly if the speaker is identified with "your [YHWH's] sentinels" (cf. Mic 7:7 and Isa 21:6). Then, as the unit moves to the emphatically contrastive and disjunctive "you vs. I" volley in vv. 5-7, the role of the addressee must be taken by the wrongdoers, who until now were referred to in the 3rd person.

The first subunit shaping this READING is the speaker's interjection that alerts the readers to the tone and basic character of the following text. This interjection also serves affective functions. It encourages the readers to identify with the speaker, to reject the speaker's opponents and their potential claims, and to pay careful attention to the text that the implied author assigns to the following speaker. The particular wording of this subunit appears elsewhere in the HB/OT only in Job 10:15.

The next section in the READING advances a description of the wrongful state of society (see Mic 7:1aβ-4a). This is achieved through two short sets of metaphors (vv. 1aβ-b and 4a) that encompass a central set of statements (vv. 2-3). The first set of metaphors points to the "harvest, but not [to] the abundance of harvest, rather the bareness after gleaning." As Luker states, "the lamenter is a lone *ḥsyd* (v. 2) in a wasteland barren of righteousness — like the leftovers of ripe, summer fruit nearly rotten when all has been picked; like solitary grapes tenaciously clinging to the vine after the vine makers have long since collected their fill" ("Doom and Hope," 198-99).

This metaphorical world leads to a set of strong rhetorical claims, centered on the basic statement that opens this subunit: there is no righteous person in the land (cf. Isa 57:1). In other words, the intended readers are asked to develop and identify with an image of the speaker's world in which every person is wicked and crooked except the speaker. The general "everyone" is then exemplified or characterized by particular references to officers, judges, and people of importance (Mic 7:3aβ-b). The king is not mentioned, as in ch. 3 (→ 3:1-12, Intention).

This description of the state of society and of the actions of representative individuals leads to an expression of confidence in YHWH's redemptive action (7:4b). A similar pattern obtains in vv. 5-7. Significantly, the particular relation between the described sin and the announced judgment in vv. 4-7 is based not on a claimed essential relationship (e.g., the judgment befits the sin, or this particular deed leads to — or seeds — this or that situation) but on a wordplay between *mĕsûkâ*, "thorn hedge," and *mĕbûkâ*, "confusion." (See Miller, 35-36; contrast with 2:1-5; → 3:1-12, Genre.)

The description of the state of society (vv. 5-6) is presented now in terms that point to the collapse of social cohesiveness and interpersonal duty and responsibility (as understood in a traditionally oriented, hierarchical society). Significantly, this is achieved by a list of instances of failure of the expected relationship that begins from symmetrical relationships (v. 5a) and increasingly moves into more and more asymmetrical, hierarchical relationships that culminate with that of the master to *'anšê bêtô*, "the people of his house" (i.e., "his servants"; for the meaning of the expression see Gen 17:23, 27; 39:14; cf. Vargon, 208 n. 55). The relation between husband and wife is considered in this spectrum as less asymmetrical than the one between father and son, or mother and daughter, but nonetheless not one of equality. (For a different approach to these verses according to which the arrangement is one of "increasing intimacy," see Mays, 152; for ancient Near Eastern parallels to this description, see Reicke, 358; and cf. *Ludlul Bel Nemeqi,* I, 84-92, *ANET,* 596-97; also cf. Ovid *Metamorphoses* 1.144-49: "Mankind is broken loose from moral bands; No rights of hospitality remain: The guest, by him who harbour'd him, is slain, The son-in-law pursues the father's life; The wife her husband murders, he the wife; The step-dame poyson for the son prepares; The son inquires into his father's years. Faith flies, and piety in exile mourns; And justice, here opprest, to Heav'n returns.")

Not only here but also in Mal 3:24 (NRSV 4:6) one finds the idea that a world in which the interpersonal responsibilities and hierarchies of the family or household are not respected cannot hold, and such circumstances are congruent with a time that is near a turning point, which in Mal 3:24 seems eschatological (but cf. Prov 30:11-14; Ps 41:10 [NRSV 9]; or even Jer 9:3 [NRSV 4] and Ezek 22:6-12; for a later understanding of these conditions as preceding and leading to divine salvation see the words attributed to R. Nehorai in *Cant. Rab.* 2.13.4; and cf. *m. Sota* 9.15; the reverberation of Mic 7:6 in Matt 10:35 and Luke 12:53 deserves a separate study that is beyond the limits of this commentary). Within the context of Mic 7:1-7, it is clear that the speaker is waiting for the turning day mentioned in v. 4.

For the position that 7:4b is a "late gloss," see, for instance, Renaud, 352-55; Wolff, *Micah,* 202 (cf. 207); but see also Hillers, *Micah,* 85-86.

Genre

The unit evokes some basic features of a lament, particularly in the description of the woeful and wrongful conditions, and given the opening interjection (cf. Gerstenberger, 10-11) and some features usually associated with a complaint, such as the affirmation of confidence in spite of the present conditions (cf. ibid., 11-14).

As such, it (1) shapes a set of circumstances that are depicted in the most negative terms from the perspective of the speaker, (2) characterizes directly or indirectly the speaker as a pious person opposed to the evildoers, (3) characterizes the speaker as one with full confidence — despite the circumstances — in the saving or restoring action of YHWH, and (4) attempts to develop in the audience an emotional attachment to the speaker. (The unit, however, shows only some of the elements that are typically found in a complaint; see Gerstenberger, 11-14.)

The words that the implied author assigns to the speaker on this occasion are well embedded within the book of Micah rather than in an independent, real-life, communal or individual ritual of complaint. Moreover, these words create a great degree of tension and ambiguity regarding the identity of the speaker. They imply an audience that is not only listening to the uttered words themselves but is able to turn the page (as it were) in the book, so as to read the preceding and the following words. This is an audience of readers and rereaders of the book. As it stands, as an integral part of the book of Micah (which is equated with YHWH's word; see 1:1), 7:1-7 is certainly another READING that the intended readership of the book is supposed to read, reread, ponder about its possible multiple meanings, and, above all, consider as an integral part of YHWH's word (i.e., of the book of Micah). Whether there was a forerunner of this unit that had a different setting and genre cannot be determined. In any case, the book of Micah did not ask its intended rereaders to deal with that question, nor is there any reason to believe that the literari who were the primary readership of the book actually read, reread, and meditated on the text from a perspective that was strongly influenced by their own understanding or reconstruction of the redactional process that they thought led eventually to the precise text within the book of Micah that they were reading and rereading. There is no reason to assume that they rejected so clearly the request of the implied author of the book.

Setting

A number of scholars (e.g., Reicke, Kapelrud) have brought into the discussion of this text's setting proposals regarding (1) a hypothetical precursor of the present READING that was related to (a) a possible liturgy of an Autumn Festival (whose character at least is debatable), or (b) any other liturgical occasion to be reconstructed from a particular understanding of the text that assumes from the outset a liturgical setting; and (2) the identification of the speaker in the text with the king or his representative.

These proposals clearly deal with issues that stand beyond the limits of what can be known with any reasonable degree of certainty. Moreover, they seem to ignore the world created within the book of Micah itself. Neither the basic narrator nor any character in 7:1-7 mentions the king; there is no refererence to any particular liturgical or historical occasion as the setting of the speaker's words. There is certainly no specific description of the when, where, or any other element of the setting (within the world of the book) in which the speaker uttered these words. As on other occasions in the book of Micah, the text is presented here with no particular attachment to historical events, and as such it allows the readers to understand it against multiple possible backgrounds.

This lack of anchoring to particular events, not only in the "historical world" but also even within the world of the book, is sharply contrasted with the clear anchoring of the text to its literary environment within the book. Thus one may notice that (1) the multiple identities that the speaker of the text may take are carried out by the interrelation of this text with its preceding and following units within the book, and (2) a double-duty verse is present at the conclusion of this unit.

As for the actual setting of the reading of this READING, it is no different from all others in the book. It points to a circle of literati who were the bearers of high literacy in their society, and who took the role of brokers of the knowledge imparted by the book of Micah in general and this READING in particular to those unable to read and reread by themselves (→ 1:2-16, Setting).

Intention

The primary intentions of this READING include the communication of an understanding of past events in terms of the wrongful character of the monarchic society, an emphasis on the divine justice that will come (and had come), and the affective identification of the readers with the speaker that serves also the purpose of moral and theological instruction by example. This READING expresses and communicates trust in YHWH not only despite a situation described as an extreme case of social disintegration, but also as a response or even as the only worthy response to such circumstances. As such it conveyed a message to the readers who lived under a less despairing situation. The intended readership of the book would hardly have imagined themselves as being under the circumstances hyperbolically associated with monarchic Judah and that were, within their discourse, commensurate to the divine actions against Judah and Jerusalem in 586 BCE. This message is consistent with and complements the one advanced in the next READING, 7:7-20, which conveys a confirmation of YHWH's overlordship (or patronage) of Judah, Jerusalem, and Israel in spite of, and in response to, postexilic conditions.

Although setting social norms is not the primary intention of this READING, it clearly reflects and reaffirms some main ones. The text conveys an image of what family (and servant-master) relationships should be, from the perspective of the authorship and intended readership. According to that image, one should be able to have confidence in a loved one, to speak freely with one's spouse; sons should treat their father with respect; daughters (before marriage) should obey their mother, and daughters-in-law their mother-in-law (after marriage; cf. Ruth); the entire family and household should stand united and structured around an accepted hierarchy headed by the father of the family. For the ancient Near Eastern background of the position of the daughters-in-law, see Ningal's words to the bride Inana before her wedding to Dumuzi, "Verily your father is (now) a stranger only. Verily your mother is (now) a stranger only. His mother you will respect as were she your mother! His father you will respect as were he your father" (Jacobsen, 21).

Bibliography

E. S. Gerstenberger, *Psalms, Part I* (FOTL XIV; Grand Rapids: Eerdmans, 1988); H. L. Ginsberg, *The Israelian Heritage of Judaism* (New York: Jewish Theological Seminary of America, 1982); T. Jacobsen, *The Harps That Once . . . Sumerian Poetry in Translation* (New Haven: Yale Univ. Press, 1987); L. M. Luker, "Doom and Hope in Micah: The Redaction of the Oracles Atrributed to an Eighth-Century Prophet" (Ph.D. diss.,

Vanderbilt University, 1985, UMI order 8607519); B. Reicke, "Liturgical Traditions in Mic. 7," *HTR* 60 (1967) 349-67; J. T. Willis, "A Reapplied Prophetic Hope Oracle," in G. W. Anderson et al., *Studies in Prophecy* (VTSup 26; Leiden: Brill, 1974) 64-76.

READING CONVEYING A CONFIRMATION OF YHWH'S RELATIONSHIP (PATRONSHIP) TO JUDAH/ZION IN SPITE OF ITS LOW WORLDLY STATUS, 7:7-20

Structure

I. Expression of trust in YHWH in spite of the enemies' upper hand ... 7-10
  A. Opening statement characterizing the speaker ... 7
  B. Short address regarding the relationship between "I" and YHWH, and between "I" and "my" enemy ... 8-10
II. Reference to future salvation for Jerusalem, Judah, and Israel, and to judgment for the enemies ... 11-13
  A. The future day: focus on Jerusalem, Judah, Israel ... 11
  B. The future day: focus on the relation between the nations and Jerusalem ... 12
  C. The future desolation due to YHWH's judgment against the enemies ... 13
III. Prayer for the deliverance of the speaker (Israel, Judah, Jerusalem) and for the humiliation of the nations and their future fear of YHWH ... 14-17
  A. Regarding Israel, Judah, Jerusalem ... 14-15
  B. Regarding the nations ... 16-17
IV. Hymn of praise to YHWH and request regarding patronship ... 18-20
  A. Characterization of YHWH by means of a rhetorical question ... 18a
  B. Characterization by a (formally) negative statement ... 18b
  C. Characterization by a (formally) positive statement ... 19a
  D. First request ... 19b
  E. Final request ... 20

The first and the last three verses in this READING serve double duty. Vv. 18-20 conclude this reading but also conclude the book of Micah (→ 7:18-20). As mentioned above, 7:7 belongs to this READING but also to the preceding READING. Among other functions, this verse bridges this and the preceding READING, and anchors this particular READING to the ongoing book of Micah (notice the opening *waw*, "and"). The expression of trust in v. 7 not only opens 7:7-20 but also alerts the readership of a significant shift in the general atmosphere that characterized the previous units (cf. Hagstrom, 103; Shoemaker, 208-9; Luker, "Doom and Hope," 203-4; also cf. Gunkel, 123-25) as it summarizes the normative position regarding YHWH and trust in YHWH in the face of strong adversity. A clear statement of trust and of normative behavior is consistent with and perhaps even suggestive of images of a brighter future, rather than with descriptions of an extremely sinful past or present.

These images of the future are materialized in the second subunit (vv. 8-10). They are presented in terms of two related pairs of relationships: that between YHWH and the speaker and that between the speaker and its enemy, both of which are constructed from the perspective of the speaker. The speaker is given here an explicitly feminine voice that, within this literary context, is likely to be understood as (Daughter) Jerusalem, (Daughter) Zion, or both; in any case, it points to Israel. Thus the text is constructed to lead the readership to identify itself with the speaker.

Regarding her relation with YHWH, the speaker's words here communicate and encapsulate main theological tenets: her basic understanding of her present — and of the present of the readership — as due to her sins, her trust in YHWH, her right attitude (now), which includes (1) continuing to bear the "anger of YHWH" (v. 9) in the present, and (2) her trust that YHWH will bring her a luminous future. These tenets are central to the postmonarchic community within which one finds the primary readers of the book of Micah.

Her relation with her enemy, on the one hand, is one of expected reversal. Whereas in the present the enemy (also a fem. voice) enjoys the upper hand, the situation will be reversed in the future described in this unit (see v. 10bβ). On the other hand, the speaker assumes already, in the present, a position of clear superiority over her enemy that is due to her superior theological understanding of the situation. She tells her enemy not to rejoice, that her (i.e., the enemy's) future is calamity and humiliation; and above all she easily recognizes that her enemy has failed to understand the real underpinnings of the present and future circumstances, as she quotes her enemy saying to her: "Where is YHWH, your God?" (v. 10). Significantly, this combination of a lower worldly status than the other nations and a claim of superior knowledge — and ideological or theological superiority in general — is consistent with the world of the postmonarchic rereaders who are asked to identify themselves with the textually inscribed speaker. It is worth noting that references to "her enemy" open and close this subunit. The readers are asked to understand the enemy, who is "the other" in this case, and to learn about themselves within this discourse.

The unit itself (7:7-10) is built around contrasts, word pairs (some of which are split pairs), and more or less common expressions. The purpose of the contrastive pairs is to convey a salient image of reversal, here always from a negative to a positive situation from the speaker's perspective. Thus one may notice the obvious contrast between *nāpaltî* and *qāmtî* ("I fall" or "I have fallen," and "I shall rise up"; see v. 8; cf. Prov 24:16; contrast Ps 36:13 [NRSV 12]; Am 5:2; cf. Ps 20:9 [NRSV 8]), *hōšek* and *'ôr* ("darkness" and "light"; see vv. 8, 9; cf. Isa 9:1 [NRSV 2]; 58:10; Ps 112:4). Perhaps a more subtle, implicit contrast between "sitting" (v. 8) and the implicit "treading upon" (v. 10) is also communicated.

Beyond contrastive pairs, there is the presence or influence of the split pair *mišpāṭ* and *ṣĕdāqâ* ("judgment" and "justice" or "deliverance") in v. 9; the associative connection between *ṣĕdāqâ* and *'ôr* ("light") in v. 9 (cf. Isa 59:9; Ps 89:16-17 [NRSV 15-16]; see also Ps 88:13 [NRSV 12]; Mic 7:8-9); and that of the pair *mišpāṭ* and *rîb* ("complaint"; cf. Deut 25:1; 2 Sam 15:2; Ps 35:23; Lam 3:35-36, 58-59).

Many of the main topoi and similes in the unit also occur elsewhere, for instance, the call for a seeming winner not to rejoice, and even the particular expression *'al-tiśmĕḥî*, "do not rejoice" (followed by a vocative that points to a fem. noun), appears in Isa 14:29 (cf. Mic 1:10; Hos 9:1; Obad 12). A simile very close to the one present in *mirmās kĕṭît ḥûṣôt* ("overtrodden as the mire of the streets") in Mic 7:10 occurs in Isa 10:6 (regarding *hāyâ lĕmirmās*, "become an overtrodden land," see also Isa 7:25; 28:18). Phrases very similar to *'ayyô yhwh 'ĕlōhāyik* are placed in the mouth of "the unjust other" in Joel 2:17; Mal 2:17; Pss 42:4, 11 (NRSV 3, 10); 99:40; 115:2 (also cf. 2 Kgs 18:34//Isa 36:19). Significantly, in all these cases "the other" incriminates him- or herself with his or her own words, as it were. In this regard, the pattern of occurrence of *hā'ōmrâ* ("who says") is noticeable: it occurs only in Isa 47:8; Zeph 2:15; and Mic 7:10, three instances in which the "enemy" is given a voice (constructed as fem.) so as to incriminate herself. In sum, the text draws from a cultural reservoir of lexical connections, topoi, and similes that is available to postmonarchic communities.

Whereas the identity of the speaker does not change throughout 7:7-10, the enemy is referred to in the 2nd person (as the formal addressee; see v. 8) but also in the 3rd (v. 10). The reference to the enemy in the 2nd person in relation to the call not to rejoice because of the speaker's disgrace in 7:8 (cf. Isa 14:29; also cf. Mic 1:10) is probably due to the affective functions of direct speech. A similar topos is developed differently in Pss 30:2 (NRSV 1); 35:15, 19, 24; 38:17 (NRSV 16), in which YHWH rather than the enemy is the addressee (cf. Vargon, 211). Although it is a common topos in the HB/OT that one should not rejoice over the fall of an enemy (e.g., Zeph 2:10; Obad 12; Prov 24:17; Pss 35:19, 24; 38:17 [NRSV 16]; Lam 2:17), it is worth stressing that in the world of this address the speaker (i.e., Zion, Jerusalem) will be allowed to gloat over her enemy; notice the explicit "my eyes will gloat over her" in v. 10. (For *rā'â b* meaning "gloat over" see Obad 12; Pss 22:18 [NRSV 17]; 54:9 [NRSV 7]; 118:7; cf. the Mesha inscription, lines 4, 7, *ANET,* 320; see also Barthélemy et al., 3:700; Ben Zvi, *Obadiah,* 143, 146; regarding asymmetric tit-for-tat situations, see, e.g., Ben Zvi, *Obadiah,* 174-75).

The actual addressee of the speaker as opposed to the formal addressee in v. 8 is not marked in the world of the text, but, in any case, the readers are those who are supposed to overhear what the speaker had to say within the world of the text. Given the issues that are discussed under Genre, it is important to notice that (a) the addressee in this section is not YHWH, and (b) that the speaker is a female voice. YHWH is not the usual speaker in a dirge or lament, and female voices do not act as speakers in dirge/laments in the Psalter (cf. Gunkel, 125-26).

The second unit in this READING (7:11-13) continues the thread of the first (7:7-10) and further emphasizes the contrast between the future fate of Zion/Jerusalem (and in any case, by implication, Israel) and her enemy. It stands apart from the former unit by the rhetorical shift of Zion/Jerusalem from speaker (vv. 7-10) to addressee and because of the tight textual coherence created by the close repetitions of *yôm* ("day") in vv. 11-12. Sound repetitions also contribute to this sense of textual coherence (see vv. 11, 12; and the repetition of *m* and *n* in v. 12).

Micah 7:11-13 focuses first on the restoration of the female character who had been the speaker in the previous section (7:7-10). The expression *bnh gādēr*, "to rebuild fences," here also "to rebuild walls," points clearly to the opposite action of *prṣ gādēr*, "to breach fences [or walls]" (cf. Isa 5:5; Pss 80:13 [NRSV 12]; 89:41 [NRSV 40]; Qoh 10:8). It serves to convey a sense of security that in Ezra 9:9 is seen as an element of national redemption. On the one hand, *bnh gādēr* serves to evoke the pastoral image of Israel, because *gādēr/gĕdarâ* is reminiscent of sheepfolds (cf. 1 Sam 24:4; Zeph 2:6; etc.; and cf. the pastoral images in Mic 7:14 and 2:12-13) as well as that of "gardens/ vineyards" (cf. Isa 5:5; Mic 4:4); on the other hand, it retains the military fortification image (cf. Ezek 13:5; Ps 89:41 [NRSV 40]). Moreover, as the removal or lack of *gādēr/gĕdērâ* introduces the disgrace or downfall of Israel (cf. Isa 5:5; Ezek 22:30), its rebuilding points to the restoration of the fortunes of the nation (or the city that stands for the nation, as here; cf. Ezra 9:9). Whereas the image of building the "fences" or "walls" points to security and may convey enclosure, the next section in the verse, *yirḥaq-ḥōq*, "the border shall be far extended" (on the location of the *atnach* in this verse, see Hillers, *Micah*, 88 n. e), points clearly and emphatically — notice the repetition of consonants — to territorial expansion (on *ḥōq* pointing to "border," "limit," see Isa 5:14; Prov 8:29; Job 38:10; and see *DBHE*, 275; *DCH*, 3:299, no. 6; *HAL*, 1:346, no. 7; cf. Hillers, *Micah*, 88; for partially similar expressions to the one in Mic 7:11, see Isa 26:15). For a somewhat different approach to this verse, see Renaud, 360; Mays, 160-62.

There has been considerable debate about the precise meaning of v. 12. The most likely interpretation of this verse is something akin to: "the day shall come when they shall come to you from (the cities) of Assyria to the (fortified) cities of Egypt, from (the land of) Egypt [there is here a connotation of 'fortress'] to the Euphrates, from sea to sea and mountain to mountain" (cf. Barthélemy et al., 3:778-79; Mays, 160-62; Hillers, *Micah*, 87-88; Luker, "Doom and Hope," 104, 133). This understanding of the verse assumes a double-duty verbal form *(yābô')* that is associated with two subjects: "the day" (i.e., the day will come), and an impersonal or indeterminate form, which in English is better rendered by "they." The choice of the sg. rather than a pl. form of the verb in v. 12 is absolutely necessary to allow for this double-duty role. This understanding of v. 12 assumes an additional polyvalent term: *'ārê māṣôr* (v. 12a) or *māṣôr* (v. 12b), which according to this interpretation and translation of the verse points both to Egypt (cf. Isa 19:6; 2 Kgs 19:24//Isa 37:25) and to fortified cities (see Ps 60:11 [NRSV 9]; cf. 108:11). Again, the precise choice of words — in this case, the choice of the rare *'ārê māṣôr* over the more common *'ārê mibṣār*, "fortified cities" — is also absolutely necessary for the text to exhibit a double meaning. A similar situation obtains in v. 14. There the word *šēbeṭ* ("staff" or "tribe") serves as a double-duty form that leads to two readings: "shepherd your people with your staff" (cf. Mic 5:3), and "shepherd your people, your tribe" (see Ps 78:71). Also here the precise wording of the text is important. Had the noun *šēbeṭ* been preceded by *ʾet* (the *nota accusativa*) rather than by the preposition *b*, the text of v. 14 would not have conveyed a double meaning to the readership.

The question that remains open is whether "they" in v. 12 refers to the children of Israel who are dispersed among the nations (cf. Isa 11:11-12; also cf. Mic 2:12-13; 4:6-7; Pss 67:22-23 [NRSV 21-22]; 106:47; etc.) or to the nations themselves (cf. Isa 2:1-4; Mic 4:1-4; but also cf. Joel 3:5 and Zech 14:16-19). This type of ambiguity is not unique to Mic 7:12 (see Zeph 3:10; cf. Ben Zvi, *Zephaniah,* 227-30). It is possible that the scenarios that obtain in the worlds of Joel 3:5 and Zech 14:16-19 and the circumstances described in Mic 7:13 and 7:17 might suggest that a reference to the "nations" rather than "dispersed Israel" is more likely in v. 12. Still v. 12 exhibits a lasting ambiguity regarding the identity of "they," and, accordingly, this verse creates an additional level of polyvalence in an already polyvalent verse. (For a significantly different approach to vv. 11-13 and v. 12 in particular, see Vargon, 217-19.)

Although v. 13 is formally ambiguous as well (whose land is to be desolate?), the context clarifies the issue. There is no lasting ambiguity here: it is not the land of the speaker addressed in these verses (i.e., that of the Jerusalemites, Israelites) that will be desolate, but that of their enemies, because of the nations' deeds. Thus v. 13 serves to a large extent as an interpretive key attached to a potential reading of v. 12: "they" may refer to the nations who will come to Jerusalem, but in no case does the text advance the kind of blissful scenario present in 4:1-4.

In sum, 7:11-13 focuses first on the restoration of the Israelites (v. 11) and concludes with the desolation of the enemies (v. 13). It advances an image of the reversal of the present conditions of the speaker in vv. 7-10 (and the addressee in vv. 11-13) in a way that is fully consistent with the main thrust of vv. 7-10. Yet, whereas in the relationship between YHWH and Jerusalem Israel plays an explicitly central role in vv. 7-10 and is implicitly central to vv. 11-13, it is still not mentioned in these verses. This relationship comes to the forefront again at the beginning of the next subunit, 7:14-17.

Micah 7:14-17 consists of a prayer that includes two related thematic sections. The first one deals with the restoration of the speaker (i.e., Israel, Judah, Jerusalem). The prayer focuses on the particular relation between YHWH and Israel. It begins by asking YHWH to lead or shepherd *(rʿh)* Israel, and then moves to emphasize this relation of patronship by the threefold repetition of "your" (i.e., YHWH's) in the opening verset in v. 14, which describes the speaker as "*your* people, *your* tribe, and the flock of *your* inheritance." Moreover, the reference to YHWH's territory ("inheritance") creates a thematic link to the territorial expansion hinted at in 7:11b ("the boundary shall be extended"). Significantly, the explicit references in v. 14 are to Bashan and Gilead, which were certainly not included in the actual territory of Persian (or, for the sake of argument, Neo-Babylonian) Judah. There is also a possible pun on the word *karmel,* "garden land," but also "Carmel" (cf. Isa 35:2).

Images of a future in which postmonarchic Jerusalem-centered Israel will expand and include the territories associated with the northern kingdom of Israel appear elsewhere in prophetic literature. Moreover, they lead into the conclusion of a prophetic book not only in Micah but also in Obadiah. (On Obad 19-21, see Ben Zvi, *Obadiah*, 197-229.) These images point to a dream of future power by the presently powerless. They also construct a territorial map of the future in which both the nations and Israel have a portion. Significantly, the area that will be Israel's is based on the outline of the history of Israel expressed in biblical literature. In other words, the text assumes an intended readership for which this construction is a given (notice the explicit reference to *kîmê 'ôlām*, "as in the days of old," in v. 14).

What will become of the nations at that time? They will be stricken for sure (v. 13), but how would they relate to the actual ruler of the world who is the patron of Israel (v. 14)? Vv. 16-17 answer that question. The nations will be smitten and humiliated so that they will acknowledge and fear YHWH, the patron of the speaker ("the Lord *our* God," v. 17), which acknowledgment in turn brings to the forefront the particular status of this client/speaker (→ 4:1-5, Intention).

Verses 14-17 are held together not only by thematic concerns but by a number of stylistic devices that contribute to the textual coherence of these verses. First, the speaker throughout the prayer is a human voice that is to be identified with the "we" that represents Israel (see v. 17), and the addressee is always YHWH, as one would expect in a prayer. One may also notice the pun on the Hiphil and Qal forms of the root *r'h* ("show" and "see," respectively) that contributes to the bond between the two subsections of this prayer (see v. 15b and 15a, and the shifts of people and objects: Israel will be shown marvelous things, whereas the nations will see disgrace). See also *yir'û* and *yir'û* ("they shall feed" and "they shall see," respectively) in vv. 14 and 16 (cf. Vargon, 220).

Verse 15 is best understood as a speaker's quote of YHWH's speech elsewhere. It serves as a kind of proof text to reassure the speaker and those who overhear the prayer of YHWH's patronage of Israel. The reference to "him" rather than the expected "you" in "I will show him" in v. 17b conveys a sense that the textually inscribed speaker cites an utterance that existed before and was originally external to the words now pronounced in the world of the book. Yet one may notice that the more common "them" was not placed in the mouth of the speaker. Had this been the case, the text could have been interpreted as pointing to the nations (i.e., "them" = the nations), because of v. 16. That is, the words of the implied author attributed to YHWH in v. 15 are likely constructed to convey some sense of original independence from the other words of the speaker, but at the same time they show that the text of v. 16 was likely in the mind of that implied author. (For a different perspective on v. 15 see Hagstrom, 100-102, and bibliography there.)

In this subunit the motif of the nations being shamed (vv. 16-17a) is linked to that of YHWH's being honored by them and their behavior toward YHWH as a powerful deity and patron (v. 17b). A similar thematic development occurs in a preceding subunit within this READING. The link in vv. 10aβ-b is between the nations actually shaming YHWH in public by reportedly asking Jerusalem, "Where is YHWH, your God?" and their own shaming at the hands of YHWH (v. 10b; see 10a). The difference between the two cases is that the nations are constructed as not only humiliated and shamed by YHWH's action in the present subunit but as "fearing YHWH."

The next section (7:18-20) moves from petition to praise of YHWH. Such praise conveys a sense of assurance that it is in YHWH's power and will to fulfill the request (cf. Pss 10:15-18; 22:28-32 [NRSV 27-31]; etc.; cf. Gunkel, 141-42). Aside from thematic links, it is closely associated to the preceding subunit by the continuity of the speaker, a human voice that is to be identified with the "we" that represents Israel (see vv. 19, 20). It also begins with a reference to YHWH in the 2nd person (v. 18; cf. v. 14), and then moves to references to YHWH in the 3rd (vv. 18-19; cf. 17), but concludes — most likely for affective reasons — with a reference to YHWH in the 2nd person (v. 20). One may notice also the reverberating reference to YHWH's *nahălâ* ("inheritance"; see vv. 14, 18) and the basic construction of Israel's immediate past and present as the result of justified, divine anger, and that of the future in terms of YHWH's deliverance (cf. v. 9a with v. 18).

The stylistic variety in vv. 18-19a (i.e., rhetorical question, negative and positive statements) conveys and calls attention to a unified message: a characterization of YHWH as a patron who is willing to forgive the sins of the client (i.e., of Israel). It is precisely this request for forgiveness that is brought to YHWH, in the 2nd person now, by the speaker representing Israel in v. 19b. Yet the main goal of the speaker must be forgiveness not for its own sake but as a necessary step to the establishment of a steady relationship of patronship that is expressed in terms of the split pair *hesed* and *'ĕmet* (on *hesed* pointing to "patronship" see Lemche; Hobbs; on split pairs see Melammed).

Finally, one may also mention reverberations of significant wordings, terms, or elements of the imagery of other READINGS in the book (cf. 7:14-17 with 2:12 and 3:12; cf. 7:18 with 2:12 and 5:6, 7; or regarding particular terms, cf. 7:13 with 1:7; 7:14 with 4:14; 7:14, 18 with 2:2). One can easily discern a trajectory in the last three examples. There a simple term (*šĕmāmâ, šēbeṭ, nahălâ,* respectively) that appears in previous READINGS within a setting that suggests a negative connotation, in this READING connotes an image that is positive from the perspective of the speaker and the implied author. Yet a positive reference to *yĕmê 'ôlām,* "days of old" (5:1 [NRSV 2]), again connotes a positive image in 7:14. In both cases "days of old" are constructed in positive terms, from Israel's perspective. (For an analysis of links between Micah 7 and other sections in the book, though from a different perspective, see, e.g., Luker, "Doom and Hope," 212-17; Willis, "Structure," esp. pp. 34-38; for the net of links between chs. 1–5 and 6–7, see Hagstrom, 115-22.) These links prove neither a single nor a Mican authorship. Instead, they point to (1) the textual coherence of the book, (2) the book being most likely written so as to be read and reread by the intended authorship as a unit, and (3) a book that creates an image of "the speaker" and of the implied author as a coherent character.

Genre

Gunkel considered 7:7-20 to be a prophetic liturgy composed of a dirge of Zion, followed by a divine oracle that answers the dirge, followed by a dirge of Israel, which in turn is followed by a hymn of assurance. He thought that "the poem was rendered as a 'liturgy' by different singers on one of the 'days of dule' in Jerusalem" about the time of Trito-Isaiah (Gunkel, 146-48). His position has been influential in much of later research (e.g., Reicke; Willis, "Structure"). Yet there is no reference in the world of 7:7-20 to any kind of performance of this text in a liturgical setting, and certainly not to its being sung by different singers on any day or type of day.

Moreover, even if one grants that "the alternation of dissimilar tunes, the oscillation between individual and collective, and the different speakers and audiences of these verses" are found in many psalms (Willis, "Structure," 36), it does not follow from this observation that 7:7-20 as it stands was performed in a liturgical setting, or that it had to exist independently from the book in general and the literary units that stand in its immediate textual vicinity in particular, as an oral prophecy patterned as a liturgy.

Most important from the perspective of a commentary on the book of Micah, none of these observations leads to the conclusion that the intended rereaders of the book were required to understand this text mainly in the light of an unmentioned oral performance rather than in the light of the *Sitz im Buch* of 7:7-20. The comparison with the individual psalms is striking in this regard. Each psalm is marked as an independent unit in a way that Mic 7:7-20 is not (indeed, from the viewpoint of textual coherence, individual psalms provide a closer parallel to the book of Micah as a whole than to 7:7-20); moreover, clear references to performance are attached to many psalms, but none is to Mic 7:7-20.

The only conclusion that one may reach on the basis of the occurrence in this unit of some rhetorical and structural devices similar to those found in some psalms is that these devices were known to the author and, more importantly, to the intended readership of the book of Micah and of 7:7-20 as part of that text. This conclusion is not surprising given the postmonarchic character of the book and many of the psalms, and the relatively small group of literati able to produce these types of literature (cf. Ben Zvi, "Urban"). Moreover, recourse to some features of known types of discourse or genre (and their frequent defamiliarization) is most common in the book of Micah; see below regarding hymn and lament.

In sum, 7:7-20 is a written text whose intended readership is clearly asked, by textually inscribed markers, to understand it as an integral part of the book of Micah, that is, YHWH's word as associated with the figure of Micah. This being the case, 7:7-20 is a "Prophetic" Reading, not an independent oral unit, be it a prophetic oracle structured as a liturgy (e.g., Willis, "Structure," 34) or any other kind of actual prophetic utterance.

For rhetorical purposes the implied author set up some subsections of the unit in ways that were likely to evoke in the readership of 7:7-20 features associated with a dirge, lament, or complaint (see 7:7-13; cf. Luker, "Doom and

Hope," 203-6, among others; but notice some amount of defamiliarization; see above, Structure), with a prayer (see 7:14-17; cf. Mays, 163, among others), and with a hymn (see 7:18-20; cf. Reicke, 365, among others). In addition, some typical motifs that are found in requests for help made by vassals or clients to their patron do appear in 7:7-20, particularly in 7:16-17 (see Barré). Yet despite the fact that in ancient Near Eastern documents the vassal is usually a king, there is no convincing reason to assume that the readers of 7:7-20 were asked to understand the figure of the speaker in 7:7-20 as either a royal figure (Jotham? Ahaz? Hezekiah? see 1:1) who is not mentioned at all in ch. 7, or as a prophetic figure who sets out to imitate the actual role of the king in a cultic drama, for which there is no support either in the text or in the actual circumstances of the postmonarchic communities within which one is to find the intended readership of the book of Micah. For a different approach, see, for instance, Willis, "Reapplied," 75.

Setting

The actual setting of the reading and rereading of this READING is no different from all others in the book. It points to a circle of literati who were the bearers of high literacy in their society, and who took the role of brokers of the knowledge imparted by the book of Micah in general and this READING in particular to those unable to read and reread by themselves.

Proposals regarding the association of this text with proposed liturgies of penance and confession, with liturgies of fast days, including the possibility of that of the Day of Atonement, have been advanced (see Gunkel, Reicke). For the reasons mentioned above, one should not accept these proposed settings.

Proposals that a hypothetical forerunner of 7:7-20 was a prophecy of hope uttered in the northern kingdom, or in relation to the northern kingdom (see Willis, "Reapplied," and bibliography there) not only suffer from the speculative character of the particular redactional history of the text that they reconstruct, but also do not address the setting of 7:7-20 as a written text to be read and reread by those able to do so as an integral part of a larger text, namely, the book of Micah. For markers within the text that suggest that the intended readership of Micah was supposed to approach 7:7-20 as part of the entire book, see the clear markers that open and close the book (i.e., 1:1 and 7:18-20), and those of textual coherence throughout the book and in 7:7-20 (→ 7:18-20, Genre).

As for the setting of the words of the speaker or speakers in 7:7-20 within the world of the book, there is no clear reference to the time, place, or circumstances within which the speaker or speakers uttered the words contained in 7:7-20. Nor is there any indication that the intended readers should have understood them in relation to a particular place, time, or specific historical events. It is clear, however, that voices assigned to the speakers identify themselves with those whose God is YHWH, that is, with Israel and Israel's city, Jerusalem (cf. 1:9). One may notice, in this regard, the self-references of the speakers as YHWH's tribe, the flock of YHWH's inheritance. From a formal perspective these self-references strengthen the already strong contextual suggestion that "the city" is to be understood as YHWH's city, Jerusalem (cf., e.g., Isa 60:14; Pss 46:5 [NRSV 4]; 48:9 [NRSV 8]; 87:3; 101:8; Samaria is never referred to as YHWH's city).

It is also evident that within the world of the book, (1) Israel/Jerusalem (i.e., the speaker) is in a situation of distress, (2) the "city" has neither "fence" nor security, (3) Israel/Jerusalem expects a gathering of exiles, (4) the nations fare much better than Israel/Jerusalem, (5) Israel/Jerusalem has sinned against YHWH but now trusts in YHWH, its patron, and in YHWH's justice and salvific acts, (6) Israel/Jerusalem is hoping for a reversal of its status vis-à-vis the nations, and (7) Israel/Jerusalem hopes for a territorial expansion that will include areas that were associated with northern Israel. Given that the affective power of the text is associated with the ability of the readers to identify with the speaker, it is noteworthy that these circumstances reflect the self-understanding and discourse of postmonarchic communities of Israel (or, geographically, Judah or Yehud), within which one is to find the readers for whom the book of Micah was intended. Against this background, precisely the lack of accurate references mentioned above, including any particular identification of the "enemy," is helpful in terms of maintaining somewhat the monarchic setting associated with the book of Micah within the literary world created by this book (→ 1:1), while at the same time striving to maximize the identification of the postmonarchic readership with the speakers' voices.

Intention

The primary intentions of this READING include (1) to assert the normative position of trust in YHWH (v. 7); (2) to imagine a world in which godly speakers with whom the readership identifies request YHWH to maintain a particular relation of patronship between Israel and YHWH (notice all the references to Israel as YHWH's), and indirectly to urge the readership to do so; (3) to communicate confidence in that relationship; (4) to construct the present and the fall of the monarchic period in the past in terms of justified punishment inflicted on the sinful client by the patron; (5) to advance a characterization of that patron as one who is willing to forgive the sinful client; (6) to identify with the godly speakers in their request from the patron to act against Israel's (Judah's, Jerusalem's) enemies and the nations that do not fear YHWH, and therefore shame YHWH within the rhetorical world of the text; (7) to shape hope of a reversal of the relative status of postmonarchic Israel (Judah, Jerusalem); and in sum (8) to convey hope for a better future for the community within which the readership of the book is situated, a hope that is anchored in the concept of YHWH's patronship of Israel, and of YHWH's own honor as it should and will be displayed in the (ideal) future thought of by both the authorship and readership of the book. The conclusion of this READING and the entire book of Micah is, fittingly, an explicit request — and in this context, a note of confidence — in YHWH's fulfillment of YHWH's role as patron of Abraham, of Jacob, that is, Israel, which includes the authorship and readership of the book of Micah. (Notice the occurrence of the pair *'ĕmet* and *ḥesed* in v. 20, which explicitly point to the patron-client relationship; see Lemche; Hobbs; significantly, the preceding verse [i.e., v. 19] deals with the removal of the potential reasons that might have led YHWH to decline to fulfill YHWH's protective role as patron of Israel.)

Bibliography

M. L. Barré, "A Cuneiform Parallel to Ps 86:16-17 and Mic 7:16-17," *JBL* 101 (1982) 271-75; H. L. Ginsberg, *The Israelian Heritage of Judaism* (New York: Jewish Theological Seminary of America, 1982); H. Gunkel, "The Close of the Book of Micah: A Prophetic Liturgy," in *What Remains of the Old Testament and Other Essays* (tr. A. K. Dallas; New York: Macmillan, 1928) 115-49; T. R. Hobbs, "Reflections on Honor, Shame, and Covenant Relations," *JBL* 116 (1997) 501-3; N. P. Lemche, "Kings and Clients: On Loyalty between the Ruler and the Ruled in Ancient 'Israel,'" *Semeia* 66 (1995) 119-32; L. M. Luker, "Doom and Hope in Micah: The Redaction of the Oracles Attributed to an Eighth-Century Prophet" (Ph.D. diss., Vanderbilt University, 1985, UMI order 8607519); E. Z. Melammed, "Break-up of Stereotype Phrases as an Artistic Device in Biblical Poetry," *ScrHier* 8 (1961) 115-53; B. Reicke, "Liturgical Traditions in Mic. 7," *HTR* 60 (1967) 349-67; R. Tournay, "Quelques relectures bibliques antisamaritaines," *RB* 71 (1964) 504-36; J. T. Willis, "A Reapplied Prophetic Hope Oracle," in G. W. Anderson et al., *Studies in Prophecy* (VTSup 26; Leiden: Brill, 1974) 64-76.

CONCLUSION OF A PROPHETIC BOOK, 7:18-20

Structure

I. Conclusion		7:18-20
A. Characterization of YHWH by means of a rhetorical question		18a
B. Characterization by a (formally) negative statement		18b
C. Characterization by a (formally) positive statement		19a
D. First request		19b
E. Final request		20

For the inner structure of the subunit, → 7:7-20, Structure.

Genre

Verses 18-20 are the CONCLUSION of YHWH's word that is associated with Micah, that is, the book of Micah. Conclusions of prophetic books provide hope to their rereaders. They also set the boundaries of the prophetic book. The actual endings of the prophetic books tend to be highly particular (see, e.g., Isa 66:24; Ezek 48:35; Hos 14:10 [NRSV 9]; Jon 4:11; Mal 3:24 [NRSV 4:6]). Mic 7:20 is another example. The expression *tittēn 'ĕmet lĕya'ăqōb ḥesed lĕ'abrāhām* is usually translated "show faithfulness to Jacob and steadfast love to Abraham." It points to a request and contextually an assertion of YHWH's protective patronship over Israel, and to the status of the latter as YHWH's client. Among the common metaphors for this relationship, one may mention those of king/suzerain–vassal/subject, shepherd–flock, and the like, which are explicit in the book of Micah. Although this topos appears frequently in the prophetic literature and elsewhere in the HB/OT, the particular expression *tittēn 'ĕmet lĕya'ăqōb ḥesed lĕ'abrāhām* occurs nowhere else, as is the case in other prophetic endings. Moreover, the same holds true for *tašlîk bimṣulôt yām*, "cast into the depths of the sea," in v. 19b. These particular prophetic endings serve as one of the important devices that demarcate the extent of a prophetic book. (On these issues and the larger question of the "Book of the Twelve," see Ben Zvi, "Twelve Prophetic Books.")

Contrary to colophons, conclusions are an integral part of the text proper. (A colophon is an addendum or note at the end of a text that contains information about the preceding text and is syntactically and pragmatically marked as separate from the text proper [e.g., Job 31:40; Ps 72:20; Sir 50:27-29; numerous examples in Babylonian and Assyrian texts, and the notes at the end of biblical medieval codices].) Yet like colophons they mark the end of the text. Significantly, contrary to the usual expectations associated with colophons, the conclusions of the prophetic books, including Mic 7:18-20, contain no information about the actual or fictive author of the book, nor about any scribal aspect of the production of the book such as the name of the scribe making the copy, or the purpose of producing the copy (see Leichty; Pearce; cf. Würthwein, 172, 178, 180). (On colophons see, e.g., Lundbom, 89-95; Leichty; Lambert, "Catalogue"; idem, "Ancestors.") The preference of "conclusions" over colophons is consistent with the self-effacing character of the compositors of prophetic literature (cf. Ben Zvi, *Zephaniah,* 347-49), their self-effacing present (cf. Ben Zvi, "Urban Center"), and the communal value of the produced copy.

Setting

The setting of the conclusion of the book of Micah is the same as the setting of the book of Micah (→ Chapter 1).

Intention

The intention of the conclusion is to mark the end of the book and to provide hope to the readers of the book, in particular to reassure them of YHWH's forgiveness of Israel's sins (vv. 18-19) and of YHWH's protective role as the patron of Israel.

Bibliography

M. Fishbane, "Biblical Colophons, Textual Criticism and Legal Analogies," *CBQ* 42 (1980) 438-49; I. S. Gottlieb, "*Sof Davar:* Biblical Endings," *Prooftexts* 11 (1991) 213-24; W. G. Lambert, "Ancestors, Authors and Canonicity," *JCS* 11 (1957) 1-14; idem, "A Catalogue of Texts and Authors," *JCS* 16 (1962) 59-77; E. Leichty, "The Colophon," in R. D. Biggs and J. A. Brinkman, eds., *Studies Presented to A. Leo Oppenheim* (Chicago: Oriental Institute, 1964) 147-54; J. R. Lundbom, "Baruch, Seraiah, and Expanded Colophons in the Book of Jeremiah," *JSOT* 36 (1986) 89-114; L. E. Pearce, "Statements of Purpose: Why the Scribes Wrote," in M. E. Cohen, D. C. Snell, and D. B. Weisberg, eds., *The Tablet and the Scroll: Near Eastern Studies in Honor of William W. Hallo* (Bethesda: CDL Press, 1993) 185-90; E. Würthwein, *The Text of the Old Testament* (2nd ed., Grand Rapids: Eerdmans, 1995).

GLOSSARY

GENRES

BOOK In the context of the forms of the HB/OT literature, a written work that presents itself as a self-contained unit — with a clear beginning and conclusion — that shows a significant degree of textual coherence and distinctiveness (e.g., the book of Isaiah, the book of Chronicles, the book of Micah). The primary readership of the HB/OT books consists of those able to read them (→ prophetic book). The composition of books such as those mentioned above implies a society in which resources are available for the development and maintenance of a group or groups of bearers of high literacy, including identifying the writers and directing readers and rereaders of these books (see Ben Zvi, "Urban Center").

INTRODUCTION The literary unit at the beginning of a (→) prophetic book that provides a frame of reference, a scheme that not only allows but also strongly informs the subsequent reading of the text. In the book of Micah, 1:1 introduces the book to its readers. It conveys to them a clear message about the genre of the book (namely, "YHWH's word," likely meaning "YHWH's instruction") and its authority. In addition, it particularizes the book in relation to similar instances of "YHWH's word" by associating it with the figure of Micah the Morashtite. It also informs the readers about the background against which they are supposed to read the prophecy, and suggests its main topics. Thus 1:1 may be considered the introduction to the book of Micah. It also serves as a (→) superscription.

PROPHETIC BOOK A (→) book that claims an association with a prophetic personage of the past (like Micah) and that is presented to its readership as YHWH's word. As such, the book claims to communicate legitimate and authoritative knowledge about YHWH. Those who were competent to read prophetic books, namely, the literati, constituted the primary readership of these books. These literati were the only group in society that had direct access to such books and the knowledge about YHWH that they claim to convey. These bearers of high literacy served as brokers of that divine knowledge to those who were unable to read by themselves (i.e., the overwhelming majority of the population). Prophetic books were not intended to be read only once, but to be read, reread, and meditated upon. It is to be stressed that "YHWH's word that came to Micah" signifies a written book, to be read, reread, and studied.

PROPHETIC READING A (→) reading (e.g., Mic 3:1-12) within a (→) prophetic book (e.g., the book of Micah). As such, it is a text written to be read and reread, and that claims for itself the legitimacy and authority of a prophetic text, of YHWH's word. It was most likely understood as such by the readership or a significant portion of it.

READINGS Literary units within a larger text written to be read and reread (→ book) that show textually inscribed, discursive markers (such as openings, conclusions, inner textual coherence, thematic focus, and the like) that were likely to suggest to the intended readership of the book that they were supposed — or at least invited — to read and reread these sections of the book as cohesive reading units. The actual, primary readership was probably not too different from the intended readership and, accordingly, it stands to reason that the text was actually reread by the reading community for which it was composed in a way that resembles, at least in some form, that suggested by the mentioned discursive markers.

I must stress that readings (at least in the book of Micah) are interwoven into the tapestry of the book in such a way that they inform each other, and that their *Sitz im Buch* is neither accidental nor unimportant. Still, these readings show a degree of literary unity that sets them apart from their textual environment within the book (e.g., 2:1-5).

SET OF PROPHETIC READINGS A cluster of closely related (→) prophetic readings, usually around a certain topic (e.g., those about the future in 4:1–5:14 [NRSV 15]).

SUPERSCRIPTION The literary unit that stands apart and looks at the following text and above all characterizes it as a unit. Mic 1:1 and similar passages should be considered the superscriptions not to (→) prophetic books but to the main body of such books (in this case, 1:2–7:20). Mic 1:1 and similar superscriptions are an integral — and most significant — part of their respective books as a whole. Indeed, they provided the rereaders of these books with authoritative, interpretive keys that, to a large extent, govern the set of potential interpretations that the texts are allowed to carry. Not only do they not stand apart from the book (a position that is implied in the distinction between superscript and script) but it is misleading to characterize them in such a way. Congruent with its role within the book as a whole, 1:1 is presented to the readers of the book of Micah as a unit by itself. Significantly, because it stands apart and "looks" at 1:2–7:20 as a whole, it clearly communicates to the readers that it characterizes that section of the book in its entirety. As such, it can be considered the superscription of 1:2–7:20.